THE
CONFIDENT
LEADER

About the Author

Susan G. Wynn, DVM, is a 1987 graduate of the University of Georgia College of Veterinary Medicine. She completed an internship in small animal medicine in Washington, D.C., and finished postdoctoral research in viral and vaccine immunology at Emory University School of Medicine in 1997. Her research concentrated on the potential for canine vaccine viruses to cause autoimmune thyroiditis in susceptible animals. She remains an adjunct instructor in the School of Medicine at Emory University.

Dr. Wynn, who is certified in veterinary acupuncture, has served on ad hoc panels for the National Eye Institute and the Office of Alternative Medicine. She is the executive director of the Georgia Holistic Veterinary Medical Association, former national secretary of the International Association for Veterinary Homeopathy, and a former member of the board of directors for the American Holistic Veterinary Medical Association. In addition, Dr. Wynn co-administers the World Wide Web AltVetMed page, as well as an email discussion list for doctors on the subject. She is also an associate editor for the *Journal of the American Holistic Veterinary Medical Association*.

Dr. Wynn is the author of numerous scientific and clinical papers and lectures on the subject of complementary and alternative veterinary medicine in the United States, Canada, and England. Dr. Wynn also co-edited *Complementary and Alternative Veterinary Medicine: Principles and Practice*, a textbook for veterinarians.

THE
CONFIDENT
LEADER

GETTING A GOOD START
AS A CHRISTIAN MINISTER

ARLO GRENZ

BROADMAN
& HOLMAN
PUBLISHERS

Nashville, Tennessee

© Copyright 1994
Broadman & Holman Publishers
All Rights Reserved
4260-61
ISBN: 0-8054-6061-6
Dewey Decimal Classification: 254
Subject Heading: Church Administration
Library of Congress Catalog Number: 93-26960
Printed in the United States of America

Library of Congress Cataloging-in-Publication Data

Grenz, Arlo, 1949-
    The confident leader : getting a good start as a Christian minister / Arlo Grenz
        p.   cm.
    Includes bibliographical references.
    ISBN 0-8054-6061-6
    1. Christian education directors.   I. Title.
BV1531.G74   1994
268'.3--dc20   93-26960
                                                                      CIP

*This book is dedicated to my mom,
Violet Grenz, and to my wife, Christa Grenz.
Their love, support, and encouragement
have made this book possible.*

Contents

Preface

"**H**ow will I ever manage?" is a question that many Christian educators ask at the outset of their ministries. This book is designed to help novices answer that query with calm assurance and to approach their responsibilities with confidence.

It relates the basic principles of leadership in a rather unique style. The management process is seen through the eyes of Jim Stafford, a new and inexperienced director of Christian Education at Bethel Baptist Church. In each succeeding chapter, Jim wrestles with fresh, real-life issues that threaten to hinder or promise to help his ministry.

As he deals with these concerns, Jim learns how to set goals, make godly decisions, and train his staff properly. In addition, he also explores areas which are seldom mentioned in broad-based management textbooks. He discovers how to be creative, how to deal with success, how to recover from failure, and how to build team spirit.

By the time Jim finishes his first year of ministry, he is better equipped to tackle the tasks that lay ahead of him. After following Jim's saga, the readers of this book should feel equally prepared to grapple with the challenges that they face as they seek to serve Christ.

1

Where Do I Begin?

(EVALUATION)

As Jim surveyed his new office, he felt a rush of excitement and anticipation. "Jim Stafford, Director of Christian Education" the plaque on his door proclaimed.

What a wonderful way to begin the new year! Jim thought. *A new church, a new ministry, new friends, and new challenges. Finally, I have a chance to put into practice what I've been learning at Broadmore Bible College for the last four years.*

Jim sat in the chair behind his desk and looked around the room. He began to dream about his ministry at Bethel Church. He pictured hundreds of people becoming Christians during his stay. Visions of dedicated teachers whose skills and persuasive power would put the secular world to shame flashed through his mind. He imagined how thrilling it would be to associate with believers who had a burning desire to know God's Word.

These fanciful images soon vanished, however, and reality started knocking on the door of his mind. Feelings of inadequacy started to temper Jim's enthusiasm as he considered the needs awaiting him. He felt a little overwhelmed by the responsibilities facing him.

Some of his panic stemmed from the fact that he had little formal training for this position and that his experience was extremely limited. Deep within himself, a nagging voice demanded, *How will you ever manage?*

This question was quickly replaced by another one: *Now that you've been hired, where will you begin?*

Jim knew that he needed to obtain the church keys, unpack his books, and get acquainted with the church staff. But then what?

As Jim pondered his dilemma, he thought back to his football days at Broadmore. He remembered how Coach Timmons had launched his career at this institution by evaluating his situation. He began by testing his player's abilities to find out their strengths and weaknesses. At the same time, he inspected his equipment and facilities. He also sent out scouts to scrutinize his competition just as Moses and Gideon sent spies to analyze certain areas and defenses.[1]

The information that Mr. Timmons gained laid the foundation for his future success. It helped him determine what kind of program, players, equipment, and drills he would use to develop his winning team.

Jim realized that he needed to employ the same strategy. So he vowed to make evaluation a top priority at the outset of his ministry. His theme became: "Diagnosis precedes prescription."

RECORDS

Jim savored the silence that enveloped him as he contemplated his commitment to the evaluation process. There were no desperate phone calls beckoning for help, no complaining parents laying siege to his office, and no committee meetings stretching late into the night.

As wonderful as the quietness was, however, Jim could stand it for only a moment. Ivory-tower musings were not his style; he was a man of action.

So Jim left his office in search of the church's secretary, Shirley Higgens. He wanted to share with her his battle plans for the future and her role in them.

Locating Shirley wasn't difficult. She was at the photocopy machine in the church's main office. Jim was eager to get down to business, and he didn't see the need for taking a few minutes to get acquainted. So, as soon as he was able, he interjected the purpose of his visit into their discussion.

"During the next couple of months, I'm going to spend a lot of my time getting acquainted with the church's people and programs. Since you already know both, I'm going to rely a great deal on you for help."

Shirley beamed. She was glad that Jim recognized the important role that she played in the church's ministry. After all, as church secretary, she was at the hub of almost every activity.

At the same time, however, she felt slightly uneasy. Her current workload was already quite heavy. Now that the church had two staff members, she wondered if she would be able to satisfy both of their demands. Her worries were amplified by Jim's next comment.

"To begin with," Jim continued, "I need some information about the church, its educational program, and the community. Could you help me collect some of the following materials?"

Shirley glanced over the list that Jim gave her. It seemed interminably long. Jim wanted attendance records, organizational charts, the church's constitution, past church bulletins, meeting minutes, educational budget, church directory, church calendar, information about the city from the Chamber of Commerce, church brochures, annual reports, and a map of the church's facilities.

"Is that all?" asked Shirley with a wry smile. Her reply was not so much a question as a statement.

Jim detected her apprehension and immediately tried to calm her fears. "I'm sorry," Jim said apologetically, "I don't mean to overwhelm you. I know that it'll take a while to assemble all of this information. But if you could help me with this task, I would be extremely grateful."

There was a long, uneasy silence as Shirley stared at Jim's list. Finally, she sighed and reluctantly accepted her first assignment from this young, eager man. "Well, I'll see what I can do," Shirley offered weakly.

OBSERVATION

"That's great!" was Jim's quick response. Having taken care of the first item on his to-do list, he was ready to move on. He abruptly excused himself and headed for the door. As he left, he muttered to Shirley, "I think I'll just walk around the church for a while and get to know its facilities."

As Jim went from room to room, he imagined how Nehemiah must have felt when he explored the walls of Jerusalem before their reconstruction.[2] Like this wise and able man of God, Jim wanted to thoroughly investigate his surroundings before making any suggestions. This way, when he was ready to recommend a course of action, he could speak with authority and credibility.

Jim was amazed by what he saw. Most of the rooms were small, cluttered, and gloomy. Some bore the battle scars of rowdy students.

Others lacked the chairs, tables, and storage that well-equipped rooms should have. However, with a little work and imagination, Jim was sure that he could improve the situation.

His inspection tour lasted only an hour. It was long enough, however, to reveal some obvious needs which Jim wrote down in his ever-present, pocket notebook.

In the days that followed, Jim continued his role as observer. As he toured the hallways on Sunday morning, he noticed who was late and unprepared. In addition, he used departmental meetings to discover the needs and attitudes of his workers.

As Jim visited various classrooms and meetings, he definitely wanted to avoid the appearances of being a "snoopervisor." So he often volunteered to participate in a group's activities rather than be an impartial observer. On a camping trip, for example, he drove one of the church's vans. At a department meeting, he presented the opening devotional. During his classroom visits, he helped the regular teachers by taking attendance and assisting students with their handiwork.

Jim reaped a number of benefits from these firsthand experiences. He had a chance to get acquainted with his educational staff and discover their personalities, habits, and ideas. His workers realized that he was a team member rather than a heavy-handed boss. He also learned what types of programs, equipment, and procedures worked and which did not.

Even though his observations provided him with a great deal of information, he was keenly aware that they might also be flawed. After all, first impressions aren't always accurate.[3] Therefore, he refrained from making snap decisions based on brief, one-time visits. He did, however, use his observations as a starting point from which to investigate apparent deficiencies more thoroughly.

Jim also realized that he didn't have to make all of the observations himself. He could bring in a denominational expert or another minister of Christian education to examine his church's educational program.

Although using consultants might involve a little more money, he thought this approach might be worthwhile. Outsiders, he felt, could give the church impartial appraisals. In addition, their opinions might be regarded more highly than his.[4]

Jim also toyed with the idea of inviting several of his friends to attend incognito. They could look at the church's activities from a stranger's point of view and give him an unbiased report about their impressions.

Jim's own family became a good source of information. His daughter, Brenda, was a preschooler. His other daughter, Barbara, was involved in the children's department. And his wife, Jill, worked with the youth group. So, together, they could give him a well-rounded picture of what was happening in the church's various educational programs.

Several days after Jim had asked Shirley to compile some data on the church and the community, he arrived at his office and found a neat pile of records and documents on his desk. The attached note said, "This is just the beginning. Happy hunting. Shirley."

As Jim waded through the information he had requested, he learned much about the church's practices and procedures. He also learned that the church didn't value record keeping as much as he did. So he vowed to develop a new record-keeping system. This one would be current, accurate, systematically maintained, simple, and most importantly—used.

STANDARDIZED CHECKLISTS

After spending a morning poring over facts and figures, Jim was ready for a break. He grabbed his coat and headed downtown to visit his good friend, Bob Sparkman.

Ever since meeting Bob at a training conference two years before, Jim had tried to stay in touch with this wise and able minister of Christian education. Since Bob was older and more experienced, Jim felt that he could learn a lot from Bob. Now that they were both living in Cody, California, Jim was hoping that Bob would agree to become his mentor.

As Jim entered his colleague's office, Bob invited him to grab a cup and help himself to the pot of coffee on the table.

"How are things going in your new job?" asked Bob as Jim sat down.

"Fine. Just fine," replied Jim. "But you wouldn't believe the work that needs to be done. It's going to take a major overhaul to get things into shape."

"Just be careful that you don't move too quickly," cautioned Bob. "Remember that a good gardener prepares the soil before he plants his seed. Even then, it takes a lot of time, loving care, and attention to produce the lovely blossoms that he wants."

When Bob heard that Jim was leading his workers through the evaluation process, he asked: "Are you using a checklist as you examine your educational program?"

"What do you mean?" asked Jim.

Bob explained, "Many large denominations and Christian publishers print a set of standards to help churches assess their members, plans, and programs. When a leader compares his organization with these benchmarks, he can quickly see which areas need to be improved. "Let me show you what I mean."

Bob went over to a beat-up file cabinet and sifted through a number of papers. After a few seconds, he turned, handed Jim a neatly-typed list of questions, and suggested: "Here's something that I've used in the past. Why don't you look it over and tell me what you think."

As Jim glanced at the following sheet, he thought to himself: *This has real possibilities.*

Community

1. What kind of reputation does the church have in the community? Don't guess. Ask the neighbors.
2. How would you describe the racial, financial, and family make-up of the community?
3. Do you have special programs which are designed to meet the needs of the community?
4. Are members actively involved in the affairs of the community?
5. Is the pastor an active member of community organizations?

Outreach

1. Over the last ten years, has attendance increased, decreased, or remained stable?
2. How do you advertise the church in the community?
3. How is Sunday School promoted within the church?
4. Does the Sunday School have a list of prospective students that it is trying to reach?
5. How are visitors welcomed and made to feel at home in the Sunday School program?
6. How are visitors followed up?
7. Do teachers telephone, write, or visit their students when they're absent?
8. When special events such as birthdays and anniversaries occur in the lives of students, do teachers acknowl-

edge them with a comment, card, telephone call, or party?

9. How many pupils have dropped out of Sunday School in the last three years?

10. How are people followed up when they stop coming to Sunday School?

11. Are people coming to know Jesus Christ as their Savior through the Sunday School program?

12. Do most members want the Sunday School to grow?

13. Is the church's visitation program properly coordinated with the educational organizations—including your Sunday School?

Records

1. Are permanent, accurate, up-to-date records kept on every Sunday School student?

2. How often do teachers use the Sunday School's records to minister to their students?

3. How are records used to improve your Sunday School program?

Organization

1. Are classes too large, too small, or just the right size for effective teaching?

2. Does the Sunday School staff cooperate with each other and exhibit a team spirit?

3. Is the Sunday School properly represented in the decision-making process of the church?

4. Are the educational efforts of the church properly coordinated?

5. Do the educational workers and agencies communicate well with each other?

Staffing

1. Is each area of the educational program properly staffed?

2. How are teachers and workers enlisted?

3. Are high standards maintained in the recruitment of workers?

4. When regular teachers or workers are absent, are enough well-trained substitutes available to take their places?

5. Before each worker assumes a new position, is he provided with a complete, up-to-date job description which details his responsibilities?

6. Are workers enthused about their ministries?

7. What is the usual tenure of teachers?

8. Does the Sunday School have a systematic, effective way to evaluate workers?

Training

1. Do your teachers and workers receive sufficient training before they begin their jobs?

2. What kind and how much training is provided for the regular teaching staff?

3. Are members encouraged to read books and attend conferences to enhance their job skills?

4. Do educational leaders receive an adequate amount of training?

5. Are training seminars well-attended?

Facilities, Equipment, Supplies, and Materials

1. Is the church easily accessible to those in the community?

2. Is the outside of the church building attractive and appealing?

3. Does the church provide sufficient parking for those who attend?

4. Are classrooms attractive and clean?

5. Are facilities, equipment, and materials safe to use?

6. Are rooms sufficiently heated and cooled during the year?

7. Is the building well-maintained and in good repair?

8. Are facilities built to be flexible?

9. Does the church have enough storage space?

10. Is such equipment as tables and chairs in each classroom suitable for the age group that uses it?

11. Are there enough materials and equipment for each class to use?

12. Are rooms well-lighted?

13. Is the size and shape of each room suitable for the groups that use them?

14. If rooms are used by more than one group, are there policies which govern their coordinated use?

15. Are teaching materials evaluated periodically?

16. Are there enough up-to-date audio-visual aids available to teachers?

17. Is there an adequate method of arranging the use of shared equipment?

18. Do teachers use all of the materials with which they are provided?

19. Do students frequently use their Bibles during their lessons?

Finances

1. Does the Sunday School have adequate input into the church's budget process?

2. Are accurate records kept of all financial transactions?

3. Does the church provide enough money for its Sunday School ministry?

4. Are adequate safeguards built into your financial arrangements and procedures?

Planning

1. Are plans, projects, programs, and events periodically evaluated?

2. How creative are plans, projects, events, and programs?

3. Does the Sunday School have clear-cut goals that are known to the entire staff?

4. Does the Sunday School have adequate input and representation in the decision-making process of the church?

5. Are Sunday School's plans coordinated with plans of other organizations of the church?

6. Is the scheduling of all church activities properly coordinated through a central person or church calendar?

7. Are Sunday School activities planned far enough in advance?

BIBLE

After Jim had a chance to digest the questionnaire, Bob said, "As you examine your activities, Jim, don't forget your most obvious evaluation tool—the Bible.

"Do you remember, for example, how the Israelites used the Word of God to evaluate their practices in Nehemiah 13?"

Jim didn't. But he wasn't going to admit that to Bob. Instead he just nodded and flashed a "sure-I-know-what-you're-talking-about" smile that encouraged Bob to continue.

"If you examine that passage, you'll notice that the Israelites went through a three-step process as they compared their practices with God's will. First of all, they were attentive to God's Word. They read it aloud so that all of the people could find out how God wanted them to act. Second, as the Book of Moses was being read, they discovered that they hadn't followed God's command to exclude the Ammonites and the Moabites from their assembly. Third, once the Israelites realized the discrepancy between God's standards and their own behavior, they acted immediately and decisively to set things straight. So they separated themselves from all of the people who were of foreign descent.

"Jim, I wish more churches would be like those Israelites. Wouldn't it be wonderful if Christian leaders would ask such questions as: Are our goals consistent with the Scriptures? Do we select our staff according to godly principles? Are our methods and motivations based on biblical standards? Is our attitude toward money, recreational activities, people, and possessions pleasing to God?"

COMPONENT ANALYSIS

"Jim, I know I've been talking a lot this afternoon," Bob confessed. "But before you go, can I share with you just one more device that you might want to include in your evaluation toolbox?"

"Sure, I'm eager to learn," said Jim.

Relieved at his young colleague's willingness to listen, Bob went on. "Every Christian leader needs to conduct a component analysis at least once a year."

"You've lost me again," admitted Jim. "What do you mean by component analysis?"

Bob explained, "The component analysis method consists of a two-part procedure. In the first step, you break down an activity into its component parts. Then, in the second step, you examine each facet of that ministry and ask the question 'How can we improve this area?' The more detailed your breakdown, the better your evaluation will be.

"Let me illustrate what I mean. Let's say you wanted to evaluate your Sunday School program. Begin by dividing its activities into such categories as—recruitment, teaching, facilities, promotion, organization, and outreach.

Then dissect each of these areas into even smaller parts. For example, if you wanted to look at the area of 'outreach,' you'd want to consider:

- the reason why a visitor comes

- the visitor's arrival at the church

- the greeting that the visitor receives at the church door

- the visitor's discovery of an appropriate Sunday School classroom for himself

- the greeting that the visitor receives at the classroom door

- the building of relationships during the classroom session

- the acquisition of the student's name and address

- the follow-up after the class session is over

"Take each of these components and ask: 'How can efforts in this area be improved?' Your examination might lead you to build a bigger church sign, provide visitors with Sunday School brochures, or assign greeters to each classroom. Do you see what I mean?"

"Sure," said Jim. "Those are great ideas. I can't wait to get back to the church and try them out."

TRACKING TRENDS

When Jim arrived at his office, he had a stack of telephone messages waiting for him. People were definitely starting to realize that Bethel Baptist had a new staff member.

Before Jim could return any of the calls, however, the phone rang. The voice on the other end sounded pleasant but unfamiliar.

"Hi, Jim. This is Barry Shoemaker from Grainville Church. I'm the workshop chairman for the Cody Lake Area Sunday School Convention which is going to be held in October. At the conference, I'd like to have some of our Christian education ministers form a panel and discuss some of the trends that will be affecting them during the next ten years. We're going to call the workshop 'Facing the Future.'"

The topic intrigued Jim, and he responded eagerly. "I presume that you'll be talking about the impact that computers, videos, and other technological advances will be having upon the church."

"Actually our scope will be even broader than that," said Barry. "We also want to discuss the way our family and community structures are changing. We'll be talking also about the ramifications of some new zoning laws, tax regulations, and recent school board decisions.

"Bob Sparkman said that you'd be a great person to include in our group. So we'd like you to join us on the panel."

Jim agreed. "Sounds great! You can count on me."

"Good. I'll call you back with more details when I've recruited the rest of the team."

As Jim gently put the telephone down, he thanked God for this wonderful opportunity. Jim relished the chance to meet some of the other ministers of Christian education in the area and to establish his credentials as a resource person. He could see that this workshop would benefit his own church's ministry. Tracking trends would enable his members to take a proactive rather than a reactive or inactive stance. This would help them to seize opportunities that others would miss.

Jim's musings came to an abrupt halt, when he noticed what time it was. Thinking about the workshop would have to wait for another day. Right now, there was only one infallible prediction that concerned him—Jill's reaction if he didn't make it home in time for supper.

QUESTIONS

Two weeks later, Jim was feeling good about the progress that he was making in identifying the church's needs. Still, he thought he could use more input from the church members and the educational leaders themselves. At this stage, they knew the church's history, situation, and people far better than he did. So he decided to follow Jesus' lead and ask questions—lots of probing and pertinent questions.[5]

To tap his people's knowledge and insights, Jim used a three-pronged approach.

He set up a meeting with his educational leaders to talk about their hopes and dreams for the future.

He called individual teachers at home and talked with them about their joys and frustrations.

He made it a point to ask people in casual conversations about their attitude toward the church's educational program.

Of course, Jim realized that raising questions during the course of a normal conversation was not the only way to poll people about their opinions. The church council at his home church had decided to take a more formal approach. To discover the needs, attitudes, and priorities of their church's membership, these leaders were going to send out the following questionnaire.

Select the seven key emphases that you think our church should pursue during the coming year.

____ 1. More vibrant worship services

____ 2. Increased church fellowship

____ 3. More vital messages

____ 4. Additional staff in the following areas:

      _____

      _____

____ 5. More prayer emphasis

____ 6. Better counseling ministry

____ 7. Stronger youth ministry

____ 8. Stronger music ministry

____ 9. Stronger educational ministry

____10. Better recreation facilities and athletic programs

____11. More fellowship with like-minded churches

____12. Establishment of a Christian school

____13. Establishment of a deaf ministry

____14. Establishment of a ministry to the mentally or physically challenged

___ 15. Establishment of separate men's and women's organizations

___ 16. Establishment of a ministry to those with drug dependencies.

___ 17. Better communication within the church

___ 18. Better teacher training program

___ 19. Increased evangelistic thrust in the community

___ 20. Better parking facilities

___ 21. Improved educational facilities

___ 22. Development of a mission outreach to:

_____

_____

___ 23. Renovation of worship facilities

___ 24. Better maintenance of present facilities

___ 25. Better ministry to the financially needy

___ 26. Increased emphasis on home Bible studies

Comments:

_____

_____

_____

COMPLAINTS

Shortly after starting his new job at Bethel Church, Jim discovered another method of evaluation which, at first, left him very frustrated. One Sunday, just before the evening service was about to begin, he was approached by Mrs. Rutledge—one of his faithful preschool teachers. Before Jim could greet her, she demanded: "Why can't my son go on the young people's skiing retreat?

"It just doesn't seem right that all of Jerry's friends can go and he can't," she continued. "Frankly, I don't think you did a very good job of planning this event."

Jim was stunned. As Mrs. Rutledge shredded his ego with her cutting remarks, Jim thought: *Lady, haven't you ever heard of the verse that says, "Do everything without complaining or arguing, so that you may become blameless and pure, children of God?"*[6] *Obviously not!*

Although Jim didn't express those thoughts out loud, he wasn't about to let her comments go unchallenged. With great difficulty, he calmly tried to explain: "The camp requires knowing, in advance, exactly how many students will be coming. And, that information was due by January 24. When Jerry asked if he could go, it was already too late."

Mrs. Rutledge shot back, "Well, couldn't you have just padded the numbers and said that more people would be coming than had originally signed up. There are a lot of parents, like me, who would love to send their kids to camp—if you'd just give them a chance."

In frustration, Jim protested: "Camp Woodlands requires us to pay, in advance, for all of the students that we tell them will be coming—whether they show up or not. There are no exceptions and no refunds. So if I pad the numbers, as you want me to do, and fewer young people than I anticipate go on the trip, it's going to cost the church a great deal of extra money."

Then the crux of the problem finally came out. Mrs. Rutledge complained bitterly, "Well, I wish I had known that a couple of weeks ago. I missed your warning about the retreat's deadline because we were gone the two weekends that you announced it in the church bulletin."

In an effort to placate his aggressive church member, Jim proposed what he thought was a reasonable solution. He suggested, "We can put Jerry's name on a waiting list in case one of our other campers can't attend."

Mrs. Rutledge, however, rejected this offer as totally unacceptable. She didn't like the uncertainty that it created.

Before Jim could plead his case any further, Mrs. Rutledge left in disgust. As she stomped off, Jim could hear her mutter under her breath, "If that's the way this church is going to treat its members, I don't know how much longer I'll continue to attend. Or, maybe, I should just stop teaching."

Jim had great difficulty sleeping that night. One question repeatedly interrupted his rest, "Is this the thanks that I get for doing the Lord's work?"

The next morning, Jim headed directly for the pastor's office. He wanted to tell Pastor Grant how upset he was over the whole episode. And, hopefully, he would gain a sympathetic audience before Mrs. Rutledge could press her case with his boss.

Although Pastor Grant was sympathetic, he gave Jim some advice that Jim didn't want to hear. In a fatherly tone of voice, Pastor Grant counseled: "You know Jim, it's much easier to accept praise than criticism. However, in the long run, criticism can be much more useful. The Bible says, 'Do not rebuke a mocker or he will hate you; rebuke a wise man and he will love you. Instruct a wise man and he will be wiser still; teach a righteous man and he will add to his learning.'[7]

"Now, we can treat complaints as irritating annoyances. Or, we can treat them as opportunities—opportunities to remedy problems and serve our fellow believers. I think the latter approach is the better one. In fact, it'd probably be a good idea if we'd take the initiative more often and ask our people to share their problems and constructive suggestions with us."

At that point in the conversation, Shirley Higgens entered Pastor Grant's office with a message. To Jim's surprise, Pastor Grant told Shirley about the problem that Jim was having and invited her to stay so that they could discuss the matter.

"Shirley," Pastor Grant asked, "How do you handle criticism?"

"Well, I try to avoid it as much as possible by doing a good job," laughed the church's secretary.

"But when it comes your way . . ." prompted the pastor.

"Well, I first try to listen to the criticism. And, that's not easy. When someone criticizes me, my natural impulse is to become angry and defensive. I want to lash out and argue with my critics.

"Of course, this only makes matters worse. An argumentative response builds barriers rather than bridges. "That's why the Bible recommends a different approach.[8] It urges us to remain cool, calm, and collected. And, above all, it asks people to try to understand what is being said.

"If we take the time to listen quietly and patiently to our critics, we'll profit from the experience. Listening to criticism helps us gain information about a problem. It allows critics to vent their feelings. And, it shows people that we value them and their ideas."

Pastor Grant smiled approvingly at the church secretary and added, "It also gives us the time that we need to consider our response."

"That's right," agreed Shirley.

Jim squirmed in his chair. He felt like he was being unfairly double-teamed. If Shirley noticed his uneasiness, she didn't show it. She just continued to respond to Pastor Grant's question.

"After I've heard what a person wants to say, I guess the next thing I do is try to determine the validity of his criticism. I ask myself such questions as:

- How reliable is this person's information?

- Are his stories and supposed facts one-sided?

- What are the critic's credentials?

- What are his motives?

- Is the person's reasoning logical and godly?"

Pastor Grant leaned forward and added, "We could also ask:

- Does the person over-generalize and use such words as *always*, *everyone*, and *never*?

- Does the person have positive, constructive suggestions or is the criticism just destructive?

- Are his assumptions correct?

- Are there any inconsistencies or discrepancies in his story?

- Does his reasoning fit the facts?"

"After hearing the complaint and screening it through those type of questions," said Shirley, "it's time to examine our own lives or our group's actions and ask if the criticism is valid.

"Many times, God's people are attacked unjustly. For example, Moses and Nehemiah were often unfairly criticized just because they were trying to carry out God's commands.[9]

"However, if we're being attacked, we'd better be sure that it's not because we've done something wrong. Too frequently our wounds are self-inflicted. For example, Jacob was the recipient of Esau's wrath—not because he was living a godly life but because he tricked, manipulated, and deceived some of his own family members.[10]

"That's why Peter tells us that if we suffer or we're treated harshly, it ought to be because of the cause of Christ and not because we've done something that's evil."[11]

"After we've done all of these things," said Pastor Grant, "then it's time to respond to our critics. If we agree with the complaint, we need to take several steps. We should:

1. Thank our critic for bringing the matter to our attention.

2. Admit that we were wrong or that the situation needs to be improved.

3. Tell him that we're sorry for what has happened.

4. Ask for God's forgiveness—if the issue is a moral one.

5. Formulate a plan of action to correct the situation.

6. Take steps to see that this plan is carried out.

7. Report back to our critic and tell him or her what action we've taken to solve the problem.

8. Learn from the experience so that we won't repeat it again."

Jim protested, "Of course, the critics aren't always right."
Pastor Grant nodded his head in agreement. "That's absolutely true. In that case, we need to:

1. Pray to God for love and strength in answering the criticism.

2. Thank the critic for bringing the matter to our attention.

3. State that we disagree with their criticism.

4. Explain our position kindly but firmly.[12]

5. Bring the conversation to a close.

6. Continue despite the opposition.[13]

7. Refuse to harbor a grudge against our opponent."[14]

Shirley added, "Of course, sometimes we won't agree or disagree with a complaint. When this happens, we need to check into the problem or tell our critic that we need more time to think about the situation."

"If we do that, we'd better make sure that we get back to the person as soon as possible and explain our findings or our decision," added Jim.

"Exactly!" said Shirley. She was relieved that Jim was finally starting to take part in their "discussion."

"There's also a fourth course of action we can take," added Jim. "When we disagree with a complaint, sometimes it's wise just to say nothing. Further arguments and explanations sometimes serve only to antagonize the critic. This strategy is especially valuable when the issue involved is trivial, the critic has made up his mind, or there's no way to correct the situation because the event has already occurred."

As the church staff ended their discussion of this thorny issue, Jim left regretting that he had ever brought this subject to his boss's attention. He didn't want to admit to everyone that he was having problems.

Jim also wondered if his coworkers' advice wasn't all too pat. It sounded like a utopian Sunday School lesson meant only for people who lived in a perfect world. *I wonder how they'd respond if I criticized them?* he thought. *Would they really take my criticism so calmly?*

Despite his misgivings, however, Jim realized that they had offered some helpful and scriptural suggestions.

He also had to admit that he could have handled his disagreement with Mrs. Rutledge differently. For one thing, he should have asked Mrs. Rutledge to come into his office where he could have discussed the matter in private. Although he objected to her tone of voice and her arguments, he should have been more sympathetic toward her feelings of frustration. Most importantly, he should have done a better job of warning parents about the deadline requirements for the skiing retreat.

In addition, he thought he could have tried harder to find out if the camp would make an exception for Mrs. Rutledge's son. Now, however, he hated to do that because it might look as if he was capitulating to her threats and emotional blackmail.

Despite his misgivings, he decided to call the camp administrator and ask if he could bring some extra campers. Surprisingly, she agreed. The camp had had some last-minute cancellations and was therefore able to accommodate Jim.

Mrs. Rutledge was amazed when Jim called later that day to tell her the good news. Through this experience, she had discovered that Jim was really trying to do his best to minister to all of the church's young people. Likewise, Jim had learned an important lesson: complaints can be disguised opportunities to learn and to improve.

While Jim was still getting acquainted with his congregation and maintaining the regular church programs that he had inherited, he continued to evaluate his situation. As he did, he was encouraged by much of what he saw. He knew, however, that he had a lot of work to do.

After a couple of months of scrutinizing his church's educational program, Jim took stock of what he had learned up to that point. He began his review by taking out two sheets of paper. On the first one, he wrote simply "Methods." On the second sheet, he wrote "Results."

Under the first category, he wrote down the basic tools that he had used to make his evaluation:

• observation	• forecasting
• checklists	• questions
• the Bible	• criticism
• component analysis	

Under the second category, he jotted down the following notes.

- **Opportunities to seize:**

  We're located one block from Christopher College; yet we have no ministry to young single adults.

  We have many unchurched children in our neighborhood.

- **Needs to meet:**

  Quite a few of our shut-ins would like to hear tapes of our services.

- **Resources to utilize:**

  Nancy North is able to sign for deaf children.

  We have a fine gym that is underutilized.

  Holly Smith is a coach at Christopher College.

  Dan Rivers is an excellent artist who works at a graphics company. Currently, he's not serving anywhere.

- **Trends to consider:**

  We have a growing number of young couples with young children.

  Fewer people are becoming involved in the church's evening activities.

  An increasing number of mothers are now working.

  Many of our members are taking adult education courses in the evening.

- **Strengths on which to capitalize:**

  We live in a new community into which many people are moving.

  We have many people who are musically talented.

- **Expectations to fulfill:**

  Pastor Grant wants the Sunday School to grow.

  The congregation wants to expand the number of church programs that we offer.

- **Problems to fix:**

  Our classrooms need to be painted.

  Storage cabinets need to be provided in our classrooms.

  Mike Todd's classroom gets too hot in the summer.

- **Weaknesses to eliminate or minimize:**

  Our Sunday School is making little effort to reach new members.

  Our teachers have never been taught how to lead a child to Christ.

  Few teachers make an effort to get acquainted with their students outside of their classrooms.

It was an impressive list. Jim's hard work had been amply rewarded. However, Jim knew that if he wanted to make a difference in the life of his church, his real ministry of improvement had just begun. Now he had to translate his assessments into specific goals and lay out a strategy for reaching those targets.

POINTS TO PONDER

1. Why are first impressions sometimes wrong?

2. Why is it important to size up a situation before trying to change it?

3. How long should a new staff member wait before he starts to make major changes?

4. Was it a good idea for Jim to give into Mrs. Rutledge's complaints?

5. Why is it easier to be a critic rather than an agent of constructive change?

6. What steps can churches take to help new staff members get their ministries off to a good start?

7. What steps can new staff members take to learn the names and the personalities of their church members?

PRACTICAL PROJECTS

1. Evaluate your church's Sunday School program and then develop a list of recommended changes.

2. Examine your church's educational records. List several ways they could be improved.

2

Where Am I Heading?

(GOAL SETTING)

Dynamic leaders have dynamic goals. They have a burning vision for what they want to accomplish for God in the future. And, what's more, they're actively working to realize these dreams. What do you and your group want to accomplish during the next year? the next three months? the next month? the next week? The answers to these questions define your goals and will have a significant impact upon your activities and performance.

As Jim read these stimulating words in one of his favorite Christian education magazines, he leaped to his feet and shouted: "Things have got to change. Tomorrow is D-Day, destination day."

Jill, who was busy in the kitchen, answered nonchalantly: "Jim, did you say something?"

Despite his wife's inattention, Jim continued to share his thoughts. "So far, in my ministry, we've maintained a rather low profile. We've spent a lot of time getting acquainted with the church—its people and its programs.

"That's been fun. But, now, it's time to enter a new phase. It's time to sharpen our focus and establish our goals. It's time to aggressively tackle the long-term needs and opportunities that our church faces." Jim's voice began to rise with each new phrase.

"After all, I don't want to spend my entire ministry running around and extinguishing one problematic 'fire' after another or mechanically maintaining the status quo. It's time for action!"

Jill, who by this time in their marriage had grown accustomed to such impromptu inspirational messages, calmly agreed. "You're absolutely right. Now, let's sit down to eat before the food gets cold."

Barb and Brenda came bouncing down the stairs in response to Jill's call. They were ready to enjoy their mother's cooking.

But Jim's thoughts were far from dinner. He was mentally choosing his targets and forming his plan of attack. Jim could hardly wait to share his ideas with Pastor Grant.

CHARACTERISTICS OF GOOD GOALS

His opportunity came the next morning. About ten o'clock, Jim sauntered over to the tall coffee urn which was a frequent meeting place for the church's staff.

"Well, Jim, how are things going?" inquired Pastor Grant as he got his coffee. His question seemed casual and perfunctory, but it gave Jim the opening that he needed to discuss some of his concerns.

"Great," Jim responded enthusiastically. "In fact, if you have some time, I'd like to talk to you a little about the church's educational ministry."

"Sure, let's go back to my office."

As Pastor Grant ushered the young Christian education director into his book-lined office, he asked, "What do you have on your mind?"

Jim struck a positive tone. "During the last couple of months, I've had a chance to get to know our people and programs quite well. And, in the process of evaluating our educational program, I've discovered that we have some very effective ministries. At the same time, however, I've noticed that we have a few problems that need some attention.

"So, this year, I'm going to try to accomplish basically five things in the educational arena. I want to provide better facilities, improve our teacher training, increase our outreach, expand the number of adult Sunday School classes, and improve our recruitment efforts."

Pastor Grant marveled at the eagerness of his young assistant. It reminded him of his first pastorate and the way he had entered that ministry with so much idealistic zeal.

With an approving nod, he complimented Jim. "That sounds great! I can see that you've discovered some of our most urgent needs. Now, let's get down to specifics. What are your goals for this year?"

Jim was a bit perplexed. "Well, like I said . . . I want us to provide better facilities, improve our teacher training, increase our outreach . . ."

Pastor Grant interrupted Jim midway through his recitation. "Jim, let me just stop you for a moment and clarify what I meant when I used the word *goals.*"

Reading the puzzlement on Jim's face, Pastor Grant went on to explain, "To me, a *goal* is a specific, measurable statement of what you want to achieve in a relatively short period of time.

"What you've described to me are your objectives. An *objective* is also a statement of what you'd like to accomplish. However, it differs from a goal in three important respects: it is a broad statement, it cannot be measured, and it does not have a termination point.

"Most leaders begin their ministries with a broad idea of what they want to achieve. For example, they may want their people to study their Bibles more frequently, to establish a witness in a foreign country, or to expand an organization's facilities.

"However, that's simply not enough. If they're sharp, these leaders will soon realize that they'll fail—unless they spell out the specifics of their dreams.

"Why? Because vague desires will never galvanize their people into action. In addition, if a goal is too broad, people won't be able to determine if they've really accomplished what they set out to do.

"Let's take your objectives, for example. You said that you wanted to increase your outreach efforts. How will you know when you have reached that objective? Will you have succeeded if only one new person comes to Sunday School? What about five new people?

"Or, did your objective imply that you want to distribute a new brochure, lead more children to Christ, or conduct a witnessing workshop?

"What do the words *increase* and *outreach* really mean to you?

"I guess what I'm saying, Jim, is that the first and most important characteristic of a good goal is that it is specific and measurable. You have some good ideas but you need to sharpen your focus.

"You can make your goals more precise by observing a few important guidelines. First begin your goals with specific action verbs. *Improve, help, increase, develop, and expand* are too vague. Instead, use more tangible verbs like *build, conduct, write,* and *purchase.* These words describe exactly what you expect people to do; and they describe actions that you can observe.

"Second each goal should have a deadline. If you talk in terms of 'someday I will do this' and 'someday I will do that,' that 'someday' will never arrive. So add a phrase which clearly spells out the date on which you expect to complete your goal. Answer the questions: 'When?' 'How often?' or 'How long?' You can attach a time limit to your goals using such phrases as: 'by May 15,' 'on June 6,' 'once a month,' or 'during the month of July.'

"Sometimes, you can also add a time element to your goals by spelling out the conditions under which the goal will be achieved. For example, suppose that you want your teachers to be able to share the gospel message with a child. Your goal then could be: '*When children ask their teachers how to become a Christian*, the teachers will be able to explain the five steps to salvation as they are outlined in our Sunday School tract.'

"Now, let's take a look at some of your other objectives and see if we can transform them into goals by adding some dates and times. You said that you wanted to provide more training for our teachers. Whom do you want to train and what kind of topics would you like to discuss with them?"

"Well, I hadn't thought much about that yet," admitted Jim. "Ah. . . . I think our adult teachers could really benefit from a class on teaching methods."

"Good," affirmed Pastor Grant. "When would you like to conduct these training sessions and for how long?"

"Well," Jim stammered as he thought out loud, "Ah . . . it'll take us a while to lay the groundwork for that. So . . . well, I guess we could hold them in the fall after we give our teachers a chance to become familiar with their new responsibilities. . . . Ah . . . I suppose we would have to talk to our leaders and ask them about the timing for the whole thing, wouldn't we?"

Pastor Grant could see that his new team member was having difficulty making his goals more specific. So the pastor made a suggestion to help Jim out.

"For purposes of illustration," Pastor Grant advised, "why don't we just pick November as your training date. Then you could state your goal something like this: 'On the ninth of November, we will conduct a two-hour training workshop on teaching methods for all of our adult teachers.' How does that sound?"

"Well, that sure is a lot more specific than 'We will improve our teacher training program,'" agreed Jim.

"There's a third way in which you can sharpen your goals," Pastor Grant continued. "With some goals, you can specify a definite quantity that you want to achieve. For example, you can say: 'We will send out one hundred Sunday School brochures.' 'We will add four new preschool teachers.' 'We will increase our average Sunday School attendance to two hundred.'

"You mentioned that you wanted to improve the church's educational facilities. How would you like to do that?"

Without hesitation, Jim volunteered: "Well, for one thing we need to purchase twenty new chairs for our senior adult class."

"Don't forget to add the deadline for that goal's accomplishment," reminded Pastor Grant.

"That's right," beamed Jim. "How's this? By March third, we will buy twenty new chairs for our senior adult Sunday School class."

"Now you're getting the idea," exclaimed a delighted Pastor Grant.

"With some goals, you can spell out the quality that you expect or how well you want the job to be done. For example, a public relations director at a camp could establish a goal like: 'All brochures and correspondence will be sent out with absolutely no spelling errors.'

"Each of your goals should also identify the person who is responsible for its attainment. Even if a project is a team effort, the group needs to know who is going to be in charge; that is, who is going to be held accountable for the goal's success. As managers are fond of saying, 'Everybody's business is nobody's business.'

With some goals you can indicate where the goal's achievement will take place by adding such phrases as 'every house within a mile's radius' or 'at the Alexander Bell School for the Deaf.'

"Boy, it sure looks like you've given this subject a lot of thought," Jim replied with a tone of admiration. "Are there any other things that I should keep in mind when setting goals?"

"I'm glad you asked," Pastor Grant responded with a smile. "Just before you came on staff, our church had a planning retreat. And, it just so happens that I conducted a workshop on goal-setting during that time."

Pastor Grant reached for a big black binder and removed a blue piece of paper which he slid across his well-polished desk toward Jim.

"Here's a handout that I developed for my workshop," the senior pastor remarked. "I hope it'll be helpful. In addition to talking about specific goals, it lists several other characteristics that effective goals should have.

"Take a look at it. Then, after you have a chance to refine your goals, come back to me and let's discuss what you want to see happen in the Christian education area during the next year."

Jim thanked Pastor Grant, returned to his office, and examined the sheet in more detail. As Jim read it over, he noted that the pastor had made the following points.

1. *Effective goals glorify God.* Throughout history, there have been powerful leaders who have set and achieved very ambitious goals. Unfortunately, many of these goals have been evil. They were built on the motivations of domination, destruction, greed, and self-glorification. The Bible tells us, as Christian leaders, that our goals ought to reflect a different kind of motivation. It says, "Whether you eat or drink or whatever you do, do it all for the glory of God" (1 Cor. 10:31).

2. *Effective goals are challenging.* The Bible says, "Where there is no vision, the people perish" (Prov. 29:18, KJV). Daniel Burnham adds, "Make no little plans; they have no magic to stir men's blood."

    Anemic goals are ineffective for at least two reasons. First of all, "Ho-hum," business-as-usual goals don't excite people. You can't arouse a church's enthusiasm with a goal to increase giving by twenty dollars over a five-year span. People want stimulating goals that will challenge them to do their very best.

    Small goals don't require us to depend on God. God is willing to give us even more than we want or than we think is possible (Eph 3:20). Yet we seldom tap His tremendous power because our faith is too weak. We don't set our sights high enough and then, amazingly, we ask why the presence of God isn't evident in our ministry. The answer may be that we haven't had the courage to dream dreams and see visions that only God could bring about.

    So let your mind soar. Don't limit God with your feelings of inadequacy. Seek His will and then trust Him to supply the resources that you'll need for the task.

3. *Effective goals are realistic and attainable.* When unrealistic goals are set, people become so overwhelmed that they're easily discouraged. Some don't even attempt to achieve a hand-me-down goal because they

believe that their assignment is too hopeless. If people do try to tackle a formidable task and fail, they become reluctant to undertake similar projects in the future.

It's unreasonable to expect a soprano to sing bass in a quartet. It's equally unrealistic to expect a group to evangelize the world in two days. However, missionary organizations can set realistic goals that attempt to win less people over a longer period of time and still be a success in the eyes of God.

How do you resolve the tension between setting challenging yet realistic goals? That's a difficult question to answer and demands a personal reply. If you're new to goal setting, you should probably start with modest expectations. However, if you're an experienced goal setter who has experienced God's blessing in your endeavors, then you should aim high—even when your expectations seem rather ambitious to others. Keep in mind that even overwhelming tasks can be made more manageable by breaking them down into smaller steps. As one maxim says, "Inch by inch, anything is a cinch."

4. *Effective goals are simple and concise.* Instead of trying to include every idea in one long cumbersome goal, aim for brevity. You can clarify complex goals in three ways:

   (1) Use simple, understandable words and phrases.

   (2) Limit yourself to one goal per statement.

   (3) Make your statements short enough to be easily memorized.

5. *Effective goals are compatible and consistent with each other.* The best way to achieve this compatibility is to begin with your primary goals and work backwards. If your primary goal is to start six neighborhood Bible clubs for children, you'll have to set a number of secondary goals to support this main goal. Your secondary goals could include: (1) select and prepare a series of twelve Bible club sessions, (2) enlist six people to lead the Bible clubs and six families to host the club meetings, and (3) prepare a flyer and distribute it to all of the homes within a mile radius of the Bible club site.

GROUP GOALS

Jim emerged from his office with a glint of anticipation in his eye. Before leaving the church, he said to Shirley, "Tomorrow I'm going up to Sherman Woods. I'm going to spend the day thinking and writing out my goals for the year. If anyone calls, tell them I'll be back on Friday.

"Oh, and set up an appointment with Pastor Grant for Friday morning. I'd like to share my goals with him when I get back."

Early the next morning, with Pastor Grant's handout and his evaluation notes in his briefcase, Jim headed toward his favorite campground. After some time of reflection and many revisions (as evidenced by the wadded up balls of paper in a nearby trash can), Jim started to smile with satisfaction.

"Setting goals isn't as difficult as I first thought," said Jim to himself. "All you have to do is spell out the three essential parts of a good goal: the deadline, the expected results, and the person who is responsible for the realization of the goal."

Before leaving the serenity of the woods, Jim looked over the following list of his group goals one last time.

Area	When?	What?	Who?
PROGRAMMING	Sept. 15	1. Start a single's group for students who attend Christopher College.	Phil Tagger
	Sept. 15	2. Start a new Sunday School class for deaf children.	Nancy North
	Nov. 1	3. Develop an athletic program which utilizes our church gym.	Holly Smith
	May 12	4. Provide tapes of the morning and evening services for shut-ins and other interested individuals who request them.	Tom Brown
OUTREACH	Dec. 22	1. Increase average Sunday School attendance to 300 people.	Mary Black
	Mar. 3	2. Design and print a brochure that describes all of the educational ministries in the church.	Jim Stafford
	Nov. 9	3. Conduct a three-hour workshop entitled "How to Lead a Child to Christ."	Jim Stafford
	Dec. 31	4. Persuade each teacher to call or send a postcard to a student whenever he is absent or has a birthday.	Mary Black
TEACHER TRAINING	Nov. 9	1. Conduct a three-hour workshop on "Teaching Methods" for present and potential adult teachers.	Jim Stafford
	May 12	2. Write a leader's manual for the VBS director.	Jim Stafford
	Sept. 15	3. Provide a teacher training book for each of our new teachers at the outset of their teaching ministry.	Kelly Rivers

Area	When?	What?	Who?
MATERIAL RESOURCES	Sept. 15	1. Build storage cabinets in the children's classrooms.	Susan White
	Sept. 15	2. Examine and repair all equipment in the resource center.	Kelly Rivers
	Nov. 1	3. Paint all of the classrooms.	Jim Stafford
	June 2	4. Install an air conditioner in Mike Todd's classroom.	Susan White
	July 7	5. Purchase 20 new chairs for the senior adult class.	Dennis Hall
STAFFING	Sept. 15	1. Recruit two more assistant teachers for the kindergarten class.	Rose Adams
	Oct. 6	2. Personally talk with every new member about his opportunities for involvement in the church's educational program.	Chad Blue
	Sept. 15	3. Have Sunday School teachers create their own teachers' covenant.	Mary Black
TEAM RELATIONSHIPS	Dec. 31	1. Pray for each education worker at least once a week.	Jim Stafford
	Dec. 31	Hold a leadership meeting once a month.	Jim Stafford
	Nov. 22	3. Conduct an appreciation banquet for all of the educational workers.	Jim Stafford
FINANCES	Dec. 22	1. Raise $500 for our Christmas missionary project.	Linda West
	May 5	2. Review and revise our financial policies and procedures manual.	Katie Miller
	Dec. 31	3. Increase our Sunday School offerings by 5%.	Linda West

PERSONAL GOALS

Jim relaxed and savored his accomplishment for a moment. It was a good feeling to be able to set down his agenda for the year. Yet, something still bothered him.

"If organizational goals are so important in the life of my church," he thought, "why haven't I written down any personal goals for myself?"

Jim opened his briefcase, pulled out his thin notebook, and began to write with renewed intensity. When he was finished, the list of his personal goals looked like this:

Spiritual Goals

1. Read the entire New Testament twice this year.

2. Memorize one new scripture verse each week.

3. Conduct a ten-minute, daily devotional time with the family.

4. Spend at least fifteen minutes in prayer each day.

5. Read one Christian book each month that is unrelated to my work.

Physical Goals

1. Weigh 180 pounds by the end of the year.

2. Walk thirty minutes, three times a week.

3. Be able to swim thirty continuous laps in the YMCA swimming pool by the end of this year.

Social Goals

1. Write or call my parents, my brothers, and my sister at least once every two weeks.

2. Join a computer club this year.

3. Invite one or two families from the church over for coffee and cake once a month.

4. Write a letter to one missionary every month.

5. Meet at least one new couple each month and get to know their occupations, the names of their family members, and where they grew up.

Mental/Educational Goals

1. Attend an adult education course this year to learn German.

2. Read one book on Christian leadership once each month.

Financial/Material Goals

1. Save $2,000 in our family's savings account this year.

2. Buy a new bedroom set this year.

3. Paint the living room.

Travel/Recreational Goals

1. Spend two weeks vacationing in Oregon this year.

2. Visit Yosemite National Park in August.

Professional Goals

1. In September, start working on my Master of Divinity degree.

2. Become the publicity chairman for this year's Cody Lake Area Sunday School (CLASS) Convention.

PRINCIPLES OF GOAL-SETTING

Early Friday morning, Jim strode into Pastor Grant's office with an air of excitement and expectation. He proudly presented a neatly typed sheet to the senior pastor and announced, "Here are my goals for this coming year. I went up to Sherman Woods yesterday and worked on them all day."

Pastor Grant peered at the piece of paper for an unbearable length of time—at least in Jim's eyes. Pastor Grant's initial smile gradually faded as he read through the goals. Finally, Jim couldn't control his eagerness any longer. Before Pastor Grant could finish, Jim blurted out, "Well, what do you think?"

Before answering Jim's leading question, Pastor Grant deliberately paused (as if to ponder how he was going to break some bad news). "Well, Jim I see that you've put a lot of work into outlining your vision for the future," remarked his boss. "You've followed my handout's guidelines very well. All of your goals are clearly and precisely framed."

Jim appreciated the encouragement, but he could tell from Pastor Grant's expression and tone of voice that his goals didn't quite measure up to his senior pastor's standards.

After hesitating slightly, Pastor Grant continued with his positive evaluation a while longer. "Jim, I'm glad that you've written your goals down on paper. That's one of the cardinal principles of good goal setting. It shows me that you've made a strong commitment to these goals. Once you've documented your vision, it becomes hard to discard or revise your goals just because you are not meeting your target dates.

"I'm a little concerned, however, because . . ."

Here it comes, thought Jim apprehensively.

"Your goals look rather ambitious, especially the ones that you've set for your own personal life," observed Pastor Grant. "Frankly, in your zeal to set these goals, I think you've given yourself an impossible task. You're just trying to do too much."

Jim felt hurt. He had listened to Pastor Grant's advice about goal setting. Then he had spent a whole day carefully crafting each of his goals. And now, instead of greeting his efforts with applause, Pastor Grant was treating them with skepticism.

Jim struggled to listen to this needed, but unwanted advice. He fought to control his emotions and apply a lesson that he had learned only a short time earlier: "when criticism comes your way, listen and learn."

"I've learned through hard experience," Pastor Grant continued, "that you have to *limit the number of goals that you pursue at one time.* Otherwise, you'll end up terribly frustrated because you won't have enough resources and energy to bring your visions to fruition. Oh, you may achieve partial successes in some of your efforts. But so many goals will remain unfinished that you may decide that goal-setting is a useless pursuit.

"Sit down with these goals—and they are good goals—and prayerfully rank them in order of their priority. Then select those goals on which you want to concentrate. This doesn't mean that your other goals will never be pursued. What it does mean is that you'll tackle the important jobs first."

As he looked at his goals, Jim knew that Pastor Grant was right. He realized that his list included more things than he could possibly expect to achieve in one year. So he vowed to set his priorities by examining his goals in light of several crucial questions.

1. Which goals are really important in God's eyes?

2. Which goals are most likely to succeed?

3. Which goals need to be accomplished before other goals can proceed?

4. In what areas are we especially qualified to do the job because of our location, facilities, or talents?

5. Which goals will stimulate the most interest in our people and, therefore, receive the most support?

6. Which goals will produce the most results with the least amount of invested resources?

7. Which goals allow us to minister to the most people?

8. In which areas have we already been effective?

9. In which areas are most of our people already involved?

10. How urgent is the need?

11. Which of these goals can be accomplished more effectively by someone else? Are other groups or individuals already meeting needs in the areas that we are examining?

12. What will happen if we do not attempt this goal?

13. In which areas can we achieve the quickest results?

14. What contribution does this goal make toward achieving our long-term goals?

15. Five years from now, will anybody care that we achieved this goal?

"Do you have any other suggestions?" probed Jim. The question rushed out before he realized how dangerous this question could be to his ego.

Pastor Grant welcomed the question because he wasn't through with his evaluation yet. He still wanted to make a few more recommendations to his energetic associate.

"Well . . . let me ask you a question, Jim. Have you asked any of your team or family members how they feel about your goals?"

"Well, no, not really."

"If you're planning to invite one or two families over for coffee and cake once a month, for instance, you'd be wise to check that out with Jill."

"I see what you mean."

"This brings me to a third principle that you need to keep in mind when setting goals," counseled Pastor Grant. *"A good leader should always involve his people in setting their own goals.* When you do that, three things will happen. (1) Your team members will be more likely to accomplish their goals. (2) Your group's goals will be more realistic. (3) Your people will have a much clearer understanding of what is expected of them.

"In addition to the three principles which I've already mentioned, let me just quickly cover three more *First, develop a plan for achieving your goals.* Goals that aren't supported with plans and actions are not really goals at all. They're merely dreams and desires. They're never meant to be accomplished.

"I know a lot of people who have had big dreams, ambitious plans, and good intentions but they've failed miserably. They've failed because they didn't have the courage to work out the specific details of their ideas. If you want to reach your goals, you have to spell out exactly what you and others must do to bring them about.

"Second, support your goals with the resources that are required to get the job done. It's easy for a leader to make promises about what he wants to do. Promises cost people nothing. However, if you really want to realize your goal, you'll have to 'put your money where your mouth is.'

"Third, establish goals that are suited to our church's unique situation. Sometimes, when one group discovers that another group is doing something well, it often copies that organization's program—detail for detail. However, this approach often fails because it doesn't take into account the mimicking group's special abilities and circumstances.

"For example, our church can't possibly provide a large, age-graded choir program like First Church can. For one thing, their congregation is three times larger than ours. But we can capitalize on the fact that we're close to Christopher College; First Church can't possibly meet the needs of those students as well as we can."

After discussing his goals with Pastor Grant, Jim left feeling a bit overwhelmed. There was so much yet to learn. However, he also felt that he had made a great deal of progress since his first feeble attempts at goal setting. He was sure that he was on the right road to a successful ministry.

ATTAINING GOALS

Some people equate setting goals with their achievement. However, Jim knew that nothing could be further from the truth. Although he had already written down his goals, he still had a lot of work to do before he could see his dreams become reality.

As Jim worked at home that evening, he started to take some of the initial steps that would propel him toward his goals. For example, *he convinced himself that his goals were attainable.* He remembered how the Israelites, on the brink of conquering The Promised Land, had faltered because of their fears.[1] They thought the power of God was no match for the strong fortresses and giants that they faced. Because they didn't believe that they could accomplish what God had already promised them, they were doomed to wander in the wilderness for forty years.

Jim was certain that the same thing could happen to him if he wasn't careful. If he thought that his goals were unachievable, defeat would surely follow. Therefore, he thanked God in advance for their attainment, committed his way to the Lord, and stepped out in faith.[2]

Jim also told God that he was willing to "pay the price" that was necessary to accomplish God's will. Making this pledge was important to Jim because he had seen so many of his friends start their Christian commitments with a flash but end them with a fizzle. He wanted to be different.

Jim took Jesus seriously when He declared that His followers must be willing to take up their crosses to follow Him.[3] Jim remembered how Jesus, instead of welcoming potential disciples with open arms, often put barriers in their way. These roadblocks served to discourage and deter the fainthearted.

The Lord constantly reminded His fickle crowd of admirers that no builder constructs a tower and no king goes to war without first considering the cost that is involved.[4] There are simply no victories in God's kingdom without sacrifice.

As Coach Timmons used to remind his players: "No pain, no gain." Despite that constant admonition by his coach, Jim had seen many talented athletes fail because they weren't willing to invest the necessary time and effort in their pregame practices. He vowed that this would never happen to him in the spiritual realm.

To keep his goals in front of him, Jim started placing reminders everywhere. He taped one list of his goals to his bathroom mirror—despite Jill's protests. He place a second list on his desk at the church and a third one in his car. He even wrote down a couple of his major goals on small cards that he placed in his pocket calendar. All of these reminders kept Jim's thoughts and actions focused on his goals.

Jim also heeded the advice of Paul who told Christians to bring their requests before the Lord.[5] Jim claimed God's promise to answer prayer[6] and spent some time each day asking God to bless his goals.[7]

To give himself added incentive, *Jim also promised to reward himself every time he achieved one of his major goals.* His prizes would consist of things like taking some time off from work, buying a new outfit, or treating his family to a special dinner. He also decided that the size of his reward would be commensurate with the size of the goal that he achieved.

In addition *Jim used a technique called "visualization."* This method helped him picture how his goals would look once they were achieved.

For example, Jim wanted to develop a singles' group that would minister to the students who attended nearby Christopher College. He sat back, closed his eyes, and relaxed. Then he created a mental image of how this singles' group would look, sound, and act. He saw their smiles. He heard their laughter. He pictured the group's members seated in a circle eagerly discussing the Word of God.

From previous experience, Jim knew that if he repeatedly imagined his fulfilled goals, his subconscious would begin to act upon his desires. In time, it would introduce fresh ideas into his mind about how to make the group's meetings more exciting. It would also sensitize him to recognize opportunities, when they occurred, for promoting the group.

Jim knew that this technique's effectiveness depended on two things: (1) how often he visualized his goals and (2) how vividly he pictured them in his mind. The more frequently he practiced this method and the more strikingly he painted his mental images, the more likely he was to reach his goal.

During the rest of the month, Jim took several other steps toward the realization of his goals. In an effort to motivate himself, *he shared his goals with a few select people. He asked them to hold him accountable for the accomplishment of his goals and prompt him with encouragement when he became discouraged or when inertia set in.*

Jim was careful, however, to choose the right type of people for this task. He knew that some people are perpetual fire extinguishers. They enjoy dampening other people's spirits and enthusiasm. And they like to remind others of their past failures.

He didn't want to share his ideas with those kind of people. That would have only invited defeat.

Instead, he looked for people who really cared about him and wanted him to succeed—people who would show a loving interest in his endeavors but not let him "off the hook" too easily. Even then, he shared his ideas with these "cheerleaders" only after he had thoroughly thought through his goals and made a successful start.

Jim knew that delays could be deadly. So, *at the earliest possible moment, he took some immediate steps to reach each of his goals.* For example, since one of his goals was to lead a workshop on child evangelism, he purchased four books that dealt with that topic. Although this step may have seemed insignificant to others, it paved the way for further progress. The momentum that Jim established by taking this initial step moved him beyond wishful thinking and into the adventure of achievement.

Periodically, Jim also reviewed the progress that he was making toward the achievement of his goals. At the beginning of every week, he set aside time to read his goals out loud. As he read each goal, he asked two important questions: "What have I done so far to achieve this goal?" and "What steps do I still need to take toward this goal's realization?"

Now, that Jim had determined where he was heading, he was ready to move on to the next step in the leadership process. He needed creative strategies for reaching his goals.

POINTS TO PONDER

1. What are the advantages and disadvantages of goal setting?

2. Why do some leaders fail to set goals?

3. What steps can a leader take to encourage his church and the rest of his team members to set goals?

PRACTICAL PROJECTS

1. Pretend that you are the leader of one of your church groups. Then write down, following the guidelines mentioned in this chapter, at least five goals that your group could achieve by the end of the year.

2. Write out two personal goals that you would like to achieve in the next three months.

3. Write an outline of a one-hour workshop designed to teach others how to set goals.

3

New and Improved

(CREATIVITY)

Jim watched, in amazement, as Dan Rivers put the finishing touches on a stage set for an upcoming youth musical. This capable artist had transformed their church's plain platform into a plush tropical paradise—complete with waterfall, cave, and sandy beach.

Dan stopped to admire his work and then turned to Jim for his unbiased critique. "Well, what do you think?"

"It looks fabulous!" said Jim. "Boy, I wish I had your creative talent."

Dan humbly minimized his contribution. "It's not really that difficult to let your imagination soar."

"It is for me," Jim replied. "My creative skills, if I ever had any, are extinct."

"Nonsense!" retorted Dan. "Everybody, including you, Jim, has the ability to be innovative.

"Just watch children when they play. They take their parents' clothes and use them as props in make-believe dramas. They convert cardboard boxes into ships, tanks, and forts. Pots and pans become hats, shovels, and musical instruments.

"Unfortunately, as we grow older, we lose our creative mind-set. We're told to color within the lines. Teachers police our paintings to ensure that our trees are green and brown rather than purple and orange. Our educational training demands 'correct' rather than creative answers.

"By the time we become adults, our pliable spirits have solidified. We're afraid or too lazy to try anything new. Our self-imposed rules imprison our minds."

"Sounds pretty hopeless to me," groaned Jim.

"Not really," replied Dan. "All you have to do is to fan the creative spark within yourself."

"How can I do that?" inquired Jim.

THE CREATIVE PERSONALITY

"First of all, you have to cultivate the traits of a creative person," explained Dan.

"What kind of traits are those?" asked Jim.

"Well, for one thing, creative people are dissatisfied with the status quo."

"Do you mean that you have be a grumbler to be creative?" laughed Jim. "If so, there sure are a lot of creative people in this world!"

"No, not at all," responded Dan. "Creative people differ from constant critics in one important aspect. They don't just complain about problems; they go around solving them. Creative people look at difficulties as opportunities to grow and challenges to overcome.

"So, if you want to become a creative church leader, you need to acquire a healthy dissatisfaction for things as they are.

"Start to scrutinize each facet of your work. Look for areas that can be improved, things that can be changed, and needs that can be met.

"And, don't wait for problems to come to you. Actively seek them out."

"Okay, I've got the idea," said Jim. "Give me another characteristic on which I can work."

"Well, Jim, creative people also have the intense curiosity of a young child. You should know all about that—since you have two young girls. Preschoolers like Brenda have a tremendous need to explore. They peek into and around structures. Every object within their grasp is subject to a thorough taste test. They push and pull everything that moves to see what will happen.

"Before children can read, they pump adults for information with their incessant cry of: 'Why?' 'Why?' 'Why?' As children grow older, they continue to explore their environment by taking things apart to see how mechanisms work.

"You can develop that kind of exploratory spirit too. All you need to do is probe ideas and the world around you with the questions, 'What if?' 'Why?' 'Why not?' and 'How?' When you do this, you start to see your environment with the fresh eyes of a child who is looking at things for the very first time. This revived sense of wonder will encourage you to investigate and experiment in areas that have become all too familiar.

"As a newcomer, Jim, you're in a better position to do this than the church's 'old timers.' They've grown too comfortable with the church's practices and procedures. However, the longer that you're here, the more you'll have to guard against the creeping paralysis of familiarity. Otherwise, you'll start to flash SOS (same old song) signals wherever you go.

"Creative people challenge assumptions. They never restrict themselves with straightjacket phrases: 'We've never done it that way before,' 'That's just the way it is,' or 'It can't be done.'

"Thomas Edison exhibited this trait. Because this determined experimenter was willing to question the conventional wisdom and the man-made barriers of his day, he was able to open up new doors of opportunity for his descendants that exceeded even his wildest dreams. When we remove the artificial boundaries which surround us, we can do the same."

"Dan," Jim interjected. "I saw an example of that kind of 'assumption bashing' at our county fair the other day. While Jill and I were walking around the fair grounds, we had a chance to see some entries in a contest for young artists. In that contest, children were given a piece of paper with an outline of a pumpkin and some instructions which said: 'Color me pretty.'

"Most of the children assumed those directions meant that they had to use paints or crayons. However, one girl challenged those assumptions. She 'colored' her pumpkin by gluing colorful seeds and yarn to the outline that she was given. In my opinion, her picture was much more beautiful and definitely more creative than all of the rest."

"Exactly!" replied Dan. "When we challenge our assumptions, we'll become more creative.

"A simple, two-step process can help us erase artificial boundaries and free us to develop innovative approaches. When we start a new project, we should make a list of all of the things that we're taking for granted. Then, we should ask the question: 'What could we do if these assumptions weren't true?'"

"Let me see if I can dress up that principle in work clothes," said Jim, as he tried to slow Dan's torrent of information.

"If, for example, Pastor Grant and I want to invigorate our church's worship service, we should begin by listing any preconceived ideas that we have. Ideas like:

- We must conduct our worship services only on Sunday.

- We must make announcements in the service.

- We must take an offering at every service.

- We must meet in the main auditorium of our church.

- Only pastors can preach the sermon.

- We must include one 'special number' in each service.

- We must start our worship services with a choir invocation.

- Only the church's pastors should baptize new Christians.

"Then, once we've jotted down these 'givens,' we should sit back and dream about how the church might operate if none of these presuppositions were true. After that, we should select the best ideas that come out of this dream session and use them to enhance our congregation's worship."

"Precisely," said Dan. He paused for a moment and then continued to flood his young friend with ideas.

"Another quality that creative people possess is an ability to generate a large number of ideas in a short period of time. If you were to ask a creative person how many uses he could find for a common brick, he could produce double or triple the amount of answers that another person might suggest. This ability is very important because the more ideas you have, the more likely you'll be able to come up with an idea that will meet your needs.

"Unfortunately, after most people think up one plausible solution to a problem, their idea factory comes to a grinding halt. This kind of premature 'closure' plugs up the pipeline through which further ideas could flow.

"You can prevent this blockage in at least two ways.

1. Set quantitative goals for yourself. For example, if you want to reduce the heating costs here at our church, make an agreement with yourself that you'll come up with at least thirty potential ways to achieve that objective before you start to decide which ideas are best. This will force you to look beyond the first apparent solution.

2. Don't evaluate your ideas at the same time that you're trying to generate them. Wait at least a day or two before looking at them with a critical eye. Otherwise, you'll feel like you're trying to drive with your brakes on.

Lastly, creative people are also well-rounded individuals with diverse backgrounds and interests. They use this broad base of knowledge to bring together seemingly unrelated fields when solving problems or developing new ideas.

"To broaden your background and expand your horizons, you can expose yourself to different cultures, travel widely, pursue different hobbies, and read a wide variety of literature. These activities will help you to overcome the narrow perspective of a specialist who concentrates on just one particular field.

"This is especially important for pastors and church staff members. Too often, they develop what's called 'tunnel vision syndrome' because they have no lives outside of their ministries."

The hour passed quickly as Jim and Dan continued to talk about the principles and problems of the creative process. However, the whine of the city's siren reminded them that it was time to break for lunch. Jim wished they could discuss this topic further. However, he knew that it was more important to put his limited knowledge to work than to acquire more knowledge that would just remain padlocked in his mind.

CREATIVE TECHNIQUES

After a short lunch at Toni's Pizza Parlor, Jim quickly returned to his office. He was eager to apply some of the concepts that Dan had taught him. He decided to revive his dormant creativity by designing a new educational brochure for the church.

Attribute Listing

After Jim retrieved Bethel's outdated educational pamphlet, he began to list its various components. As he did, he tried to be as thorough as possible because Dan had told him: "The chances for change increase in proportion to the number of ideas that you produce."

By the time he had finished, he had noted seventeen elements.

Color	Lack of Sound or Motion
Shape	Arrangement of Elements
Size	Number of Pages/Folds
Texture	White Space

Text Size   Front Cover
Font   Graphics
Topics   Weight
Words   Cost
Content

Then Jim began to think of ways that each of these components could be changed or improved. For example, as Jim considered the brochure's color, he asked: "Should I change it? Make it lighter? Make it darker? Add more colors?"

When Jim considered the brochure's shape, he asked: "Should our brochure be made in the shape of a circle, a church building, an animal, or a person's head?" "Should it have holes in it?" "Should it have a three-dimensional look?"

Checklisting

After a while, Jim's stream of ideas slowed to a mere trickle. At this point, he pulled out of his top desk drawer a checklist that Dan had given him. It consisted of a set of prepared questions that Alex Osborn had designed to stimulate creative thought. As Jim slowly began to ponder each of the following questions, his idea production began to increase once again.

Put to other uses?	New ways to use as is? Other uses if modified?
Adapt?	What else is like this? What other idea does this suggest? Does the past offer [any] parallel? What could I copy? Whom could I emulate?
Modify?	New twist? Change meaning, color, motion, sound, odor, form, shape? Other changes?
Magnify?	What to add? More time? Greater frequency? Stronger? Higher? Longer? Thicker? Extra value? Plus Ingredient? Duplicate? Multiply? Exaggerate?
Minify?	What to subtract? Smaller? Condensed? Miniature? Lower?

	Shorter? Lighter? Omit? Stream-line? Split-up? Understate?
Substitute?	Who else instead? What else instead? Other ingredients? Other material? Other process? Other power? Other place? Other approach? Other tone of voice?
Re-arrange?	Interchange components? Other pattern? Other layout? Other sequence? Transpose cause and effect? Change pace? Change schedule?
Reverse?	Transpose positive and negative? How about opposites? Turn it back-ward? Turn it upside down? Reverse roles? Change shoes? Turn tables? Turn other cheek?
Combine?	How about a blend, an alloy, an assortment, an ensemble? Combine units? Combine purposes? Com-bine appeals? Combine ideas?[1]

In thirty minutes, Jim had stockpiled quite a number of options. After considering each one, Jim decided that he would:

Make the brochure in the shape of an open Bible.

Replace its mundane title, "The Educational Program of Bethel Church," with a new caption: "Learning to Live and Love."

Substitute modern clip-art for the old pictures.

Have a professional printer produce it.

Change the brochure's color from black and white to black print on blue paper with a splash of red on the front page.

Print the brochure on parchment paper rather than ordinary typing paper.

Add several paragraphs that would mention the impor-tance of personal and family devotions.

Eliminate a section that talked about the church's history.

Rearrange the information so that the church's preschool program would be featured on the first page. Since Bethel was renovating its preschool facilities to attract more young couples, Jim wanted to give this ministry plenty of visibility.

Change the wording so that it would appeal to the non-Christian parent as well as the regular church attender.

Reduce the brochure's size so that people could easily slip it into their shirt pockets.

Change the cluttered look of the brochure by introducing wider margins and more space between sections.

Attach a plastic bookmark, with a summary of the church's activities, to the back of the brochure. Hopefully, it would remind people of the church's educational ministry.

After Jim had finished designing his new brochure, he looked at it with pride. A previously limp and out-dated document had been transformed into a dynamic, winsome promotional piece.

Dan might be right, Jim thought to himself. *Maybe my wilted creative skills can still be revived!*

Brainstorming

When Jim was hired, the church had a small children's choir program called The King's Kids. Because of discipline problems and the resignation of the choir's leader, the group had started to falter.

Although this group wasn't mentioned in Jim's job description, Pastor Grant came to him and asked if he would be willing to direct the choir. Since Jim had a musical background and an intense love for children, he decided to accept the challenge.

Under Jim's guidance, the choir began to blossom. More members were enlisted. A new staff was recruited. Meetings were made more interesting. Higher standards were imposed. And, troublemakers were dismissed.

Now Sid Simms, the adult choir leader, had come to Jim with a proposal that would greatly enhance the choir's ministry.

Jim explained the opportunity to his musical team later that evening. "Sid has asked the children's choir to sing a few numbers during the church's Fourth of July celebration. What do you think? Are we ready for that?"

Sue Johnson, the choir's pianist, didn't hesitate for a moment. "I think that's a terrific idea! We have plenty of time to prepare. The children want to perform. And, a lot of people who wouldn't normally come to our festivities will come to hear their children sing."

The rest of the choir team concurred.

Jim was pleased at his group's eagerness. As he passed out several music books, he said: "Good. Let's take a look at the songs that Sid wants us to sing and start planning for that program this evening. Then, we'll tell the choir about the good news at our next meeting.

"Now, we could simply sing these pieces straight through," explained Jim as the choir team examined the music in front of them. "However, I don't think that would be very appealing or have much impact. I want to present our songs in such a way that people will sit up and take notice. We need to arouse our audience's emotions.

"This is where you come in. I'd like to spend next thirty minutes brainstorming the situation. Let's see if we can come up with some ideas on how to make our presentation really effective.

"Before we begin, however, let's review some of the basic rules that we need to observe during our discussion.

>*"All criticism is strictly forbidden.* Even poor ideas can trigger good ones. So let's not attack each other's suggestions. We'll evaluate our ideas later.

>*"Wild and zany ideas are not only welcomed; they're encouraged.* Offbeat suggestions can free our minds from the restrictions and assumptions that we normally impose upon our thinking. Most of us are reluctant to voice our ideas until we're sure that they'll be accepted. However, if we can overcome that reluctance, we'll produce a lot more alternatives.

>*"Quantity is desired.* Rather than looking for *the perfect solution*, we should try to produce as many options as possible. The more ideas we generate, the more likely we'll be able to find the useful ideas that we're seeking.

>*"Let's try to build on each other's ideas.* Every time one of us makes a suggestion, the rest of us should feel free to improve upon that idea or combine it with one

of our own. This 'piggybacking' procedure will serve as a springboard to other possibilities."

After explaining the basics of brainstorming, Jim turned to his assistant choir director and asked, "Clint, could you record our ideas on the overhead projector? This way, we'll have a record of our suggestions. And, looking at our comments on the screen may prompt even more ideas."

After Clint had agreed, Jim said: "Okay, let's begin. How can we present our four patriotic songs in an interesting manner?"

The question acted like the starter's gun at a fifty-yard dash. The group responded immediately with a torrent of ideas.

"Let's present three of the songs as a medley."

"The children could 'rap' one of the songs."

"Let's fire cannon shots while we sing the last verse of 'The Battle Hymn of the Republic.'"

"We could slow that song down to half-speed on the second verse for variety."

"Or, we could substitute a waltz tempo for the march tempo in the fourth verse."

"Let's create a military outpost as a backdrop for these songs, complete with tents, a campfire and uniforms."

"Maybe the children could unfurl a huge flag during our last song."

"Aw, that would cost too much," protested Mike West.

"And besides, the kids can't handle a heavy flag like that."

Jim broke into his team's discussion. "Remember, Mike, evaluation is strictly forbidden at this stage."

During the rest of the session, Jim tempered his input.

He didn't want to dominate the discussion. In fact, he had thought of temporarily leaving the room while the group generated its ideas. He knew that his presence might hinder the group's output.

Despite this possibility, however, he had decided to stay and guide the group's efforts. In addition to occasionally enforcing the rules of brainstorming, he tried to encourage members and stimulate ideas with compliments: "That's great," "Keep going," and "What else does that bring to mind?"

When the conversation lagged, Jim induced more submissions by restating the problem in a slightly different way or prompting his team with questions and ideas.

After about twenty minutes, the group's output started to dwindle. So Jim brought the brainstorming session to a close and thanked the participants for their help. Before moving on to other choir business, he let them know how much he appreciated the large number of options they had produced.

The next day, Jim presented Shirley with a dozen overhead transparencies. They contained all of the ideas that the choir leaders had generated the night before. He asked her to group and type these ideas on several sheets of paper.

Once that was done, Jim redistributed these notes to his choir leaders and asked them for further input. Amazingly, his team came up with sixteen more suggestions by the end of the week.

Jim was pleased by his group's efforts. It had definitely thought up more ideas than he could have generated by himself.

Jim allowed a couple of days to pass before he examined the group's suggestions once again. Then, he evaluated them ruthlessly and selected the best ideas by carefully screening each alternative with questions like:

- Is it Christ-honoring?

- Is it feasible?

- Will it enhance our performance?

- Will people react favorably?

- Will it effectively accomplish the goal which we are trying to achieve?

- Is it an efficient solution? In other words, is it simple and direct?

- What will it cost us in terms of time, money, equipment, and manpower? Will the results justify the cost? Could we get more results in some other area if we applied a similar amount of resources?

- Is this the proper time to introduce the idea?

- Will there be any side-effects (negative or positive) that are not readily apparent?

- Do we have the skills and knowledge to implement the idea?

- Do we feel enthusiastic enough about the idea to persistently pursue it even if it runs into difficulty?

Although Jim decided to use only 40 percent of the ideas that were offered, he felt that the process and the product had been well worth the time and the effort.

Analogies

"Jim, we're not going to make it," lamented Mary Black as she entered Jim's office. "We're simply not going to make it."

The church's Sunday School director was obviously upset about something. However, her abrupt entrance didn't provide any clues about the source of her concerns. Fortunately, Jim didn't have to wait long before Mary explained the reason for her frustration.

"One of our goals for this year was to increase our Sunday School attendance by 20 percent over last year. Well, I don't think that's going to happen."

"In fact, our attendance may drop slightly. Three church families will be leaving this month because Buxby Paints is closing down their manufacturing plant. Two elderly couples will be retiring and moving out of the community. In addition, we're losing two more families because of company transfers.

"And, if that isn't enough, our tried and true methods for reaching nonChristians don't seem to be working any more. Last year, our February Fun Fest brought a lot of new children into our program—at least for a little while. This year, however, it should have been dubbed our February Flop.

"We're going to have to do something drastic if we ever expect to reach our attendance goals."

Some people would have been discouraged by Mary's statements. Jim, however, had learned to take her outspoken, roller-coaster personality in stride. He knew that her comments stemmed from a desire to do her very best and to meet the high standards that she continually set for herself.

Like Mary, Jim had become increasingly pessimistic about the Sunday School's ability to grow. Losing several faithful families in the next couple of months certainly wouldn't help.

However, he felt that this wasn't the time to discuss his doubts and fears. Neither was he ready to abandon his goals so early in the year.

So, he tried to console and encourage his energetic worker.

"Don't worry," countered Jim. "We still have nine more months to go. And, I'm sure we'll be able to reach our goals by then.

"Maybe we can use some creative techniques to develop the new strategies that we need. For example, analogies are usually a fertile source of fresh ideas."

"What do you mean?" asked Mary.

"Well, analogies draw comparisons between two ideas or objects," explained Jim. "We use them every day. For example, we compare a heart to a pump, the structure of an atom to the solar system, or an eye to a camera.

"When Jesus lived on earth, He used analogies to drive home a point. At the outset of His ministry, for example, He compared believers to salt and light.[2] He later compared the kingdom of heaven to a treasure, a pearl, and a net.[3] To emphasize the importance of reaching the lost, He likened people to wayward sheep, missing coins, and prodigal sons.[4]

"We, as Christian leaders, can also use analogies to make us more effective in our endeavors. For example, in our case, we might want to ask: 'What is our outreach program like?'

"I guess we could compare it to:

- a magnet

- an adhesive with gripping power

- a farmer who harvests a crop

- a salesman who offers people his merchandise

- an advertiser who promotes his product

- a dog whistle

- a carnival barker who invites people into a tent show

- a mother who tries to convince her child to eat his vegetables

- a doctor who treats a patient

- a fisherman who entices his catch with bait

"After we've made comparisons, we need to ask ourselves: 'What implications does this have for our outreach efforts?' As we think about that question, we might come up with some interesting conclusions.

- Harvesting is a long-term process. So is developing relationships with people who can benefit from our Sunday School ministry.

- In a long-term process, we need to sow seeds and then be patient enough to let them grow instead of trying to harvest them before they've even begun to sprout.

- We should have some way of determining when people are 'ripe' or ready for the Sunday School experience.

- Just like a carnival barker, we need to tease people's curiosity and let them know what we have to offer.

- We need to go where potential prospects congregate just like fishermen seek out productive fishing holes.

- We need to use different enticements to attract different people just like a fisherman uses different lures for different fish.

- Like a salesman, we need to go back to the customers who have bought our product in the past and ask them to buy it again. If they no longer want to buy from us, we should ask them 'Why?' and then make any needed improvements so we don't lose other customers.

Jim paused a moment to see if Mary was following his train of thought. Then he continued. "So far I've been talking about *natural analogies*. However, we can also use *vicarious analogies* to generate new ideas."

Once again, Mary seemed bewildered by Jim's terminology. "Okay, I'll bite. What are vicarious analogies?"

"Vicarious analogies are created when a person puts himself into someone else's shoes," responded Jim. "For example, if we're having problems getting along with our mate, we should try to see the conflict from their point-of-view."

"But how does that apply to our attendance problem?" interjected Mary.

"Well, let's try to imagine how we would feel if we were visiting our church for the first time. What would entice us to come to our church? How would we feel once we arrived? What kind of questions would we have? What would be our first impressions? How would we find our way to our Sunday school class?"

"Boy, I've never thought of doing anything like that before," said Mary. "And, honestly, I don't know if this approach would help us much."

"Well, try it this week and see what kind of ideas you can generate," urged Jim.

"Okay, I'll see what happens," said Mary as she stood up to leave. "You know, the pressure of goal-setting is starting to get to me. I sure hope your ideas work."

ENCOURAGING CREATIVITY

After Mary left, Jim began to think about how he could encourage others in his team to become more creative. He knew that it would be a difficult task. People who aren't accustomed to thinking creatively don't change overnight. However, he still felt he could boost his team's creative output.

In fact, that's why Jim had asked Dan Rivers to suggest several ways that he could develop an atmosphere in which innovation could thrive. Dan had responded with a letter which Jim had just started to read before Mary Black had come into his office. Now he turned his attention back to Dan's note. It looked like it had some terrific suggestions:

Dear Jim,

"Thanks for the stimulating conversation that we had the other day. I enjoyed it. Maybe we can get together again sometime and discuss the subject of creativity over a cup of coffee.

"I gave your question a lot of thought last week and would like to suggest the following ways to stimulate the innovative urges in your team members."

1. *Ask for and expect creative ideas.* When you assign people a given task, ask them to use creative approaches in their work.

   When you ask people to submit plans to you, tell them at the outset that you want their suggestions in rough form only (for example, a list of alternatives or some simple sketches). This will keep them from doing a lot of difficult, detail work which they may have to redo or discard if you don't like their basic concepts.

   If they bring you proposals which have no new or fresh ideas, ask them to try again and be more creative the second time.

   Ask them to give you an outline of their plans far enough in advance so that there is time to make revisions, if necessary.

2.   *Compliment people when they try new methods and ideas.* Usually, innovative concepts are greeted with distrust and a lack of enthusiasm. Surprise your coworkers. Tell them how much you appreciate their imagination and flair. You'll find that praising people for their creative ideas produces better results than criticizing them for a lack of creativity.

   You might also want to praise creative people indirectly. Tell the other members of your team about the originality that some of their coworkers have displayed and how much you value those efforts. Publicly acknowledging these triumphs will show people that you put a premium on creative ideas.

3.   *Prime people's pumps by asking questions that stir their creative juices.* For example, ask them "what if" questions. Find out what they would do if they were the group's leader or what they would do if certain barriers didn't exist.

4.   *Allow creative people a great deal of input in the decision-making and planning processes.* When you delegate a task, don't issue top-down, fully detailed instructions. Instead, tell them the goals that you want to achieve and then let them work out their own strategies and details.

5.   *Support creative people by supplying them with the resources needed to put their innovative ideas into action.* You may even want to set aside part of your budget for creative opportunities that come up during the year.

6.   *When a new idea is suggested, delay your first reaction—if it is a negative one.* Many ideas don't survive because somebody prematurely criticizes them. Instead of dismissing a suggestion outright, be a good listener, have faith in the person who has recommended the idea, and assume that the proposal can be accomplished. If the idea needs refinement, tell the person so. If the suggestion has potential, give the person the resources to experiment with the idea, develop it, and try it on a small-scale basis.

7. *Recruit creative team members.* This will save you the time and effort that it takes to train novices to be innovative. Hopefully, these imaginative people will also serve as role models and infect others with their creative attitudes.

8. *Creative problem-solving takes time.* Discourage crash programs. Give your team members the time that they'll need to work on a problem. Of course, this doesn't mean that you shouldn't impose time limits. Reasonable deadlines can stimulate people to produce, as long as they're established far enough in advance.

9. *Don't be too harsh when people try to do something creative and it doesn't work.* Instead, thank them for their efforts, emphasize the things that did go right, and encourage them to try other imaginative projects in the future.

10. *Train your workers in the creative process.* Studies have shown that people who are trained to use their imaginations score much higher on creative tests than those who are not.

In the margin of his letter, Dan had scribbled a note which said: "Jim, if you need some help in this last area, I'd be willing to conduct a workshop on creative methods."

Jim didn't want to pass up that offer. So he quickly took out his to-do list and jotted down a note to himself: "Phone Dan about creativity workshop."

Then he continued reading the next section of the letter.

"Jim, if you're going to demand creative strategies from your fellow workers, you're going to have to be a good example to them. To increase your creative output, take the following suggestions to heart."

1. *Establish goals.* Put pressure on yourself by setting deadlines for the production of new ideas. Or, set quotas which specify how many ideas you want to discover during your creative sessions.

2. *Create incentives for yourself.* Write down the general benefits that you'll receive from being a creative leader or from completing a creative project. When you've successfully produced a number of creative ideas,

reward yourself. Take some time off, buy some new clothes, or take your wife out for a evening of fun and relaxation.

3.   *Broaden your horizons.* Since you'll be drawing upon your personal experiences and information for creative solutions, try to expand and diversify your reservoir of information. Make an effort to do things that you don't normally do. For example, you might try travelling to new places, taking new routes or modes of transportation to work, listening to new types of music, reading unusual books or magazines, playing new sports, or attending workshops that discuss topics which are totally foreign to you.

4.   *Think visually.* Because words can restrict your flow of ideas, learn to doodle as you think. Make a diagram of your problem or proposal. Relax, close your eyes, and form mental images of your dilemmas before you begin to solve them.

5.   *Practice your creative skills.* Your physical muscles can be developed through rigorous exercise. So can your creative muscles with flair.
        The best way to develop your creative skills is to actually put them to use. Play games that allow you to rearrange items into new patterns. Try hobbies that tap your artistic flair. Use your imagination wherever you find yourself—in your cooking, in your leisure times, in your home repairs, and in your interpersonal relationships. All of these activities will build your confidence so that you can tackle larger, work-related projects.

6.   *Expose yourself to creative people.* If you're constantly around negative individuals who criticize creative work rather than developing innovative approaches, you'll tend to develop the same mind-set. However, if you spend time with people like me, our wacky ideas and creative attitudes will start to rub off on you.

Yours in Christ,

Dan Rivers

THE PROS AND CONS OF CREATIVE STRATEGIES

By the end of the week, Jim was tremendously excited about injecting new ideas, methods, and activities into the church's educational program. He was anxious to present some of his innovative thinking to the church council that week.

When the group asked for his monthly report, Jim enthusiastically showed its members the new educational brochure that he had designed. He thought that the pamphlet would be accepted immediately. After all, it wasn't controversial, both Pastor Grant and Shirley liked the new design, and the congregation had hired him to improve the outreach efforts of the church.

However, the council was deeply divided about his proposal. Some people thought a colored brochure was too expensive. Others felt that the brochure would be too hard to produce if it were shaped like a Bible. Still others had reservations about how it was going to be distributed.

Because of their reservations, the church council asked Jim to come back with another proposal—at the next meeting. When they did, Jim thought to himself: "We'll never make any progress this way."

Although there were many other issues on the agenda that night, Jim spent the rest of the evening sulking. All he could think about was the rejection that he had suffered at the hands of these supposedly spiritual people.

By the time that he returned home, he was emotionally bankrupt. "How can I do my job if the church leadership straightjackets my ideas?" grumbled Jim to Jill as they were getting ready to go to sleep. "At this pace, it's going to be years before we'll see any improvements in our programs."

Jill tried to reassure her husband. "Don't give up. Being creative is important. After all, God is creative in His dealings with people.[5] So, you're just trying to follow His example.

"Creativity can keep people from falling into a rut. It can keep churches in tune with changing times. It can provide relevant programs. And, it can excite people. Isn't variety supposed to be the spice of life?"

"Sure, but developing creative ideas also has plenty of disadvantages," argued Jim. "It takes a lot of time and effort to develop new programs. Some people think trailblazers are a bit strange. And, when you try something new, you set yourself up for failure because people change so slowly."

Jim was just about to go downstairs and prepare a cup of hot tea to sooth his shattered nerves when the telephone rang. Jim immediately recognized Mary Black's boisterous voice on the other end.

"Jim, I tried putting myself into the shoes of our elderly members, mothers with young children, and singles—just like you suggested," she gushed. "As I thought about their needs, feelings, and reasons for not coming to Sunday School, I came up with a zillion new ways to promote our program. Can I stop by the office tomorrow and share them with you?"

By the time Jim ended his conversation with Mary, he was feeling much more upbeat. In fact, in the days that followed, his determination to use creative methods grew. And, the more he fanned his creative spark, the easier his creative efforts became. Some days, he had so many new ideas that he had difficulty choosing which creative strategy he would employ.

POINTS TO PONDER

1. Why are people reluctant to accept new ideas?

2. Why do people fear those who act and think differently than they do?

3. What are some of the advantages and disadvantages of creative thinking that this chapter does not mention?

4. What is the difference between logical and creative thinking?

5. Share with your classmates a creative idea that you've employed in your ministry and how you implemented it.

PRACTICAL PROJECTS

1. Describe at least three creative techniques that are not mentioned in this chapter.

2. Research, list, and describe the four or five major steps in the creative process. Is the creative process always as neat as psychologists seem to think?

3. List ten creative ways to encourage people to delve into the Bible. Don't include sermons, Sunday School, VBS, midweek clubs, or other common methods.

4

She Loves Me,
She Loves Me Not

(DECISION MAKING)

Jim glanced down at his menu before looking up at his colleagues with quiet desperation. "Decisions, decisions, decisions," he groaned. "I've been wrestling with decisions all day long. When will I get up? What will I wear? What will I do with my time? How will I spend my money? and now. . . ."

"And now. . . you have a few more decisions to make," added the good-natured waitress towering over Jim and his three companions: Doug Saxby, Bill Chamberlin and Vance Jordan.

"What can I get for you?" she asked the group. This question was followed by other questions: "Would you like soup or salad with your meal?" "What kind of dressing do you want?" "Would you like your sandwich on rye, wheat, or sourdough?"

After their waitress had retrieved her menus and made her exit, the group's mood became notably more serious. Doug announced with authority, "OK, let's get down to business. We have some more decisions to make. The church council has appointed us to recommend a computer system at their next meeting.

"In order to carry out that mandate, we need to ask some basic questions: Why do we want a computer? What kind of jobs do we want it to perform? Who will be using it?"

Jim jumped into the conversation with enthusiasm. "To begin with, we want our computer to help us with our business letters, training handouts, newsletters, and our church directory. We also want it to keep track of our membership, visitors, and financial records."

"I hate to change the subject," said Bill, "but shouldn't we first ask those who are going to be using the computer system to help us in its selection?"

Jim agreed. "That's a good idea. We should definitely get their input or, better yet, we should include them on our committee."

"But our secretary and treasurer, for example, don't know anything about computers," Doug protested.

"That may be true," Bill quickly countered. "But unless they have a chance to voice their ideas, they may not like the system that we choose. And, if they don't support our proposal, it'll never be approved."

Vance leaned forward and complained, "I don't know why we're spending so much time investigating different computers when Sid Simms offered to donate his computer to the church. We could save ourselves a lot of money by using it."

Jim smiled nervously. "Well, we certainly appreciate his generosity. And, we should consider his computer along with all of the others that we'll be examining. But let's not make a premature decision before we determine our needs."

"But, if we don't move fast enough," Vance protested, "he might give it to someone else. After all, we could use it on a trial basis. Later on, if we didn't like it, we could . . ."

Doug interrupted. "To do that, we would have to invest a lot of time learning how to use that antiquated machine. Furthermore, we would have to buy disks, software, and a printer to go with it. What if we did all of that and then found out it still didn't meet our needs? Besides, Sid has a habit of donating things to the church and then trying to control how people use his so-called 'gifts.'"

PREREQUISITES TO GOOD DECISION MAKING

The meeting was off to a rough start. Everybody seemed to approach the issue from a different angle. For the next ninety minutes, the computer committee sat, ate, talked, listened, and debated. Finally, their plans and procedures started to crystallize.

As they considered their task, the group realized that their deliberations would require a lot of work. They also concluded that they needed to take a few initial steps to arrive at a sound decision.

1. They needed to involve the people who were going to implement their decisions in the decision-making process.

2. They needed to generate as many alternatives as possible. The more options they had, the better their decision would be.

3. They needed to collect as much information as they could. Although the committee recognized that they would never have all of the facts they wanted, they resolved to be as thorough as possible. The quantity and quality of their data would determine the caliber of their decision.

4. They needed to recognize their prejudices from the outset. Maybe they would never be able to divorce themselves totally from their biased opinions. If, however, they were aware of their prejudices, they were more likely to render an impartial verdict.

Doug concluded the meeting by asking each member of the group to research a particular aspect of the problem. Vance volunteered to look at computer software. Doug and Bill agreed to investigate computers and monitors. That left Jim to explore the current crop of printers on the market.

Once the assignments were made, Doug brought the meeting to a close. "Okay. We've made a good start. Can we get together next week and share some of our findings?"

"Sure. Let's meet right after this Sunday evening's service,'" suggested Vance. He hated to spend any more nights at the church than was absolutely necessary. His wife was already asking if she should send his mail there.

"Well, I suppose that means I'll have to attend the evening service for a change," Doug admitted sheepishly.

"I suppose so. Variety is the spice of life," chuckled Bill.

"Before we go, let's ask God to help us in our deliberations," Jim proposed.

"Our young preacher has a prayer for every situation," quipped Doug with a twinkle in his eye. Bill and Vance glanced uncomfortably at each other. However, Jim ignored the comment and made his petition to God.

As the others began to leave, Doug leaned over to Jim and began to tease him again. "Well, Jim, I guess we'll have to put on our thinking hats for this one. Neither the Bible nor prayer will be able to tell us which model of computer to buy, will they?"

Jim glared at Doug with a mixture of disgust and hurt. Jim knew that the committee was fortunate to have Doug on their team. He was an astute businessman with a keen mind and a host of valuable connections. However, Jim was appalled by his flippant attitude toward spiritual things. He also resented the fact that Doug made fun of his youth so frequently.[1]

Keeping a tight reign on his anger, Jim just smiled, turned and talked to Bill about his latest camping trip. It wouldn't do any good to argue with Doug. His mind had the flexibility of a concrete pillar.

On his way home, though, Doug's remarks began to irritate Jim once again. He asked himself, "Am I really trying to interject too much spirituality into a simple business decision?" "Is God only interested in 'big' and 'religious' decisions?"

Jim didn't want to sound too "high and holy." At the same time, though, he felt that Christians should pay close attention to several spiritual prerequisites before making any decision. Otherwise, they wouldn't be able to arrive at a good and godly conclusion. And, that was true even if it only concerned the purchase of a simple business machine.

The Bible urges decision-makers to live in tune with God.[2] It also says that they should possess an intense desire to know God's will,[3] display a willingness to obey God's direction once it's found,[4] and bathe their decisions in prayer.[5]

LOGIC AND REASONING

After supper, Jim told his wife about the meeting and about Doug's comments. Jill didn't respond as favorably as Jim would have hoped.

"Don't take everything so seriously," she said. Her condescending tone of voice made it sound as if she was addressing a child.

"You know how Doug likes to joke with people. After all, the Bible tells us to love God not only with our hearts, souls, and strength but also with all of our minds.[6] All I think he was trying to say is that God gave us brains and He expects us to use them.

"Do you remember how you decided to take this job? God didn't send you a mystical vision. You had to use your God-given intellectual abilities."

Jim remembered the decision all too well. And now, he was a little embarrassed because his approach didn't seem very spiritual.

After the church had offered him a job, Jim constructed a simple balance sheet on which he jotted down the pros and cons of accepting the staff position. Then he made his decision based on a prayerful consideration of the following factors.

PROS	CONS
The senior pastor seems like a very friendly and intelligent person.	The climate in Cody is very cool and damp.
The church is a new, energetic church with a good reputation.	We'll have to move to a large, metropolitan area.
The job will make good use of my skills and talents.	I'll have to work with young people and that isn't my forte.
My wife has a job offer from a hospital in Cody.	We'll have to move farther away from Jill's parents and my sister.
Cody has a fine seminary where I could begin work on a Master of Divinity degree.	My wife's work hours will be terrible.
Cody has a fine school system which would benefit both Barb and Brenda.	My salary will be lower than I would like and the church is offering very few benefits.
	Housing and insurance costs will be expensive.

Jim pondered his decision for a moment. "Had he made the right choice?" "Was he truly 'called of God' to work at Bethel Church?"

Jim didn't have time to linger over these questions. Brenda and Barb squatted at their father's feet and begged for his attention. It was time to tell them a story and put them to bed.

After the girls were asleep, Jim retreated to his study to finish some church work that he had put off for a number of days. Once again, he spent much of his time trying to make decisions. Within thirty minutes, he had determined who would lead the church's home Bible studies during the summer, how tapes of the church services would be distributed, and where the youth would hold their big car rally next month.

Before going to bed, Jim wrestled with one final decision. He tried to decide what kind of tape recorder his youth group should buy for their classroom. In front of him lay a criterion sheet. This tool was similar to a balance sheet, except that Jim used it when he considered multiple alternatives. It looked like this:

CRITERIA	Option #1	Option #2	Option #3
Attractiveness	good	great	poor
Cost	$60	$120	$45
Durability	good	very good	poor
Size/portability	good	fair	good
Stereo speakers	no	yes	no
Dubbing	no	yes	no
Dual tape deck	no	yes	no
Sound quality	good	very good	poor
AM/FM Radio	no	yes	no
Record radio program	no	yes	no
Microphone	fair	fair	poor
Pause control	yes	yes	no
Bass/Treble controls	no	yes	no
Batteries required	4	8	4

As Jim stared at his sheet, he thought again about Doug's comments. Jim was discovering that the decision-making process that he was using seemed secular. He wondered, *Where does God's will fit into the construction of these balance and criterion sheets?*

Then Jim realized that the answer to that question lay in his Christian values. Even though the advantages and disadvantages in a certain course of action might be about the same, not all of the factors were equally important.

As Jim digested this thought, his mind flashed back to the story of the good Samaritan.[7] When the Samaritan came across a man who had been beaten and robbed, he wanted to help. However, he also had to consider the disadvantages of taking care of this helpless victim. If he stopped and cared for the injured traveller, he would be unable to do other things on his schedule, it would cost him money, he would have to overcome his racial prejudice, and he would have to jeopardize his own safety.

A Levite and a priest had already weighed the pros and cons of assisting this pitiful figure. They had decided that the disadvantages outweighed the advantages.

However, the Samaritan had a different set of values. He placed saving a human life at the top of his priority list. So he decided to stay and help the stranger.

Jim knew that he would face similar value judgments in his ministry. For example, he might have to decide whether counseling a needy person outweighed spending time with his family. If his salary didn't improve, he might have to decide whether it was better to earn "a good living" or to continue in full-time church work. Tomorrow, he would have to decide whether he should spend more money on curriculum materials or the Sunday School's outreach efforts.

As Jim thought about how he used his reasoning powers, he realized that God does want Christians to exercise their intellectual skills when making a decision.

However, Jim also realized that logic has its limits. After all, people's perceptions can be clouded by sin.[8] When that happens, a person's spiritual blindness can lead to flawed decisions.

Also, God's wisdom doesn't always make sense to people. In fact, sometimes it is plainly contrary to worldly wisdom.[9] Jim thought about Isaiah 55:8-9:

> For my thoughts are not your thoughts, neither are
> your ways my ways," declares the Lord. "As the heavens
> are higher than the earth, so are my ways higher than
> your ways and my thoughts than your thoughts.

Jim tried to imagine Joshua explaining his game plan for demolishing the walls of Jericho;[10] the Israelites must have listened with disbelief. *How,* Jim wondered, *did Gideon justify his drastic troop reductions before attacking the Midianites?*[11] *Military experts also must have been astonished when David chose to attack Goliath with a sling rather than with conventional weaponry.*[12]

*How could any of those decisions be explained logically? They couldn't.
So Jim concluded: It's important to have a sanctified outlook when making
choices.*

In fact, that's why Paul said:

> Do not conform any longer to the pattern of this world, but be trans-
> formed by the renewing of your mind. Then you will be able to test
> and approve what God's will is—his good, pleasing and perfect will
> (Rom. 12:2).

This is also why God warns his followers not to rely on their own
cleverness and cunning but to look to Him as the source of their wisdom.[13]

ADVICE

The members of Jim's committee were experienced computer us-
ers. However, they still wanted to solicit the opinions of others before recommending a computer system to the church.

Jim was happy about that. Their actions were clearly in line with
the Bible's teaching which says: "Where no counsel is, the people
fall: but in the multitude of counselors there is safety."[14]

There were several reasons why Jim believed so strongly in this
scriptural admonishment.

- The advice of others can be a tremendous source of
  ideas and insights. The more options that a leader has,
  the more likely he will make a wise decision.

- When people are emotionally involved with a pet
  project or a cherished idea, it's hard for them to see its
  potential pitfalls. Outsiders, however, can usually provide a more objective view.

- Talking with others about upcoming decisions helps
  leaders clarify their own thoughts and feelings about
  the options that are being considered.

- Outside counsel provides leaders with expertise and
  experience that they don't possess themselves.

- When people are consulted during the planning process, they are in a better position to enthusiastically

endorse and effectively implement the decisions that are made.

Even though Jim highly valued the advice of others, he still had trouble making decisions because he didn't always know whose advice to take. Sometimes, when making a decision, it seemed as if everybody had a different opinion.[15]

Therefore, Jim always scrutinized advice by asking several important questions:

- *Is the advice coming from only one source or viewpoint?* Whenever Jim sought other people's advice, he tried to get a balanced point of view. He chose counselors who were both positive and negative, young and old, insiders and outsiders.

- *Is the person's advice biased in any way? Jim remembered the story of Daniel's imprisonment in the lion's den.* King Darius had bowed to his subordinates' suggestions and made a decree which prohibited prayer to anyone except himself.[16] Little did this monarch realize that, by signing that decree, he was sentencing Daniel to death. To his horror, the king ultimately realized that the recommendation from his court counselors was flawed by their jealousy and selfish motives.

    Jim was wary of people who, like King Darius' advisers, had something to gain by making a particular recommendation. Some of the computer sales representatives, for example, didn't always suggest things that were good for the church. Sometimes, they based their recommendations on the fact that their company sold a particular product, they received a good commission on the item, or they weren't familiar with other merchandise that did a better job.

- *Is the adviser a "yes" man?* Too often, leaders surround themselves with people who agree with all of their ideas and rubberstamp their decisions. This allows leaders to get their own way and supposedly eliminates friction within their organization. However, it also causes leaders to overlook possible dangers in their plans. This is why God sometimes sends prophets to tell the unvarnished truth—even if it is unpleasant to hear.[17]

- *Does the adviser have a good track record?*[18] As Jim evaluated computer vendors, he always talked with their former customers. He wanted to know how satisfied these buyers were with their previous purchases.

- *Is the adviser knowledgeable in the area about which he is being consulted?* As Jim worked with computer dealers, he wanted to know their credentials. So he checked into their backgrounds and tested their expertise by asking them demanding questions.

- *Do the adviser's recommendations conflict with the Scriptures?* Jim didn't run into a problem in this area while shopping for computer equipment. However, he did know churches which constantly violated God's commands. They failed to heed God's word to evangelize,[19] to minister to the poor,[20] and to maintain a spirit of unity.[21]

- *Is the adviser godly?* Psalm 1:1-2 warns people not to seek counsel from those who are unrighteous. Despite this, Jim had seen many churches listen to board members who were selected because of their business expertise rather than their fervent relationship with God. Therefore, their advice was sometimes based on solely financial rather than spiritual considerations.

Even though Jim usually sought and received good advice, he realized that (in the final analysis) it was still simply that—advice. It was his responsibility to sift through the information he had gathered and make the final decision.

THE HOLY SPIRIT, SIGNS AND CIRCUMSTANCES

"How goes the battle?"[22] asked Jim benignly as Bob Sparkman wedged himself into the chair across from Jim's desk. As the words left his mouth, Jim realized that the question was unnecessary. He could tell from the way Bob's heavy frame slouched in the chair that it had been a rough week.

"Things haven't been going that well lately," admitted Bob. "I'm on a committee that's reviewing our church's insurance. We've been scrutinizing policies from various agencies and, at times, the task seems both overwhelming and confusing. Each contract has so many different options and clauses to consider."

Jim commiserated with Bob. "I can identify with that. I've been wrestling with a few tough problems myself."

As Jim and Bob swapped their experiences, Jim thought to himself: "If an experienced Christian educator like Bob has trouble making decisions, is there any hope for me?"

"Wouldn't it be wonderful," Bob wondered out loud, "if God would simply send us a vision every time we had a decision to make?"

"Like He did with Joseph,[23] Ananias,[24] and Peter?"[25]

"Right."

"Or, since we're dreaming," said Jim, "wouldn't it be great if God would give us some obvious signposts to follow?"

Bob concurred. "That's for sure. Look at the Israelites. Boy, did they have it made. All they had to do was follow a pillar of cloud by day and a pillar of fire by night.[26]

"Why doesn't God do that for us today?" "You know, one of our members wants to donate his archaic computer to the church," Jim said sarcastically. "Maybe that's a sign from God. But, I don't think so."

"Don't be such a skeptic, my friend," responded Bob. "God still works today through the Holy Spirit, signs, and circumstances."

Bob deliberately tried to change the mood of their conversation. He was becoming a little concerned about the irreverent tone that was emerging. Maybe the stress of their jobs was beginning to affect their attitudes.

"When I was thinking about going to seminary," Bob continued, "I was faced with a tremendous hurdle. I didn't have enough money. While I was thinking about how to overcome that obstacle, a lady whom I had never met before introduced herself and put me in touch with an organization that I didn't even know existed. That group gave me the money I needed.

"Through those circumstances, God confirmed what I had already felt. He wanted me to become a pastor."

Jim felt a bit dismayed when he heard Bob's comments. "Sometimes I feel so spiritually inferior. I hear preachers on television talking about some wonderful vision that they've received from the Lord. And, now you tell me about how God provided, almost miraculously, for your seminary training."

Jim hesitated for a moment and then went on, "But, you know, I've never experienced that in my life. What's wrong with me?"

"Probably nothing," answered Bob. "God uses different methods to show us His will. Sometimes He speaks through the Holy Spirit or special circumstances. However, He also shows us His will through the Bible, the advice of others, and our own reasoning abilities.

"In fact, the Bible says that seeking signs is often an indication of unbelief.[27] And, frankly, some who claim that God has given them a special revelation are plain phonies. So we need to be careful. Every method that we use to determine God's will has some subtle traps built into it.

"For example, as you read Acts, it's clear that God guided HIS servants through His Holy Spirit. The Holy Spirit instructed Philip to speak to the Ethiopian eunuch.[28] It was the Holy Spirit who brought Peter and Cornelius together.[29] And, it was the Holy Spirit who directed Paul's travels.[30]

"However, not all of the promptings that we feel come from the Holy Spirit. Sometimes our emotions can be affected by medicine, stress, or even our own health.

"Sometimes, our own selfish desires disguise themselves as the promptings of the Holy Spirit. For instance, we may announce that we feel led to build a great building or organization for the Lord. In reality, however, those dreams may stem from our own craving for fame and fortune. The Bible tells us that we have a natural tendency to follow our own inclinations and do what is right 'in our own eyes.'"[31]

"I know what you mean," agreed Jim. "I heard of a woman who was considering a trip to Europe. One morning, she woke to find that her clock read '7:47' and that she was listening to a British musical group. She immediately jumped to the conclusion that it was God's will for her to fly to England on a 747 jumbo jet."

"Exactly," said Bob. "She read her own feelings into this 'so-called' sign. That's why signs and circumstances can be uncertain guides in determining God's will.

"Open doors, for example, don't always mean that we're doing God's bidding if we go through them. For example, on two occasions, David had a chance to kill Saul.[32] He could have viewed these opportunities as open doors, especially since his friends urged him to take Saul's life. But David rightly felt that it was wrong for him to harm God's anointed servant.[33]

"We may have the opportunity to steal, speed, or cheat without being caught. However, these 'open doors' are clearly invitations to do evil rather than good.

"Just as open doors don't always indicate God's blessing, seemingly closed doors don't necessarily indicate that God wants us to stay out of certain ministries. People often feel 'the leading of the Lord' to quit their jobs when they begin to encounter difficulties, when they have to do unpleasant tasks, or when they see few results.

"However, we know that problems are sometimes the price we have to pay for doing God's will. The prophet Isaiah, for example, was told to speak to a nation that would be deaf and blind to his message.[34]

"If anyone would describe a potential ministry in those terms today, we'd be reluctant to accept God's challenge. We'd conclude that God had shut the doors of opportunity. However, despite the dismal prospects of an 'unsuccessful' ministry, Isaiah preached to Judah with a fervency that was rooted in his deep conviction that God had called him to that demanding and unfruitful task."[35]

THE BIBLE

At that moment, Doug Saxby strode into the office. "Hi Jim. Sorry, I don't mean to intrude. I just wanted to drop off some interesting information about computer printers that I thought you should see."

"You're not interrupting at all," said Bob as he glanced at his watch. "In fact, I was just about to leave. Boy, time flies when you're talking about the Lord's work."

As Bob raced off to his next appointment, Jim invited his coworker to stay. "Have a seat, Doug. Let's see the brochures that you brought." As Jim leafed through the materials, Doug apologized again for breaking into Jim's conversation with Bob.

"Oh, don't worry about it," responded Jim. "Bob and I were just having a philosophical discussion about decision making."

"Well, if you two have discovered how to make all the right moves, maybe you can help me," mused Doug.

"Oh?" exclaimed Jim, as his interest perked up. Doug impressed him as a self-assured businessman who never sought the advice of anyone. Now, it seemed as if he needed a sounding board.

"Pastor Grant's sermon on stewardship last Sunday really pricked my conscience," conceded Doug. "God has blessed me so much, and yet I don't feel that I've plowed back enough of my finances into the Lord's work. That has to change. I want to use my money to help build God's kingdom. But, I'm not sure where to begin."

"Well, Doug, I could use a little extra cash," said Jim with a hearty laugh. "Seriously, I think the Bible could really help you out in this area. It may not tell you exactly which organization or person needs your money. However, it's filled with instructions about how to acquire and use money."

"Really?" stammered Doug. "I thought the Bible was a theological book. I didn't realize that it dealt with such . . . well, practical matters."

Jim reassured his visitor that it did. "The Bible has a lot to say about relevant, everyday issues. It tells us what our attitude towards adultery ought to be. Yet countless Christian leaders ruin their lives and their organizations every year because they don't obey the Scriptures.

"The Bible tells us how we ought to treat other people. Yet sometimes there seems to be as much fighting in the church as there is in the world.

"The problem is not that the Bible is silent about these and other relevant matters. The problem is that we don't listen to what it has to say. As someone has said, 'It's not the things I don't *understand* in the Bible that bother me; it's the things I *do understand*.'

"Here, let me give you a book called *Your Money Matters* by Don Woodson. It lists almost every scripture verse in the Bible that deals with money and possessions. Take it home and study the passages. When you're through with it, I'd like to get your reaction."

Doug thanked him for the book, briefly discussed the articles that he had brought by Jim's office, and then excused himself. By the time Doug and Jim had finished their conversation, Jim's attitude toward this aggressive community leader had changed. Before, Jim had been a little scared of Doug and his intimidating style. But now, Jim realized that Doug was just another fellow Christian who was struggling with the same problems that he was.

STANDARDIZED DECISION MAKING

Jim noticed that he was already way behind his afternoon schedule. However, he felt that his time with Bob and Doug had been well spent. He was also glad that the decision-making process wasn't always as difficult as their conversations seemed to indicate.

Jim knew that many of his decisions were actually quite routine.[36] They occurred over and over.

To handle these recurrent decisions, Jim knew that he could use one of four basic strategies.

1. *He could develop policies.* Policies are broad guidelines that govern a group's actions on a particular subject. They try to

anticipate questions that may arise and provide answers to these inquiries before they occur. For example, Bethel Church had established policies concerning the use of its van, the presence of sick children in its preschool program and the use of its kitchen facilities.

2. *He could establish procedures.* A procedure is a standardized series of steps designed to accomplish a recurrent goal. For example, Jim's church had developed procedures which explained how to order Sunday School supplies, run a fire drill, and conduct a house-to-house religious survey.

3. *He could create rules.* A set of rules is a standardized code of conduct. Because Jim's church association wanted to protect its children at camp, for instance, it posted a list of rules on the gate outside its swimming pool.

4. *He could be guided by customary practices.* Practices are traditional ways of doing things. For example, Pastor Grant didn't have to struggle with the church's order of worship each Sunday. Neither did he have to wonder if the church was going to have a "sunrise service" on Easter morning. These were already long-established and well-accepted traditions.

When Jim used these standardized methods of handling routine decisions, he reaped several benefits. In addition to the time and mental energy that he saved, he was also able to treat people and issues in a fair and consistent way.

In addition, when Jim's novice team members followed his guidelines correctly, he was able to get twice as much done. Jim could delegate some of his work and still be sure that his ideas were being implemented the way that he wanted them to be.

Despite these benefits, Jim felt that standardized decision-making was sometimes a hindrance to his ministry.[37] He found that routines trapped his people in a rut that restrained their flexibility, initiative, and creativity. Shirley was right when she defined a rut as nothing more than an open-ended grave.

To avoid this problem, Jim encouraged his leaders to periodically review their practices, policies, procedures, and rules. He wanted to make sure that they were up-to-date, understandable, streamlined, and helpful in accomplishing their goals.

TIMELY DECISIONS

As the computer committee considered the enormous amount of information it had collected, Jim became more and more frustrated. It seemed like the group was incapable of making up its collective mind.

They had already struggled with their task for five weeks. However, they still weren't ready to make a recommendation. In the meantime, technology was changing and new products were being introduced.

How long are we going to have to wait, Jim wondered, *before we're able to make a reasonably sound decision?*

He knew, of course, that some people were like Mary Black, the church's energetic Sunday School director. She habitually made snap decisions which she regretted later. She often behaved like Abraham and Sarah who, in their haste to have a son, raced ahead of God.[38] Jim realized that the antidote to this kind of impulsive behavior lay in the psalmist's admonition: "Wait for the Lord; be strong and take heart and wait for the Lord."[39]

On the other hand, some people were like Pastor Grant. He was a snail of a decision-maker. Before moving ahead, he always tried to make sure that he had accumulated all the facts, thoroughly considered every option, and developed a fool-proof plan. He sometimes delayed decisions so long that crises occurred, time was wasted, and opportunities were lost. That thoroughly frustrated Jim.

In Jim's eyes, his slow shepherd needed to step out in faith more often. After all, when the Israelites entered the Promised Land, the Jordan River didn't dry up until the priests who carried the ark of the covenant actually moved forward and placed their feet into the water.[40]

As Jim thought about this issue, he decided that there were at least seven factors which determine the speed at which a decision should be made. These elements could be expressed in questions like these:

- *What will the decision cost us in terms of resources?* If an organization is going to construct a new building, the project will require a great deal of money, manpower, time, and effort. Therefore, the matter should be given considerable thought. On the other hand, if a decision involves only a few dollars, it can be made rather quickly.

- *Can the decision be easily reversed?* It's obvious that a person who is going to have a leg amputated needs more time than one who is trying to choose what kind of clothes he is going to wear. Why? Because one choice is permanent and the other is not.

- *If a decision can be changed at a later date, how much will it cost us to make that change?* Sometimes a decision can be reversed but that reversal will be expensive and difficult to implement. If that's true, a person needs to weigh his options carefully before he makes a decision.

- *What is the decision's long-term impact on our organization?* If Jim signed a five-year service contract for the church's office equipment, he'd have to consider the ramifications of his decision much longer than if he was planning to sign a contract for three months.

- *How urgent is the matter?* A fireman doesn't have the luxury of waiting a week before making a decision. Emergency situations call for quick, decisive action. However, people can often avoid crisis decision making by anticipating problems and dealing with them before they occur.

- *What is the worst thing that will happen if the decision is postponed?* If a delay would significantly cripple his efforts, Jim would have to make up his mind quickly. If it would not, he could make up his mind at a more leisurely pace.

- *How complex is the decision?* The greater the issue's complexity, the more time Jim would need to finalize a decision.

IMPLEMENTING DECISIONS

After deliberating two months, the computer committee finally came up with its recommendation. Once the decision was made, Jim told the group that it was useless to procrastinate or second-guess their conclusions.[41] It was time to act.

In the past, when Jim had been unsure of an idea, he would try it out on a small scale. These trial efforts often indicated whether his plans would work or not. They also helped him to refine his approach and techniques.

In this case, however, Jim felt certain that they were on the right track and ready to move. The rest of the committee agreed.

Of course, Jim knew it wasn't wise to engrave their plans in stone. Just as sailors keep a watchful eye on the air and water currents around them, the group needed to keep their eyes open for problems, new opportunities, and changing circumstances. More than likely, they would still have to make a few adjustments in implementing their plan.

Jim also recognized that, despite their best efforts, the computer committee might fail or make one or two mistakes.

Despite occasional failures, however, Jim believed that the committee and the church as a whole could accomplish more by taking a risk and daring to do something great than by never trying to do anything at all. He liked the slogan that he had seen on a plaque recently: "If you want to have a fruitful ministry, you must realize that the good fruit is always out on a limb."[42]

POINTS TO PONDER

1. What kind of decisions do you face during a typical week—both at work and at home?

2. Would you seek God's guidance when choosing a tape recorder? Why or why not?

3. To whom do you go for advice when you have to make an important decision? Why?

4. How could leaders speed up the decision-making process at your church?

PRACTICAL PROJECTS

1. List the criteria that you would use in selecting:

   - A company to pave your church's parking lot.
   - A printer for your church's computer system.
   - The date and time for a training workshop.

2. Interview three pastors and ask them what role prayer has played in their decision-making.

5

Which Way Is It to Portland from Here?

(PLANNING)

"It looks like somebody's planning to go on a trip," observed Holly as she strode into Jim's tiny office.

"That's right," replied Jim as he gathered up the numerous tour books, maps, brochures, and magazine articles cluttering his desk. "Our family is going to Portland for a vacation this year," he explained. "So I was using my lunch hour to do some preliminary planning for our little excursion."

"I wish I could go with you," sighed Holly. "I hear there's plenty of things to see and do."

"Maybe too much," responded Jim with a weary nod of his head. "We're looking forward to our sightseeing spree. But there are so many details that we still have to work out before we go. When should we leave and return? How far should we travel each day? What will we see and do? How much can we spend? And, where will we eat and sleep?

"We want everything to go smoothly, get the most for our money and make sure that our time is well spent."

"It sounds a little like planning for our annual Sunday School picnic, doesn't it?" joked Holly.

"I suppose you're right. And, I guess that's why you're here, isn't it?" Jim asked. "Let me just finish cleaning up this mess and then we'll be ready to begin." As Holly quietly sat down, Jim quickly deposited his mountain of information into his briefcase.

PRELIMINARY PLANNING

After Jim retrieved a file marked "Sunday School Picnic," he picked up the conversation where he had left off. "I'm glad, Holly, that you've agreed to coordinate the Sunday School picnic this year. I know that you'll do a fine job."

"I'm not so sure about that," confessed Holly. "I've never done this before and it's quite an undertaking. I'm not even sure where to begin."

"Well, let's begin by making some initial decisions," suggested Jim. "First, we need to determine the date and time of the picnic."

"Well, that's fairly easy," responded Holly. "Traditionally, we hold the picnic in June. That's because it still rains too much in May and, by July, a lot of our people are already on vacation."

"Well, would you mind challenging tradition and holding it in September?" asked Jim. "That way, we could kick off our Sunday School year with an exciting event."

Holly smiled an "Amen" grin and laughed quietly, "No problem. It certainly would give me more time to prepare."

"Good. I was hoping you'd like that idea," said Jim. He was glad that he had found a kindred spirit.

Jim leafed through his pocket calendar until he came to the month of September. Then he continued.

"I've already looked at the church and community calendars, and made some discoveries. The first weekend in September, Labor Day weekend, is out. Many of our people will be gone. The second weekend is also out; that's our county rodeo. And, we can't hold our picnic on the fourth Sunday of the month because our young people are scheduled to present a choir concert that evening. That leaves only the third Sunday in September. Is that okay with you?"

"Sure. That'll be great," agreed Holly. "In fact, we can capitalize on the excitement of our county rodeo by using a western theme for the picnic this year."

"Okay, the third Sunday it is," said Jim as he quickly scribbled this event down in his already event-filled pocket calendar.

"Before you leave this afternoon, make sure that Shirley knows about our decision," advised Jim. "She coordinates the church's calendar and irons out the conflicts between competing church activities. I'll also mention it in our next staff meeting.

"Now, what time should we begin and end the picnic?"

"Well, we need to allow the people enough time to go home after church, change their clothes, and gather their food," reasoned Holly. "I think 1:30 would be just about right.

"And, if we quit around 5:30," she continued, "we'll have enough time to clean up and get back home at a reasonable hour."

Jim jotted a quick note to himself before throwing out another question. "Where would you like to hold the picnic?"

"Three places come to mind," answered Holly without a pause. She handled Jim's questions as expertly as a professional baseball slugger handles batting practice.

"Here, I've made a chart of the pros and cons of several possibilities," said Holly as she handed Jim a neatly typed sheet of paper.

	Church	City Park	Doug's Ranch
Easy to Find	excellent	good	poor
Space	poor	good	excellent
Playgrounds	no	yes	no
Privacy for Program	very good	poor	excellent
Time Available To Set-Up	good	poor	fair
Facilities for Closing Program	excellent	poor	poor
Cost	free	expensive	free

"Are you always so organized?" asked Jim as he considered the information on the chart.

"I guess it comes from having a mom who wraps gifts at Warner's Department Store," admitted Holly. "She likes everything in neat little packages; and so do I."

Holly gave Jim some time to consider the chart and then explained her personal preference. "I think that we should have the picnic out at Doug's ranch. It's a beautiful place, and people will have no trouble finding it, as long as we provide them with a good map."

"I agree," affirmed Jim. "Doug wants to get more involved in church activities and use his possessions to help the church blossom. This would give him an excellent opportunity to do so."

"What's more, this choice dovetails with my idea of using a western motif for this occasion," added Holly.

"It would tie all of our activities together and give us a chance to use our creativity. Our food, games, clothes, decorations, music, and even our evening devotional could be centered around this theme. How does 'Lassoed by the Lord' or 'Branded by God' sound?"

Without waiting for a response to her ideas, Holly continued. "It would also give us a chance to capitalize on our church's resources. Jerry Wilder, who tours the rodeo circuit during the summer, could give an excellent testimony. Sid Simms' quartet could provide some good country and western music."

"Aren't the words 'good' and 'country' contradictory terms?" asked Jim with a broad grin.

"Let me finish," protested Holly with a warm smile that matched Jim's. "As I was saying, Sid's group could sing for us. And, since they have a great portable sound system, maybe we could use it for the entire closing program.

"Come to think of it, Doug could provide us with bales of hay to sit on. . . ."

"Whoa. I get the idea and I like it," said Jim enthusiastically. Holly's exuberance was contagious. Jim was really getting excited about an event that had been as bland as porridge in the past.

"I guess that brings us to the picnic's program," said Jim. "What kind of activities do you have planned for the picnic?"

"Well, I've already sketched out a tentative schedule for your approval," said Holly. "It looks something like this:"

1:30-2:30	Welcome, Prayer, Picnic, and Fellowship
2:30-3:00	Contests and Games (for the entire family)
3:00-4:30	Adult Games (baseball, volleyball, etc.)
	Children's Fair (with a variety of booths)
4:30-5:30	Closing Program (with special speaker)
5:30-6:30	Clean Up

As Jim looked approvingly at the outline Holly had handed him, he couldn't help wishing he had more workers like Holly. She was smart, enthusiastic, excited about the church's ministry, and fun to be with. In fact, there were times when he wished that his wife could be a little more like her.

Embarrassed by the direction of his thoughts, he squelched his feelings and turned his attention toward Holly's plans. "That's great!" exclaimed Jim with admiration. "It looks like you've given this more thought than you want to admit. Do you have a guest speaker in mind?"

"Well, as matter a fact, I have three people in mind," said Holly. "But you know these men better than I do. Maybe you can help me make that decision. Here's how I've laid out their strengths and weaknesses:"

Speaker:	Frank Evans	Paul Tyler	Ken Thomas
Proximity:	Close	Close	Far Away
Style:	Formal Evangelistic	Casual Humorous	Casual Teacher
Cost:	Average	High	High
Well Known:	Yes	Yes	No
Ability:	Good	Excellent	Good
Doctrine:	Evangelical	Evangelical	Evangelical

"Your descriptions are very accurate," commented Jim as he scanned her list. "I think we should go with Paul Tyler because: our picnic will be a very informal affair, our program will be designed basically for our own church members, and we want a quality speaker who will draw people."

"My thoughts, exactly!" beamed Holly. Jim and Holly's ideas were meshing like a well-crafted dovetail joint.

SCHEDULING

"Okay, we've made some basic decisions about the picnic. Now let's flesh out the specific details," recommended Jim. "When I'm planning an event, I usually like to follow a five-step planning process that I learned back in Bible school." As Jim outlined his approach to planning, he secretly hoped that he would be able to impress Holly with his management knowledge and skills.

Step 1, "Let's write down everything that we need to do to make this picnic a success. We can jot down each individual step on some index cards that I've printed up especially for this purpose." As Jim made this suggestion, he handed Holly a short stack of blue cards which looked like the one below.

Task:	
Person:	
Start:	End:

"I guess we could also use small slips of paper for this exercise, Jim added. "It certainly would be cheaper. But I find it's much easier to handle stiff stock like this. Okay, let's see what kind of ideas we can generate."

Both Holly and Jim began to write down their ideas furiously. After only a minute of deliberation, they had come up with the following ideas:

- Alphabetically divide the congregation into three groups and then ask families to bring hot dishes, salads, or desserts according to their group assignment.

- Provide such incidentals as ketchup, mustard, paper plates, napkins, and garbage bags.

- Ask Bill Chamberlin to arrange a crew to set up the food table and warm up the hot dishes.

- Recruit Paul Tyler to be our special speaker.

- Contact Jerry Wilder to give a testimony.

- Ask Sid Simms' group to provide the special music.

- Recruit ushers for the evening program.

- Bring offering plates.

- Bring plenty of garbage pails for trash.

- Cover the picnic tables.

- Set out the food on tables.

- Set up a pop stand.

- Organize the fair booths.

- Provide games for the children.

- Bring sports equipment.

- Clean up the site after the picnic.

- Ask Sid if we can use the quartet's portable speaker system.

Five minutes later, Jim looked at the mound of ideas that they had produced. He was gratified with the results.

He thought they had written down every conceivable step in their plan. Of course, they hadn't. As their planning progressed, Jim knew that they would have to add to this initial list of ideas. However, they had made a good start.

Step 2, "Let's take all of these ideas and sort them into some natural categories. Let's put all of the activities that deal with food into one pile, and all that deal with publicity into another pile. We'll continue to do this until all of our activities have been properly grouped."

Holly followed Jim's instructions immediately and began to sort the cards into their respective groups.

Step 3, Once that job had been completed, both of them launched into a third phase. They arrange the activities within each area in the sequence in which they hoped to accomplish them. This led quickly to a fourth step.

Step 4, Jim proposed that they assign deadlines to each of the activities. "Deadlines," editorialized Jim, "lend urgency to each task and help motivate people to finish their jobs on time."

Holly objected timidly, "But it's so hard to estimate when things should be done and how long each task will take."

Jim could identify with her concerns. "That's true," he said sympathetically. "But experience is a good teacher and, after you've done this a few times, the accuracy of your estimates will improve greatly."

Holly stared at Jim and pondered the implications of his statement. She wondered how many more projects he had in mind for her.

If Jim noticed Holly's anxious look, he didn't mention it.

He simply continued talking as if he were teaching a Sunday School class. "Two things will help us with our calculations. We need to start from the picnic's date and work backwards and we need to build slack time into our schedule. This way, if problems occur, and they will, we can solve them with a minimum amount of anxiety and pressure."

This step definitely turned out to be the most difficult. Holly and Jim spent a long time discussing the project and assigning dates to the various tasks. After they had completed this part of the project, Jim started to explain the final rung that they needed to climb on their planning ladder.

DISPLAYING SCHEDULES

"Lastly, after you've designed a game plan, it's often helpful to display your schedule in such a way that you and your team members can see where you're going and how things are progressing. This brings us to our last step. You'll need to decide how you're going to display your plans.

"There are several ways of doing this. You can use a storyboard approach. In other words, you can tape or tack these index cards to a wall or a bulletin board in the order in which the events will occur. If you follow this approach, your storyboard will look something like this."

Food	Select Menu	Decide Who Brings What	Select Food Pre-parers	Set Up Equipment
Family Games	Select Staff	Choose Games	Bring Materials	Host Com-petition
Children's Fair	Dream Up Booths	Select Staff	Find Equipment	Set Up Booths
Closing Program	Select Speaker	Select Musicians	Plan Song Service	Print Programs
Publicity	Display Posters	Announce in Bulletin	Announce in News-letter	Sell Tickets

"Gummed notes would work perfectly for this, wouldn't they?" asked Holly.

"Yes. I suppose they would," agreed Jim. Inwardly, however, he felt disappointed that anyone would prefer a substitute for his specially printed cards.

"You also might want to display your plans with a project planner," recommended Jim.

"Here's an example of what one might look like if you used it to plan your publicity efforts," added Jim as he handed Holly the following sheet.

PROJECT PLANNER

Project/Event: *Sunday School Picnic:*
Area: *Publicity*
Completion Date: *Sept. 15*
Project Director: *Tom Brown*
Goal: *Persuade 200 people to come to the picnic.*

| Done | Schedule | | Activity | Person |
	Begin	Finish		
x	8/5	8/10	1. Paint picnic banner	Dan Rivers
x	8/5	8/10	2. Paint picnic posters	Dan Rivers
x	8/11		3. Display banner and posters	Tom Brown
x	8/11		4. Announce picnic in bulletin	Shirley H.
	8/25		5. Announce picnic in newsletter	Shirley H.
	8/26	8/28	6. Prepare bulletin insert and take-home invitations	Shirley H.
	9/1	9/8	7. Distribute take-home invitations	Mary Black
	9/1	9/15	8. Sell tickets	Tom Brown June Johnson Holly Smith
	9/1	9/15	9. Announce picnic in bulletin	Shirley H.
	9/8	9/15	10. Announce from pulpit	Pastor Grant

"A third alternative would be to use a horizontal bar chart which graphically shows people how your project is progressing," said Jim.

Here's an example of one that Susan White used in presenting our nursery renovation program to the church council."

Event/Project: *Nursery Renovation*
Prepared by: *Susan White*

TASK	SCHEDULE					
	Nov	Dec	Jan	Feb	Mar	Apr
1. Design Nursery Plans	██████					
2. Seek Approval of Plans		██				
3. Obtain Special Donations			██████			
4. Purchase Materials				████▒▒		
5. Renovate the Nursery					███▒▒▒	
Finished: ██						
Planned: ▒▒						

"Then, of course, you could display your plans with a PERT diagram. This is a sophisticated charting technique which was developed for large construction projects. It shows the complex network of relationships and interactions between a set of tasks. . . ."

Jim could tell from the bewildered expression on Holly's face that she didn't understand what he was trying to say. So he cut his diatribe short with the words, "But I think that's a little too complicated for our purposes."

Jim sat back in his chair and surveyed the plan that they had outlined. It had taken a couple of hours to develop their schedule, but Holly and he were immensely pleased at their efforts.

"Well," sighed Holly. "This sure has been a lot of work but it's also been quite rewarding. Jim, you sure know a lot about planning. I wish everybody I worked with would be as organized as you are."

Jim appreciated Holly's compliment. It was like a warm fire on a frigid night.

He also enjoyed working with Holly. She was so positive and pleasant, not to mention attractive. He certainly hoped that he would be able to work with her on other projects as well.

"Well, I have another appointment in a couple of minutes," said Jim as he brought the planning session to a close. "However, I think you have more than enough ideas with which to begin. Why don't you start recruiting some of your key leaders. Then, give me a call in a couple of weeks and we'll see how things are progressing.

"Oh, just one more thing, don't forget to save your plans and paperwork. It'll help the next group that has to plan the Sunday School picnic."

CURRICULUM

While waiting for his next appointment, Jim quickly scribbled a memo to June Johnson, an elementary school teacher who had agreed to coordinate the church's upcoming VBS efforts.

Dear June,

Here are the curriculum samples that I promised you. Each set of materials has its advantages and disadvantages. As you examine them, please evaluate their suitability in the following areas.

biblical and theological content
appeal to our students in terms of interest and abilities
technical competence (the quality of their paper, print, graphics)
overarching theme
teachability
methodology
organization
literary style
teaching resources
teacher training sections
practicality
emphasis on evangelism and Christ

When you've selected the materials that you'd like to use, let me know. I can order them from Sweetwater's Christian Bookstore. It'll take about three or four weeks for delivery.

Before you purchase any other materials, please check the church's resource center. We already have a large selection of audio-visual aids and classroom supplies that your teachers can use.

When VBS is over, please return the teaching materials to Kelly Rivers, who takes care of our resource center. She usually tries to re-cycle our curriculum materials. She often laminates the pictures and songs that are included in the teachers' resource kits. This way, we can use them over and over again in our church. At other times, she gives the curriculum materials to a mission project or another church.

If you have any questions, let me know. I'll talk to you about our workshop for VBS teachers shortly.

Yours in Christ,
Jim Stafford

FACILITIES AND EQUIPMENT

As Jim was finishing this note, he heard a commotion in the hallway. He knew right away that Mary Black and her daughter, Sally, were on their way to see him. Sally's demanding wail was quite distinctive.

As Jim's guests entered his office, he offered Sally a book and some lemon drops from the oak candy dish that garnished the top of his otherwise barren desk. Some parents didn't appreciate Jim's bribes, but Mary looked grateful. Now that Sally was temporarily distracted, Mary could discuss an important matter with Jim that had been bothering her for some time.

"Jim, we just have to do something about our educational facilities. Our church looks like it is suffering through the Exodus plagues.[1]

"The rooms are dirty, drab, and dingy. Some of them aren't properly cooled or heated. And, the walls in Vance Jordan's three-year-old classroom look like his students have been using crayons to create a pop art mural.

"Now, I know that churches back in New Testament times didn't meet in fancy structures. But, doesn't the Bible say that we should be as interested in maintaining God's house as we are in maintaining our own houses?"[2]

Jim knew that Mary tended to exaggerate when she wanted to make a point. He also knew that church members could become so enamored with beautiful buildings that they would forget the reason for their existence.

Even so, Jim agreed with Mary's concerns. The facilities definitely needed to be improved. They had seen little change since Bethel Church had bought their building from another congregation over ten years ago.

Mary took what looked like a shopping list from her leather handbag and then began enumerating her concerns. "We need to replace the old, wooden chairs in the kindergarten classroom. They're ancient.

"Then we need to install an air conditioner in Mike Todd's adult classroom. Summer is coming and that room attracts heat like a clean car attracts rain.

"We also need to knock out the wall between the second grade classroom and the small storage room adjoining it. This would give us the twenty-five to thirty square feet per child that educators recommend.

"Furthermore, we should have a clean-up day sometime next month. This will give our teachers a chance to sandblast their rooms and replace their pre-WWII pictures with some new and attractive decorations."

Mary paused slightly to see if Jim was saluting the flag that she was raising. Fortunately, that unshackled Jim just long enough to insert one brief observation.

"Mary, don't forget, timing is crucial.[3] I learned in playing baseball that if you swing too early or too late, you'll strike out. Why don't we wait until this fall to hold the clean-up day? That would be a natural time for our teachers—especially the new ones—to take a fresh look at their rooms."

Although Mary wasn't known for her patience, she was willing to grant Jim that minor concession.

"The same principle," Jim said, "holds true for some of the other projects that you've mentioned. We don't want to spring those ideas unexpectedly on the trustees, Pastor Grant, or our janitor. Because we need their support and approval, let's carefully sow some seeds first and then harvest them when they're ripe for the picking."

Mary felt the energy and enthusiasm draining out of her. She wanted to accomplish great things for God. But now Jim's words of caution loomed up in front of her like an insurmountable barrier. She began to hesitate as she presented her next set of ideas. Her robust barks became timid pleas.

"Well, I don't know if the church leaders would agree with me, but I think we need to be better stewards of our facilities. Most of the time, our classrooms are empty. Couldn't we invite outside groups to use them during the day? Our church could become a place where people gather to vote, donate blood, exercise, or even learn English.

"Once people come to our church and see our facilities, maybe they'll decide to visit our worship services."

In the short time that Jim had been at Bethel Church, he had already received requests from several organizations to use the church's rooms. However, he worried about the insurance and tax implications. He was also afraid that the church would spend so much time accommodating other groups that it would forget its two major ministries: evangelizing non-Christians and equipping Christians.

However, Jim didn't express his reservations to Mary. He sensed that his previous comments had already taken some of the sizzle out of her proposals.

Mary went on, "We also need to swap our women's class and the junior high class. If we do that, then all of our young people will be in one location. In fact, I'd like to see our junior high class paint and decorate their own room just the way that they would like. I'm sure that they could come up with a comfortable, contemporary look that would be suited to their age group."

Mary ended her evaluation with a small but potent question. She asked Jim, "What do you think?"

Jim had already taken stock of the church's educational facilities and was slowly trying to improve them. He enjoyed this part of his job and felt that he could make a lot of progress in this area.

So Jim was disturbed that Mary seemed intent on intruding into his territory. He felt that her initiatives would interfere with his own plans. They'd take money away from his projects and upset the trustees unnecessarily.

At the same time, he was reluctant to throttle back such an enthusiastic worker. There were so few like her involved in the church's educational program. And, after all, Jim felt that he was already juggling more balls than he could possibly manage.

As Jim considered his response, he realized that he had partly contributed to the dilemma that he faced. He had never informed Mary about his plans to enhance the facilities. In doing so, he had neglected the very principle that he had emphasized with Mary just a short time before; that is, people need to be informed about and involved in the planning process.

So, after letting Mary know that he was on her side, he shared with her some of the steps that he was already poised to take. He told her that he would be asking the trustees, at their next meeting, to approve the building of storage cabinets in the children's classrooms and the installation of an air conditioner in Mike Todd's classroom.

By the end of the year, he was also hoping to paint the church's educational wing. Right now, however, the trustees were concentrating on the nursery's renovation which was already running a month behind schedule. So Jim felt that it would be better to approach them about this project in the fall.

In addition to sharing these plans, Jim also asked for Mary's input in some other decisions that still needed to be made. For example, they debated whether it was more important to buy chairs for the senior adult or the kindergarten classroom. Jim eventually acquiesced to Mary's demands in this area. He did so with the hope that his actions would garner her sympathy and support when they dealt with other issues later.

As they discussed the church's facilities and equipment, Jim and Mary quickly recognized that, because of their limited resources, they couldn't do everything at once. They would have to set their priorities.

So, after outlining all of the improvements that needed to be made, they divided their list into short-term and long-term goals. Some things could be done immediately while other things would have to wait.

Just as they were finishing their conversation, Sally wailed her frustration, "Mommy, I'm tired. Can't we go home?"

Mary assured Sally that they were just about to leave but turned back to Jim so that she could add a postscript to their discussion.

"I thought you might be interested in a little sign that I saw at First Church. It said:

1. If you open it, close it.

2. If you turn it on, turn it off.

3. If you unlock it, lock it.

4. If you move it, put it back.

5. If it belongs to someone else, get permission to use it.

6. If you use it, take care of it.

7. If you borrow it, return it.

8. If you don't know how to operate it, leave it alone.

9. If it doesn't concern you, don't mess with it.

10. If you break it, repair it.

11. If you can't fix it, call someone who can.

12. If you make a mess, clean it up.[4]

"Isn't that precious? I think we ought to make a copy of this list and post it not only in our resource center but also in every classroom in the church."

Convinced that Jim had been sensitized to her feelings and ideas, Mary left his office with a sense of satisfaction; but not before Sally demanded a going-away-present: two more lemon drops from Jim's confectionery.

FINANCES

It had been a long, rain-drenched day. The Staffords had spent the whole evening preoccupied with church matters. Jim had refined his Sunday School lesson, even though it was only Thursday. Jill had put together the details of an upcoming baby shower.

By the time their grandfather clock announced the arrival of ten o'clock, both Jim and Jill were ready to draw the curtain on another busy day. Jill was hoping, at last, that she would be able to relax and spend a few quiet moments with Jim—alone. Lately, it seemed like these tranquil oases were appearing farther and farther apart.

But this time, everything looked promising. Brenda and Barb had gone to sleep. The lights had been turned down low. The relaxed piano stylings of Clint Gardner were playing gently in the background.

It seemed like the stage had been set for a restful conclusion to an otherwise productive evening. However, just as they sat down, the telephone rang.

As Jim went to the telephone, Jill pleaded, "Do you have to answer the telephone?" She was annoyed at the interloper who had so rudely intruded their quiet, romantic moment.

"You never know. This might be an important call," Jim replied defensively as he closed the door of his study behind him. When he picked up the receiver, he immediately recognized a familiar voice on the other end.

"Hi! This is Holly," she announced in her effervescent tone. "This afternoon, when we were talking about the Sunday School picnic, I completely forgot to ask you about something: 'How are we going to pay for everything?'"

"Good question!" replied Jim. "I'm sorry we didn't have time to talk about it this afternoon. The church has already budgeted two hundred dollars for this event."

"How did they arrive at that figure?" asked Holly.

"Well, from what I can gather," said Jim, "the church usually increases the amount of each budget item by about 10 percent every year. Unless, of course, a group is foolish enough to drastically underspend their budget. Then the church council just slashes the group's new budget by whatever amount that the organization had left over from the preceding year."

Holly was astounded by Jim's explanation. "What if our allotment isn't enough to cover our expenses?" she asked.

"More than likely, it won't be," answered Jim. "When the church council put together the budget, they assumed that we would be having a traditional potluck picnic with a bland, local speaker and equally uninviting activities. I wasn't on staff yet. So nobody gave it a second thought. Of course, this year, I want our picnic to be different. I want it to sparkle like a fireworks display on July fourth."

"Maybe we'll have to ask the bank for a loan," teased Holly.

"I don't think that'll be necessary," snickered Jim. "Besides, the Scriptures warn us about living within our means.[5] "However, if we want to achieve our goals, we may have to look for ways to augment our income. For one thing, we could ask the church council if we can take an offering, during our evening program, to defray our expenses. We could also sell pop, chips, and 'Praise the Lord' T-shirts. Or, we could charge a small fee at each carnival booth."

"Won't some people object to that?" asked Holly.

"Maybe. But the church sells tickets to people who attend our sweetheart banquet and the money that is collected is used to cover some of the expenses for that event," countered Jim. "I don't think our situation is any different than that.

"We could also solicit individual contributions. However, the church might get upset if we do that. In principle, our church has a unified budget. This prevents people from supporting only the groups or the activities that they like. It also helps reduce the amount of control that some people like to exercise over certain church activities.

"Of course, it doesn't always work out that way. Both our women's group and our youth group have budgets outside the church's jurisdiction."

"Couldn't we ask people to donate items that we'll need for the picnic?" asked Holly.

"Sure!" responded Jim. "If Doug donates the use of his ranch, he'll save us a hefty park fee. If Sid Simms agrees to let us use his sound system, that'll save us some more money. We could also ask people to contribute food and lend us their barbecue grills."

Holly piggybacked on that idea. "Maybe we could even get some local businesses to donate food items or prizes that promote their product. I'll bet Rose Adams would even lend us her clown costume for the children's activities."

"On the expenditure side," said Jim, "we also can take several steps to keep our costs down. We can buy in bulk, watch for sales, purchase big-ticket items from a discount dealer, and compare prices as we shop."

"By the way, how will the church reimburse us for our expenses?" asked Holly.

"To insure that we stay within our budget," said Jim, "the church council requires that I approve all expenditures for the areas under my control. So, before you purchase something, make sure that you ask me first. Then I'll fill out a check request form and ask our treasurer, Katie Miller, to pay the appropriate person or company. If an item costs under fifty dollars, we can pay for it out of our petty cash account.

"Holly, when you buy things, make sure you keep all of your receipts. Otherwise, the church won't reimburse you. In fact, it might be wise to appoint somebody to be the picnic's treasurer. They could keep track of both our income and our expenditures. It's important to keep such records. They'll document your honesty, and, they'll help us when we plan next year's picnic."

"All of these controls seem a bit cumbersome, don't they?" Holly observed.

"Maybe. But they also help us keep a tight reign on our costs. That's especially important when our funds are running low, like they are right now."

Holly was surprised by Jim's financial news bulletin. "You mean we aren't meeting our budget?"

"That's right," said Jim. "So the church council has asked everybody to cut back their expenses by 10 percent. However, instead of asking every educational group to cut their budgets by that much, I've decided to postpone our children's crusade and the purchase of some sporting equipment until we're back in the black. That will give us about the same amount of savings.

"I've also asked Pastor Grant to make a special appeal to our church members. However, he's reluctant to do that because requests for money usually upset people. I think I've convinced him, though, to state in the bulletin where we stand in relationship to our budget so far this year."

"Now that I know about our church's dilemma," said Holly, "I'm going to take some of the money that I usually give to other missionary organizations and give it to the church."

"Good. I'm glad to hear that," remarked Jim. "I'm trying to do my part too. Even though it's tough at times, both Jill and I give more than a tenth of our incomes to the church.

"I, for one, think that tithing is biblical. Unfortunately, very few of our families seem to agree.[6]

RESOURCES

Holly asked somewhat skeptically, "Do you think we'll have enough money and resources to provide a good picnic?"

"Well, as Pastor Grant is fond of saying, 'If we do God's work in God's way, we'll never lack God's resources.'[7]

"Take, for example, the feeding of the five thousand.[8] A little boy was willing to give all that he had. Most people, that day, probably scoffed and said that his gift wasn't big enough to do the job. However, Jesus took that sacrificial gift and supplied a meal that thousands would never forget.

"In the Old Testament, God is called Jehovah-Jireh [9](which means 'the Lord will provide') for a very good reason. He's in the business of supplying our needs.[10] He gave the Israelites manna to eat and water to drink in the wilderness.[11] He fed Elijah when that prophet was hiding from Ahab.[12] The Bible says that He's even willing to give us more than we request—if we'll just trust in Him."[13]

Jim paused and glanced down at his watch. He was stunned by how long they had talked. So he quickly tried to bring the conversation to a close.

"Boy, it's getting mighty late. I'd better be going.

"Why don't you prepare a budget for the picnic showing me your anticipated income and expenditures? As you do that, remember a couple of things: allow for inflation, hold back enough to cover miscellaneous costs, overestimate expenses, and underestimate income. Then I'll check back with you in a couple of weeks, and we'll talk more about financing the church picnic."

By the time Jim returned to the living room, Jill was fuming. It was already 10:30 and she was tired. Not too tired, though, to ask an important question.

"Who was that?" she gently prodded.

"Oh, that was just Holly," Jim nonchalantly explained. "We had to go over some details for our fall picnic."

His explanation seemed so benign that she was embarrassed by her feelings of jealousy. Yet, she couldn't help wondering if there was more to the call than he was willing to reveal.

She was angry that he was spending more and more time with Holly—even if they were discussing church business. She asked herself, *Why can't Jim be more sensitive to my feelings and spend as much time nurturing our relationship as he spends building his precious church programs?* As they went to bed that night, more than the evening chill was in the air.

PLANNING PRINCIPLES

Two weeks later, Jim decided to give Holly a call and see how things were progressing. When he did, he was surprised by her response.

"I guess things are going well enough," remarked Holly in an uncharacteristically reserved tone. "But I sure know a lot more about planning now than when I first talked with you. Why didn't you warn me that this job would be so difficult?"

Her comment both stunned and disappointed Jim. He naively thought that his coaching session with Holly had thoroughly equipped her to plan the entire picnic. As Jim listened to Holly, he reasoned defensively that a trainee could never learn everything that there is to know in a single, brief session.[14]

Unaware of Jim's bruised pride, Holly continued: "For one thing, I learned that plans don't always work out the way that you expect. For example, I talked to all three of our potential speakers. And you know what? None of them can come.

"Then I talked to Sid about using his sound system. He welcomed my request with the enthusiasm of a child who has been forced to drink castor oil.

"And, who knows what kind of problems we'll encounter in the future. Will it rain? Will one of our leaders get sick? Will some of our equipment break down?"

"Well, I see that the principle of uncertainty is still as certain as ever," quipped Jim.

"That's for sure," said Holly. "And, because the future is so unpredictable, I'm trying to be a little more flexible in my planning.[15] But it's hard.

"I've started to write down my long-range plans in pencil rather than pen. I've begun to preface my declarations with the phrases like: 'if the Lord wills.'[16] I'm also trying to develop some contingency plans, just in case things don't happen the way we hope they will. Most importantly, since God knows and controls the future, I'm learning to commit my plans to His care."[17]

"I'm sorry to hear that you've had such a tough time getting out of the starting blocks," said Jim in a concerned voice.

"Oh, it's not really that bad," offered Holly. "I'm just glad that I started preparing for this picnic so early. This way, I'll have the time that I need to recruit my workers, locate my materials, develop some really creative ideas, handle unexpected difficulties, and still approach the picnic with a relaxed and confident attitude."

Jim was relieved to hear that, despite some early frustration, Holly was still eagerly pursuing her goals.

"Would you like to speak at one of our teacher training workshops?" he asked. "Boy, I wish I could convince my Sunday School teachers of the need for early preparation."

Holly declined the invitation and then went on to describe another lesson that she had learned. "Yesterday, I brought together my key leaders for a meeting. I described, in detail, what and when things needed to be done—just like we had outlined them in your office.

"Well, I thought my cohorts would love my easy-to-use, ready-made plan. It would certainly save them a lot of time and effort.

"Boy, was I wrong. At first, they didn't say much. However, I could tell by their body language and lack of response that they resented my prefabricated proposals. They wanted to develop their own strategies and timetables.

"When I shared this experience with one of my colleagues at Christopher College, she pointed out that I had violated one of the major principles of good management. The principle of participative planning states that those responsible for implementing a plan should participate in developing it. 'When people have a hand in preparing their own plans,' she noted, 'those plans will not only be better understood but also be more realistic, enthusiastically supported, and willingly carried out.'"

"Since our last conversation, I've learned a few planning principles myself," admitted Jim. "First of all, I've discovered that I have to dream big but keep my plans simple. Otherwise, things get so complex that I can't see 'the forest from the trees.'

"Secondly, I've discovered that plans increase in their specificity the nearer that I get to an event. In other words, I don't have to have all of the details worked out three months in advance of an activity."

Surprised by Jim's confession, Holly remarked: "It's encouraging to see that I'm not the only one struggling with my plans and preparations.

"Say, why don't you stop by my house tomorrow and I'll show you our timetable, budget, and ideas for the picnic."

"I can't make it tomorrow," said Jim. "I have to wait around here for the delivery of our new computer. Could you stop by the church instead?"

"Okay. But you'll miss the chance to sample some of my great apple pie."

THE IMPORTANCE OF PLANNING

Jim was pleased with the way that Holly's plans were progressing. He had heard that the previous picnic had been a disaster. Its 'planners' had run out of food, made a mess of the activities, and presented a lackluster closing program.

It looked like Holly, however, would be able to avoid that kind of fiasco. The key to her success would be her willingness to adequately prepare for the event. This wise investment in planning would not only save money, time and materials but also prevent chaos, improve performance, reduce stress, and help her to coordinate her team's efforts.

POINTS TO PONDER

1. In this chapter, you've indirectly encountered at least ten of the following planning principles:

    - written plans
    - an uncertain future
    - flexibility
    - divine dependence
    - participation
    - contingencies
    - early preparation
    - simplicity
    - complexity
    - investment

    How would you define each of these principles? What other principles should you keep in mind when planning?

2. How should churches handle scheduling conflicts?

3. Why are teaching facilities, equipment, and materials so important to a church's ministry?

4. What steps can an educational leader take to increase the financial support for his or her organization?

PRACTICAL PROJECTS

Select one of the following projects.

- VBS program
- evangelistic crusade for children, youth, or adults
- city-wide teacher training conference
- valentine banquet
- church picnic with game activities and a closing program
- activity for children, youth, or adults which would last an entire weekend

Then provide a timetable, a list of needed physical resources (facilities, equipment, materials and supplies), and a budget for that project.

6

Where Have All the Workers Gone?

(RECRUITMENT)

"I can't believe it!" shouted Jim as he hung up the phone. "That was Rick Thorten. He volunteered to work in our children's ministry."

"That's wonderful," responded Jill. "Your appeal for more workers last Sunday has really yielded a bountiful harvest. He's the fourth person this week who's volunteered to teach in Sunday School."

"I told him that we didn't have any openings in that area right now," explained Jim. "But, I promised to put his name on our waiting list and let him know as soon as a position opened up.

"In the meantime, he agreed to do some substitute teaching."

"Great!" remarked Jill. "Did you tell him about our three-month training course for potential teachers?"

"I sure did," said Jim. "He enrolled immediately and thanked me for offering the course."

Just as Jim was basking in the glow of another successful recruiting experience, he felt a familiar tug at his shirt.

"Daddy, daddy," said Brenda. "It's time to wake up. Supper's ready, and I'm hungry."

Jim bolted to an upright position and dusted the cobwebs from his mind. Then he groaned: "I knew it was too good to be true. It was just a dream, just a dream."

SETTING THE STAGE FOR RECRUITMENT

When Jim met with his volatile Sunday School director the next day, he longed for the warm cocoon of that dream. Mary Black was in a pessimistic mood. She was overwhelmed by the daunting task of finding all of the workers that she needed for the church's summer and fall programs.

"Recruiting people is an endless and thankless job," complained Mary. "People continually move, quit, change jobs, or ask for a reprieve from their present responsibilities."

"Some of our most faithful people even have the audacity to die on us," she said with an impish laugh.

Jim refused to be contaminated by Mary's negative outlook. "Don't forget. One of our problems is that we're growing," said Jim as he tried to interject a few positive notes into Mary's otherwise gloomy dirge. "And, that's a good problem to have."

Mary remained unconvinced as she continued her lament.

"I sure wish I could recruit like Jesus did. All He had to say to His disciples was 'follow me' and they did.[1] Of course, He was God Incarnate.

"There just doesn't seem to be any commitment out there any more.[2] Everybody seems so self-centered or indifferent. Don't people realize that we can't provide them with the programs that they want if they're not willing to help out?

Once Mary had spent her venom, Jim went on the attack.

"Recruitment has always been difficult, Mary" said Jim.[3] "When God called leaders in the Old Testament, they often responded by making excuses,[4] demanding signs[5] or running away.[6] Jesus' attempts to recruit people didn't always evoke a ready response either. Some people rejected His call outright.[7] Others made excuses.[8] Still others followed Jesus only a short time and then abandoned Him or betrayed Him.[9]

"But, you know Mary, God has a habit of supplying us with everything that we really need.[10] If we're going to be successful recruiters, we have to trust God in this area just as we trust Him in the others areas of our lives.[11]

"Let's not succumb to negative thinking and assume that nobody's interested in serving. Instead, let's cultivate a positive attitude and expect God to guide us to the people whom He's already chosen.

"Before we can staff our programs adequately, we also need to do something else: we need to pray. Jesus said to his disciples: 'The harvest is plentiful but the workers are few. Ask the Lord of the harvest, therefore, to send out workers into his harvest field.'"[12]

"While we may intellectually accept the validity of those verses, we don't often practice them. Most of the time we launch into our recruiting campaigns without ever seeking God's help.

"In fact, we began this meeting without a word of prayer. So, why don't we stop right now and take a moment to talk to God about our concerns."

As Jim prayed, Mary squirmed. She could only spend an hour with Jim. Consequently she was anxious to get on with the recruitment task.

After Jim finished praying, he continued to list the prerequisites that he thought were necessary to successful recruiting. "In addition to approaching our enlistment efforts with faith and prayer, we need to create an atmosphere that is conducive to recruitment. That means that we have to demonstrate to our members how important our educational program is.

"I'm tired of hearing our educational staff say, 'Oh, I'm *just* a Sunday School teacher.' Teaching a Sunday School class is one of the most important things that a person can do in this church!"

"I know that and you know that," said Mary, "but how can we convince our church members that that's true?"

"For one thing," said Jim, "we have to continually tell our congregation about the great things that are happening in our educational program. When our youth group helps to build a church in Mexico, let's trumpet that triumph. When our children present a program in a nursing home, let's spread the good news. When our classes grow or when they complete an important project, let's publicize it."

"Most of the time, we're not doing anything that dramatic," complained Mary. "In Sunday School, we don't major on the spectacular. We just quietly and routinely go about teaching God's Word."

"Well then," said Jim. "Maybe we have to introduce a little pizazz into our activities. I think we should plan our calendar so that we have at least two special events each month that we can promote.

"Then, we need to highlight those activities in a variety of ways. For example, we can use newsletter articles, bulletin inserts, slide shows, special services, skits, and posters.

"I'm even trying to get Pastor Grant to mention our programs and our workers a little bit more in his sermons. If something interesting has happened during the week in one of our programs, I try to mention it to him just before we enter the sanctuary. Then, he'll often refer to my comment during our worship service."

"Sneaky," said Mary with admiration.

"We could also underscore the value of our educational program by holding 'Appreciation Sundays' and 'Appreciation Banquets.' In addition, we could get Pastor Grant to have an installation service for our workers in the fall."

"Great ideas!" said Jim. He was so relieved that Mary was finally offering some positive suggestions that he neglected to tell her about his plans for the fall. He was already preparing to do exactly what she had recommended.

"I also think we need to emphasize a theology of service[13] and sacrifice[14] from the pulpit and in the classroom," added Mary. "Every church member should know that we expect them to be involved in at least one major job in the church."

"That's true," said Jim. "However, we want to emphasize the positive aspects of that theology. If it sounds like Christian service is all drudgery and duty, people won't respond. However, if we tell them about the joys of ministering to others, we'll be more effective.

"We can only do that if we, as leaders, are convinced that Christian service is important and exciting. We have to stop equating recruitment with filling slots. It's so much more than that. Our enlistment efforts provide people with opportunities to serve Christ, utilize their gifts, and change people's lives."

Mary thought to herself, *What Jim is saying sounds good. However, I wish he'd stop sermonizing and give me the names of some people that I can ask to become teachers.*

When Jim paused briefly, Mary jumped into the conversation and tried to steer it in that direction.

"I can think of one more thing that we have to do before we can recruit people," she said. "We have to conduct a needs assessment. And, it just so happens that I've already done that.

"Look at all of these slots that we need to fill," said Mary as she handed Jim a piece of paper with ten positions on it.

"Oops! Let me rephrase that. Look at all of the service opportunities that we have for people. Sorry. Old attitudes die hard," she said with a chuckle.

DISCOVERING POTENTIAL WORKERS

Jim refused to be derailed. He had an agenda that he wanted to cover, and he was determined to give Mary all of the information that he had to offer.

"Before we start looking for workers," said Jim, "I want to make one more point. If we're going to be successful recruiters, we're going to have to retain as many workers as we can from year to year.

"As I've looked through our records, I've noticed that we have to replace a quarter of our workers every year. Unless we can stop that kind of hemorrhaging, we're going to become very frustrated."

"Become?" said Mary sarcastically.

"How can we do a better job of retaining our workers?" she asked.

"First, we need to find out why people are dropping out at such an alarming rate," said Jim."

"They leave their positions for a variety of reasons," explained Mary. "They quit because they're overworked, they're tired of their jobs or they're going through a physical, emotional, or spiritual crisis in their lives. They also leave because they feel inadequate, they've had bad experiences, they feel unappreciated, their jobs have become boring, they haven't received the kind of support that they were promised, or they can't get along with their students, fellow workers, or leaders."

"That's quite a list!" said Jim. "It's a wonder that we retain as many workers as we do.

"Fortunately, however, we can take steps to prevent the very problems that you've cited. For example, if we provide our workers with proper support, correct placement, excellent curriculum materials, and good training, they're less likely to have bad experiences or to feel inadequate.

"If teachers are experiencing burnout, we can give them a temporary reprieve. Or, we can ask them to team teach. That way, they would only have to teach every other Sunday. We can also show people how to keep their jobs fresh and interesting by using creative teaching methods."

Mary still wanted to get specific names for her summer programs rather than to discuss long-range solutions. So she said, "OK, let's say we're able to retain 90 percent of our workers and grow only 20 percent. If that happens, we'll still have to harvest a bumper crop of new workers.

"Or, maybe we'll have to trim some of our programs."

Jim dreaded the thought of Mary's proposal. Now that the church had a new director of Christian education, it expected more (rather than fewer) programs. So he quickly suggested, "Let's not act too hastily. I'm sure that we'll be able to find the right people if we just make a concerted effort.

"The first thing that we need to do is to communicate our needs. Some people don't volunteer because they think we have enough workers."

"I've already asked Shirley to put a list of our needs in the church bulletin," said Mary, "and you can draw people's attention to that list on Sunday morning."

"Good," said Jim. But as he uttered his affirmation, he realized that maybe he was steering Mary in the wrong direction. He knew that pulpit appeals, sign-up lists, and bulletin inserts were often ineffective. Worse yet, sometimes they attracted eager but ill-equipped workers.

It'd probably be better and safer to ask our teachers and church leaders to recommend potential candidates, thought Jim. *However, I hate to squash my own idea—especially since Mary has already contacted Shirley. Maybe I can suggest the recommendation route later on in our conversation.*

Sensing Mary's desire for more ideas, Jim continued his original line of thought. "Secondly, we also need to look at our records and see who has helped out in the past.

"Thirdly, then we need to go through the church rolls person by person to see if we've overlooked someone. "Fourthly, we need to consider people who haven't been able to help us out in the past—such as returning college students or returning servicemen and women.

"Fifthly, let's see if our midweek club leaders and the professional teachers in our congregation can help us out. In the past, I've discovered that these two groups of people are often willing to substitute teach because of their reduced workload in the summer."

"In addition to taking these immediate steps, I'd also like to do a number of things that will help us with our long-range recruitment efforts.

"On the last Sunday in June, for example, we're going to conduct an 'Interest and Involvement Survey.' After Pastor Grant preaches on the parable of the talents, we're going to pass out some survey sheets which list all of the 'service opportunities' that we offer in the church. Then, we're going to ask people to indicate, on those sheets, where they've served in the past, where they're serving presently, and where they would like to serve in the future.

"Each one of our Vacation Bible School teachers will be asked if they'd like to teach during our regular school year."

"I've asked Chad Blue to make a presentation about the church's educational program to our new members class. He's going to discuss the importance of spiritual growth, highlight our activities with a slide show, and challenge people to get involved, both as students and as workers.

"We will have a 'time, talent and treasure' workshop this fall. It'll be designed to help people not only manage their schedules and money better but also discover their spiritual gifts. At the end of the workshop, the participants will take a spiritual gifts examination and fill out our 'Interest and Involvement Survey' sheet.

"In the fall, I'm going to conduct a workshop for potential adult teachers. Then, at the end of our class, I'm going to ask each one who is there how they'd like to participate in our educational ministry.

After taking a moment to catch his breath, Jim continued: "Now, I know I've rattled on a bit this afternoon. However, I wanted you to see the big picture and know where we're headed in this area.

"OK, let's comb through our church records and church directory and see how many potential candidates we can find for you."

Finally! said Mary to herself.

SELECTING QUALITY TEACHERS

Jim and Mary's prospecting yielded eight potential names. That wasn't as many as Mary had wanted. It was, however, a start. Maybe the involvement survey, the pulpit plea, the new members class, and some personal conversations would produce even more prospects. For the sake of her high blood-pressure and sensitive stomach, Mary hoped so.

She was just ready to leave when Jim brought up another aspect of recruiting.

"Now that we have a preliminary list of potential workers, we need to select the very best people for each position that's available. One of the reasons why we may be losing so many workers to turnover is that people are being placed in the wrong positions, positions for which they're not qualified and positions in which they're not interested."

Mary applauded Jim's idealism. However, it seemed so impractical at times.

"I understand what you're saying, Jim. But, listen, we can't afford to be *too* picky. We're working with volunteers, not hiring engineers and scientists who have several doctorates.

"If we can't find a teacher for a particular class, students won't have an opportunity to learn and visitors will never return. If we put a willing but not-unusually-talented person in that class, the students may not learn much; but at least, they'll learn something. A warm body is better than no body."

"I'm not sure that's true," said Jim. "I've learned the hard way that you can't afford not to be choosy. If you select the wrong person, your students will suffer, your workers will suffer, and you'll suffer because you'll have to deal with the problems that your ill-equipped staff creates.

"As you read through the Bible, you'll discover that godly leaders were always concerned about finding qualified workers for their ministries."[15] "As you read through the Bible," said Mary, "you'll also discover that God doesn't necessarily choose the best and the brightest to do His work. As Paul said to the Corinthians,

> Brothers, think of what you were when you were called. Not many of you were wise by human standards; not many were influential; not many were of noble birth. But God chose the foolish things of the world to shame the wise; God chose the weak things of the world to shame the strong. He chose the lowly things of this world and the despised things — and the things that are not — to nullify the things that are, so that no one may boast before him. . . . Therefore, as it is written: "Let him who boasts boast in the Lord."[16]

"Just look at the disciples that Jesus selected," said Mary. "They weren't perfect gems. Peter let Jesus down in a crisis and was even called 'Satan' by his master. Judas betrayed his Lord. And, Matthew was a despised tax-collector.

"Let's face it", Mary answered, "God turned the world upside down with ordinary, unschooled men."[17]

"You're absolutely correct," said Jim. "God set the world ablaze with low-grade fuel. "And, I know there'll be times when we'll have to work with people who are 'diamonds in the rough.' When that happens, we'll need to spend a lot of time challenging them, training them, guiding them, and encouraging them.

"However, I still think we have to be cautious. I don't want poor teachers turning off young people or heretical teachers spouting false doctrine."

"I agree," said Mary. "I don't want those kind of teachers either. How high should we set our standards? What kind of workers should we be looking for?"

"Well, every job has a different set of qualifications," said Jim. "However, in general, we should be looking for people who are gifted, trained, experienced, dependable, and team players. And, above all, we need workers who love people and love the Lord.

"To make sure that you recruit those kind of people for your team, I think it's important to check the references of any person that wants to teach."

"You mean I should call up their present and former employers?" asked Mary with a bewildered look.

"Not exactly," said Jim. "Although that might not be a bad idea. What I mean is: it's wise to discuss potential teachers with Pastor Grant, with church leaders, and with me before you place them in a position of leadership. We might know something about the person that you don't; and, what we know may make you reluctant to enlist that person.

"There's also another way to ensure high standards in your teaching staff."

"I know," groaned Mary. "You want me to get the teachers together and develop a covenant for everyone to sign. I'll get that done eventually. It's just that I've spent so much time recruiting people lately that I haven't had time to tackle that project.

"Which reminds me. I better be on my way. I promised to call Sally Hobart back this afternoon and find out if she could sub for Terry Martin on Sunday."

CONDUCTING A RECRUITMENT INTERVIEW

Jim realized that Mary probably wasn't the only one struggling to staff her program adequately. So, immediately after she left, he wrote a memo to all of his educational leaders. He wanted to let them know what steps he was taking to help them in this difficult task.

He also wanted his workers to know how to recruit people correctly. So, in his memo, he included the following three-part outline.

The Enlistment Interview

A. When you enlist people, follow this procedure:

1. Make an appointment to meet with them.

2. Pray about your approach before you go.

3. Explain the importance of the position.

4. Tell them why you'd like to see them serving in that capacity.

5. Give them a written job description as you explain to them the responsibilities of the position.

6. Share with them your expectations and goals.

7. Indicate when you'd like them to start and how long you'd like them to serve.

8. Show them the equipment, materials, and supplies that they would use.

9. Tell them what training opportunities are available to them.

10. Discuss with them any additional physical, financial, and human resources that are at their disposal.

11. Assure them of your prayers and support.

12. Describe the class to them if you're approaching them about a teaching position. Tell them such things as: the approximate number of students that they'll have, the age of the students, the location of the class, and the time that the class begins.

13. Explain to them how their job fits into the overall educational ministry of the church.

14. Answer their questions and address any apprehensions that they might have.

15. Invite them to observe the class in action.

16. Give them time to prayerfully consider the opportunity.

17. Follow up the person to find out their response.

18. If they accept the position, reconfirm the date and time that they're expected to begin, introduce them to the members of the class and to other workers, and give them the training and materials that you promised. Also, check back with them periodically to see how things are going.

19. If they decline to serve, resist the urge to "twist their arms." Leave the door open for other opportunities. And, if they'd like to serve somewhere else, help them contact the appropriate person.

B. As you meet with people to discuss a particular position, follow these guidelines:

1. Don't minimize the position by telling them that the job is easy or that it won't take much time.

2. Don't try to recruit people in the church's hallways.

3. Enlist people face-to-face.

4. Anticipate excuses and be ready with responses.

5. Avoid strong-arm tactics or questionable pleas, such as: "Please, do this as a favor to me," "If nobody's interested in helping out, I'm going to resign." or "If you don't accept the job and the program falls apart, it'll be your fault."

6. Capitalize on the following meritorious motivations:

   - "It allows me to use my gifts, talents, and training."
   - "I'll have a chance to change lives."
   - "Other people have ministered to me. Now I want to do my part and minister to others."
   - "It'll give me a chance to meet people and participate in a ministry with my friends."
   - "I'll learn more as a teacher than as a student."
   - "I'll be helping the church grow."
   - "I'll have a chance to say 'thank-you' to God for all the things that He has done for me."
   - "I want to make sure my children have the best Christian education possible."

7. Enlist people for a limited time frame.

8. Stress the spiritual aspects of the job.

9. Be enthusiastic and positive.

10. Be honest. Avoid creeping involvement where people agree to one job only to discover that you want to expand their responsibilities little by little.

11. Describe the class or the position realistically. Mention both the opportunities and the problems that they may encounter.

12. Give them enough time to prepare for their new position.

C. As you recruit people, employ these principles:

1. Begin recruiting as early as possible. Otherwise, people will make plans that will interfere with their ability to accept certain positions. It will also allow you to approach the task in a more relaxed manner.

2. Recruit aggressively. God never waits for people to come to Him and volunteer. He always takes the initiative and recruits the leaders and disciples that He wants. We should do the same.

3. Avoid overworking your most faithful people. Some overeager individuals have never learned to say no. Therefore, we repeatedly ask them to help us out. Eventually, however, their overcommitment leads to "burn-out," unfulfilled responsibilities, damaged relationships, and inadequate performance.

4. Coordinate your recruitment efforts with the rest of our educational team. On occasion, I've noticed two or more of our leaders vying to enlist the same person. To avoid the bitterness that ensues, I'm going to suggest (at the next meeting of our Christian Education Board) several ways that we can work together in this area.

DISCOVERING PEOPLE'S SPIRITUAL GIFTS

Wally Ashcroft was new to the church and to the community; he was also a stranger to Jim. So Jim was surprised when Shirley said Wally was coming over to see him. Jim was even more surprised by what this Utah transplant had to say once he arrived.

After Wally took a seat in Jim's office, he shared the purpose of his visit. "Mr. Stafford, I'd like to help out in the church some way, but I'm not exactly sure where I should be serving. Do you need some teachers?"

Jim thought to himself, *An actual volunteer. I can't believe it! I thought they were an endangered species.*

Jim was immediately tempted to plug Wally into Thelma Neuhart's second-grade class. This capable teacher desperately needed more helpers. However, he resisted the urge. He wanted to find out more about this newcomer before he made any recommendations.

After Jim and Wally had spent some time getting acquainted with each other, Jim said: "Tell me. What are your spiritual gifts?"

"What do you mean by 'gifts?'" responded Wally. A quizzical look crept across his face.[18]

"Well, the Bible tells us that when we become Christians," explained Jim, "God gives each one of us at least one spiritual gift that we can use to help our fellow believers.

"Let me see. I think I have a handout that will help me explain this concept."

Jim rummaged through his file cabinet until he came to a folder marked: "STAFFING: Spiritual Gifts." From that file, he pulled a neatly-typed sheet of paper with the following information on it.

SPIRITUAL GIFTS		
Name	**Scripture**	**Description**
Prophecy	Rom. 12:6 1 Cor. 12:10,28-29 Eph. 4:11	An ability to proclaim God's Word so that it exposes evil and challenges people to change their lives.
Serving (Helps)	Rom. 12:7 Eph. 4:12 1 Cor. 12:28	An ability to recognize and meet the practical needs of others.
Teaching	Rom. 12:7 Eph. 4:11 1 Cor. 12:28– 29	An ability to discover, organize and explain biblical truth in a way that people can easily understand.
Exhortation	Rom. 12:8	An ability to correct, counsel, encourage, and stimulate people so that they will grow spiritually.
Giving	Rom. 12:8	An ability to contribute material resources to others and the Lord's work.
Leading	Rom. 12:8 1 Cor. 12:28	An ability to organize, mobilize, and guide people in the accomplishment of a task.
Mercy	Rom. 12:8	An ability to be gracious and help alleviate the hurting of others.
Word of Wisdom	1 Cor. 12:8	An ability to apply God's Word in practical, helpful ways.

Word of Knowledge	1 Cor. 12:8	An ability to perceive, understand, and organize the truths of God's Word.
Faith	1 Cor. 12:9	An ability to see possibilities that other people miss and trust God to accomplish great things.
Healing	1 Cor. 12:9,28,30	An ability to cure diseases.
Miracles	1 Cor. 12:10, 28–29	An ability to perform supernatural feats.
Discernment	1 Cor. 12:10	An ability to distinguish between what is true and what is false, what is godly and what is ungodly.
Tongues	1 Cor. 12:10, 28,30	An ability to utter divinely-inspired speech.
Interpretation of Tongues	1 Cor. 12:10,30	An ability to understand someone who is speaking in tongues and translate what they are saying.
Apostleship (Missions)	1 Cor. 12:28–29; Eph. 4:11	An ability to cross cultural barriers to share the gospel.
Evangelism	Eph. 4:11	An ability to share the gospel in such a way that people make Jesus the Lord and Savior of their lives.
Pastoring	Eph. 4:11	An ability to care for, lead, protect and nurture Christians.
Hospitality	1 Pet. 4:9	An ability to care for needy people by providing them with fellowship, food, or shelter.

As Wally looked over the list, Jim added a few precautionary notes. "Some people might say that this list isn't exhaustive or they might argue with its definitions. However, I think it will give you a good starting point from which to launch your exploration of the subject.

"On the reverse side of that sheet, you'll find some good principles that Christians should keep in mind as they exercise their spiritual gifts."

Wally turned the sheet over and noted that it made the following points.

1. Every Christian has been given at least one spiritual gift(s) (Eph. 4:7; 1 Cor. 12:7,11; 1 Pet. 4:10).

2. Spiritual gifts are varied. No gift is required of every Christian or given to all believers (Rom. 12:4-6; 1 Cor. 12:4-11,14,29-30; 1 Pet. 4:10).

3. Every spiritual gift is dispensed sovereignly by the Holy Spirit (1 Cor. 12:7-11; 4:6-7; Rom. 12:6; Heb. 2:3-4; Eph. 4:7). This principle, in turn, has several corollaries: (1) the possession of a particular gift should not lead to jealousy, pride or boasting (1 Cor. 4:6-7; 8:1; 12:27-30; 13:1-4); (2) specific gifts can not be learned; (3) people should not try to force a particular gift on another person; (4) having a particular gift doesn't make one person more spiritual than another.

4. Christians should exercise the gifts that God has given them (1 Pet. 4:10; 1 Tim. 4:14; 2 Tim. 1:6; 1 Thess. 5:19-21). However, they need to exercise their gift within biblical guidelines (1 Cor. 14:1-40).

5. Every gift should be exercised in love (1 Cor. 13:1-14:1; 1 Pet. 4:7-11).

6. Gifts are given to build up fellow believers (1 Cor. 12:7; 8:1; 10:31-32; 13:1-3; 14:4-5,12,16-25; Eph. 4:11-12; Rom. 14:19; 1 Pet. 4:10). Therefore, exercising them should not cause division (1 Cor. 12:4-25; 1:10-17; 3:1-9; John 17:20-23; Ps. 133:1; Rom. 12:16; 15:5-6; Phil. 1:27; 2:2).

7. Exercising one's gifts should bring glory to God rather than to oneself (1 Pet. 4:10-11; 1 Cor. 1:26-31; 3:18-22; 10:31).

When Wally finished examining the sheet, he looked up and said, "OK. I understand spiritual gifts a little bit better now. However, I must admit: I'm still confused. How can I discover what my particular gifts are or where I should use them?" asked Wally.

"Before you do anything else, you need to pray and ask God to reveal them to you," said Jim.[19] "After you've done that, you can discover your spiritual gifts in several ways.

"I have a spiritual gifts examination that you can take. After you've answered about seventy questions and I've scored your response sheet, we should have a pretty good idea of what your gifts are.

"You could also ask another Christian who knows you well to look over the handout that I gave you and tell you which gifts they think you possess.

"You could also make a list of some of the successes that you've experienced in your life. Then, as you examined each of these achievements, you could ask yourself: 'What gifts, talents, and skills did I have to use to make these dreams come true?'

"If you're still not sure what gifts God has given you, you may want to experiment a little. We can let you try out several positions on a short-term basis. After you've done a job for three or four weeks, I think you'll know whether or not that's the place for you."

"I'm confused again," said Wally. "You seem to be using the terms 'talents' and 'gifts' interchangeably. Are they the same?"

"I'm sorry if I left that impression," apologized Jim. "According to the Bible, they're two different things." "Talents are natural abilities that people have from birth; they can be used to entertain and help a wide variety of people. Gifts are supernatural abilities that the Holy Spirit gives us when we become Christians; they should be used to help our fellow believers grow spiritually.

"But, don't worry if you can't always distinguish between the two. God wants us to use everything that He's given us: our gifts, our talents, our experiences, our education, our interests, and our resources.

"Many times, we can find our place of service by combining these components into one job.For example, in our church, we have people who are very talented musically and who have the spiritual gifts of leadership and teaching. So, they direct our church choirs.

"Judy Moore is an excellent art teacher and puppeteer. Since her daughter died of cancer last year, she's developed an intense desire to help children who are sick or hurting. So now she visits children who are in the hospital or in dysfunctional families. From what others tell me, her art, puppets, and laughter have provided some wonderfully therapeutic experiences for these children."

After Wally and Jim had spent an hour discussing spiritual gifts and the church's educational program, Wally agreed to take the spiritual gifts examination and meet with Jim again the following week.

When Wally returned, Jim had a much better idea of where this eager Christian could help out. The spiritual gifts examination had revealed that Wally possessed the spiritual gifts of teaching and service.

After considering Wally's spiritual growth, interests, talents, job experience, training, and preferences, Jim told Wally that he was uniquely qualified to begin a new ministry. Jim recommended that Wally conduct car-maintenance workshops for young people in the church and in the neighborhood. He also suggested that Wally could help repair the cars of some of the older and poorer church members.

As Jim talked about these potential ministries, Wally's eyes glowed with enthusiasm. He couldn't sing, he dreaded teaching children, and he didn't feel knowledgeable enough to teach adults. However, he enjoyed working with cars and liked the idea of helping those with special needs.

When Jim asked Wally what he thought of his suggestions, Wally could barely contain himself. "Those are great ideas, Jim. I can't wait to begin."

Wally's new ministries didn't improve Mary's situation. However, they gave Wally an outlet for his gifts and interests. They also helped the church meet some pressing needs.

As Jim reflected upon the situation, he was glad that he had taken the time to talk with Wally about his spiritual gifts. The more Jim thought about it, the more he realized that Wally would have made a lousy elementary teacher.

In the future, Jim thought, *maybe we should try harder to organize our church ministries around people's gifts rather than organizational slots.*

POINTS TO PONDER

1. What are the three biggest mistakes that leaders make when they try to recruit workers?

2. What kind of qualities should you look for in a teacher? in a leader?

3. Would you ever allow a Christian who is not a church member to teach in your Sunday School? Why or why not?

4. Why do you think God chose Moses? Nehemiah? David? Saul? Paul?

5. Why did Jesus choose twelve, unschooled, ordinary men to bring His message of love and grace to the world?

6. Do high standards encourage or discourage people?

PRACTICAL PROJECTS

1. Outline a lesson plan that you could use to enlist new church members in your church's educational ministry.

2. Interview three people who lead large organizations in your church. Ask them to share the joys and frustrations that they have experienced in the area of recruitment.

3. Write a ten-page paper that describes the perfect teacher.

7

Have You Read Any Good How-to Books Lately?

(TRAINING)

"**B**oy, I can hardly wait for VBS to begin."

"That guess-who game was a riot. My students will love it."

"Good job, Jim. You sure held my attention."

"I hope that you'll be leading some more training courses this fall. We need them desperately."

Jim smiled as his teachers paraded past him and out the classroom door. He thought that his Vacation Bible School workshop had gone remarkably well, and the comments of his teachers seemed to confirm this.

CHARACTERISTICS OF GOOD TRAINING

One of the things that his teachers really enjoyed about the workshop was its practicality. That made Jim extremely happy. He didn't want to waste time reciting pie-in-the-sky concepts that his workers might use—someday. Instead, Jim wanted to equip his teachers with tools that they could use immediately.

With that in mind, Jim had designed his workshop so that teachers could prepare their VBS lessons right during the training sessions. When they discussed "Meaningful Scripture Memory," for example, Jim showed them how to teach the exact verses that their students would be learning in VBS.

Jim employed the same technique in a session entitled "Tell Me the Stories of Jesus." During that segment, teachers practiced telling the actual stories that they would use with their children.

This approach saved the teachers valuable time, allowed them to hone their skills under guidance, and promoted a collaborative effort. The training sessions were something like a football scrimmage in which team members had a chance to run through their plays prior to the actual game.

Another way that Jim kept his workshop interesting was to involve his teachers in the learning process. Because he subscribed to the you-learn-by-doing philosophy, he asked them to do more than simply listen to lectures and take notes.

For instance, Jim didn't spend a lot of time talking about the need to win children to Christ. Instead, he broke up the group into pairs and asked his teachers to communicate the gospel message to their partners who pretended to be VBS students.

For some, this was a frustrating experience. Jim's VBS staff thought they knew how to share Christ; after all, most of them were seasoned Christians who had listened to countless evangelistic sermons. However, when it came time to actually verbalizing their beliefs, quoting verses, answering questions, and gearing their comments to children, they discovered the process wasn't as easy as they had imagined.

Another thing that made Jim's training so effective was the example that he set. While training his crew, he was always trying to model the kind of behavior that he expected from others. He was thoroughly prepared. He came to the church early enough to set up his materials. He chatted with early arrivals and involved them in interesting pre-session activities. He began his sessions on time. And, once his class began, he kept his activities fast-paced and stimulating.

To keep his workshop exciting, Jim used a variety of methods. One moment, he was lecturing or leading a discussion. The next moment, he was role-playing or holding up an audio-visual aid to drive a point home.

Jim selected each method that he used on the basis of the following criteria.

- the size of the group
- the teacher/pupil ratio
- the space and facilities that were available

- the equipment, materials, and supplies that were available

- the time allowed

- the cost involved

- the topic under study

- the receptivity of the students toward a particular method

Whatever method Jim employed, he was careful not to let it become an end in itself. He used only those methods that would achieve his learning objectives.

To make his workshop as effective as possible, Jim used the principles he had learned in Bible College:

- Use expressions that the learner understands. If you must use words or abbreviations with which the student is unfamiliar, explain your terminology as you go.

- Don't do all of the talking. Instead, frequently ask questions and listen to the responses of your learners.

- When teaching new concepts and skills, don't waste your time discussing unimportant details. Stress those points that will have the greatest impact on a person's behavior.

- Set high standards for your students and let them know your expectations.

- Don't just show people techniques and procedures. Explain *why* you would like your workers to use them.

- Adults are not children. They have a lot of experience which they can impart to others. So let them share their stories, ideas, information and viewpoints in class.

- Allow adult learners to participate in the planning of their own training program. In class, allow them to explore and ask questions about areas in which they're interested.

- Adults resent being treated like children. So don't.

- Adults will come to your class with definite, well-established beliefs and behaviors. If the new ideas that you present conflict with these preconceived concepts and patterns, your learners will usually resist them — unless you can convince them that the new ideas will improve their lives.

- Tie new information to facts that are already known.

- Adult learners are skeptical of pat answers and easy solutions.

- When people do well, applaud their efforts.

- When people have trouble learning a concept or skill, make positive and constructive suggestions.

- Never criticize, talk down to, or ridicule your trainees.

- Students come not only to learn new information and skills but also to enjoy the class's fellowship.

- Adults are whole learners. You can't divorce their spiritual lives from their physical, mental, and social lives.

- Facilities that are too crowded, hot, cold, stuffy, or breezy can inhibit learning.

Of course, nothing is ever perfect. As hard as Jim tried, no one would have described his workshop as *the* ultimate learning experience. In fact, if Jim could have conducted his workshop all over again, he would have made at least two important changes.

First of all, he would have done a better job of focusing his training efforts. Some of his topics, like storytelling and audio-visual aids, lent themselves to almost every age-group. However, some of the other methods which Jim discussed didn't really apply to all of his teachers.

For example, when he talked about using paper and pencil activities, he lost the attention of his preschool staff. They protested that those techniques weren't really relevant to them because they were going to teach children who couldn't read.

Secondly, Jim realized that he could have minimized this problem by dividing his VBS staff into smaller, age-oriented groups. Then, he could have addressed each group's training needs and special requirements.

Jim also could have improved his workshop by dispensing fewer facts. In an effort to produce fully-equipped teachers, he fed his staff too much information too quickly. By the end of the day, the teachers were suffering from information overload. They simply couldn't absorb everything.

Jim vowed never to repeat that mistake. *Next year*, he thought, *I'm going to be more selective in picking the topics that we discuss. I'm also going to spread our training out over two evenings a week apart. This will give people time, between sessions, to digest and implement what they've learned.*

Oh well. Mistakes are opportunities to learn. In the future, I'll do an even better job.

Because of that desire, Jim shifted his attention from the past to the future.[1] He didn't want this workshop to be a one-time, isolated event. He knew that training, in order to be effective, has to be regular and systematic.

TRAINING CONTENT

"How did the workshop go?" asked Jill as her husband strolled into their living room.

"Really well," said Jim. "In fact, I'm so excited about teacher training that I thought I'd spend the next hour mapping out the church's training calendar for the rest of the school year."

"How often do you plan to train your workers?" asked Jill.

"Well, I'd really like to have a training session at least once a month. However, I'm so busy right now that I don't think that will be possible.

"The Cody Lake Area Sunday School Convention is going to be held in October; so we've taken care of that month. We're swamped in September and December. It would be suicide to schedule a workshop for either one of those months. That means, for this year, all we have left is November; we'll have to squeeze whatever training we want done into that small slice of time."

"Maybe, when the church council gets together to plan next year's church calendar," said Jill, "you can designate the third Thursday of every month as your training night. That will help teachers organize their schedules, prevent other groups from pilfering those training dates, and help you to plan ahead.

"What kind of training workshops do you want to conduct in November?" asked Jill.

"Well, we have two pressing needs," said Jim. "Pastor Grant has just approved our Children's Crusade which will be held November 19-22. So, we need to train counselors for that activity.

"I also need to fulfill a pledge I made to Pastor Grant at the beginning of the year. I told him that I'd conduct a three-hour workshop for present and potential adult teachers."

"What kind of training do your crusade workers need?" asked Jill.

"I think their training should be based on the job description that we're going to give them," said Jim. "Basically, we're going to expect them to befriend the children who come, exercise discipline if needed, share the gospel with children who come for counseling, and follow up those who decide to become Christians."

"What about your adult teachers? What kind of skills, attitudes, and information do they need?" asked Jill.

"From what I've seen and heard, I'd like to encourage them to use a wider range of teaching methods," suggested Jim. "Right now, they seem to be wedded to lectures and group discussions. It's too bad because those aren't the only teaching techniques available to them. They could make their lessons much more interesting if they would just expand the scope of their methodology.

"I'd also like to see our adult classes shift their emphasis away from acquiring knowledge to putting the knowledge that they already possess to work."

"Be careful," Jill warned. "Teachers, especially older ones, aren't always eager to experiment with fancy, new methods."

"I know," said Jim. "It sure would be easier if they would be open to fresh, innovative ideas."

Jill resisted the urge to remind Jim that he had some pretty rigid notions of his own.

"Well, Jim, it looks like you've already mapped out your training strategies for November. But, I'm curious. Have you ever asked your teachers what *they* want? I think you'd get your training program off to a better start if you'd begin by dealing with subjects that really interest your workers.

"You could discover those felt needs by talking with your teachers individually or by asking them to fill out a survey sheet.

"If you really wanted to be radical, you could even test your staff to find out what they know about certain educational techniques.

"Before selecting your workshop topics, you should also check out the church's training records and find out what areas have already been covered. In addition, you should make sure that you have the expertise, speakers, teaching materials, and other resources that you'll need to conduct the workshop."

"I like the idea of surveying my teachers to find out their training needs," said Jim.

"Good. Why don't you design a questionnaire while I cook supper," said Jill. "Then we can talk more about your training program after we eat."

In a matter of minutes, Jim had constructed the following checklist:

In the fall, I'd like to conduct a workshop for present and potential adult teachers. You can help me prepare for this event by indicating what type of training you would like to receive. Please rank the following topics in order of their importance to you (1 = most important; 23 = least important).

_____ Effective Lecturing

_____ Leading Lively Discussions

_____ Teaching for Response

_____ Using Audio-Visual Aids

_____ Building Relationships with Your Students

_____ Creative Bible Learning Activities

_____ Home Visitation

_____ Age Characteristics of Adult Learners

_____ Characteristics of an Effective Teacher

_____ Motivating Adult Learners

_____ Using Bible Study Aids in Your Lesson Preparation

_____ Using the Bible in Your Classroom

_____ Developing Interesting Illustrations

_____ Techniques to Help Your Class Grow

_____ How to Lead a Person to Christ

_____ Spurring Your Students' Spiritual Growth

_____ Lesson Preparation

_____ Characteristics of an Effective Teacher

_____ Teaching Methods of Jesus

_____ The Learning Process

_____ Principles of Learning

_____ Paper/Pencil Activities

_____ Small Group Dynamics

As Jim looked at his checklist, he realized that there were many other topics that he could include. He could offer classes on missions, Bible doctrine, church history, and counseling. However, for the time being, Jim decided to limit his offerings to topics that were directly related to the teaching task and topics that weren't being taught elsewhere in the church.

It had taken Jim only twenty minutes to develop his survey sheet. However, it took another three hours before he could show it to Jill. After supper, Brenda and Barb demanded a lot of attention. Because of a flurry of late-night church meetings, it was the first time that their dad had seen them in three days.

Finally, after the girls went to bed, Jim proudly showed his finished product to Jill.

Jill looked over Jim's list, complimented him on its completeness and then made one minor suggestion.

"I know that you already have a training date in mind," said Jill. "However, next time, it might be wise to ask the teachers when they would like to meet.

"For example, I'd probably append these words to any future surveys."

Jill scribbled a brief note and then handed the following addendum to Jim:

When would you like these training sessions to be conducted?

_____   During the Sunday School hour

_____   On Sunday evening, before the worship service

_____   On Wednesday night

_____   On Saturday

_____   During a weekend retreat

_____   Other: _____

TRAINING APPROACHES

"So far, Jim, you've only mentioned training conferences and church workshops," noted Jill. "However, don't forget that there are a host of other approaches that you can use to equip people."

"Like what?" asked Jim.

"Well, you could encourage your teachers to increase their expertise by beginning a program of independent study," recommended Jill. "In other words, you could supply your workers with teaching videos, cassettes, magazines, books, and manuals. Then they could examine these materials at home at their own pace.

"You might even want to produce some of these training aids yourself. For example, you could have videotaped your workshop today. If you had done that, you would have a resource that you could distribute to absentees or future teachers."

"That's a good idea," said Jim. "I wish I would have thought of it.

"In some other ways, though, I've already implemented your suggestion. When I recruited June Johnson to lead our VBS program, I gave her a book written for VBS directors called *VBS—The Way to a Child's Heart.*

"I've also written a leadership manual for Mary Black, our Sunday School director.

"This fall, I'm also going to give each teacher a training book that is geared to their specific age-group. Then, from that point on, each new teacher will receive one of these books at the outset of his or her teaching ministry."

"To save money, you might want to circulate these and other types of training materials through the church library," suggested Jill. "If you do that, though, make sure that you encourage teachers to use them and periodically check to see if they're being read. Otherwise, they'll just sit on the shelves and gather dust."

"I'm also toying with the idea of producing a newsletter called 'Teaching Tips'," said Jim. "It would keep teachers informed about what's happening in the church's educational program and provide them with fresh ideas and techniques.

"Since our funds are a little tight, I wouldn't mail it out. Instead, I'd distribute it with our attendance records on Sunday morning and on Wednesday night. I could also leave a few extra copies in our resource center for other people who might be interested in reading it."

"In my junior-high teaching manual," said Jill, "the publisher always provides a special training section called 'TNT — Teachers in Training.' It's packed with all kinds of educational ideas. It might be fun (or maybe a little discouraging) to ask some of your workers about those suggestions and see if they're applying them in the classroom.

"Also, Rose Adams is taking a correspondence course from Kenmore Bible College. Maybe we could enroll some of our teachers in that program or, at least, use some of Rose's materials."

"You're right," said Jim. "There are quite a few ways to train people, aren't there?"

"And, we've just been talking about ideas that pertain to self-guided training," said Jill. "Think of all the other approaches that are at your disposal."

"For instance?" said Jim.

"Well, most small churches feel badly because they can't provide large, age-group workshops like bigger churches can," said Jill. "I mean it's a little difficult to tell your two preschool teachers to break up into small groups and discuss the finer points of using guided-conversation.

"That's where coaching sessions can come to your rescue. You can arrange regular, one-to-one training opportunities with your teachers in small departments.

"There are two big differences between a coaching session and a workshop: the amount of individualized attention that the teacher gets and the degree of scrutiny that the teacher receives.

"In a coaching situation, the trainer first visits the classroom and watches the teacher in action. Then, he sits down with the teacher and evaluates his performance."

"That kind of training requires a pretty good relationship between trainer and trainee," Jim observed.

"It certainly does," agreed Jill. "The trainee has to be willing to be observed and listen to constructive criticism. And, the trainer has to be a knowledgeable, empathetic person who can make positive suggestions and focus on issues that really count.

"While coaching is an approach that has to be handled with sensitivity, I don't think that there's any better way to discover problems and develop solutions in the classroom."

"There's another problem with that method," objected Jim. "It's time-intensive; and I don't have much time to spare."

"Then, you need to use approaches that enlist the help of other people," suggested Jill. "For example, you could develop an apprenticeship program where experienced teachers guide prospective teachers in developing their teaching skills.

"In the beginning, the novice could sit and observe the experienced teacher in action. Then, the apprentice could gradually start helping out in a few areas. Maybe he would tell the Bible story one Sunday and lead the singing the next. By the end of the program, the trainee should be able to take over the entire class himself.

"In order to implement that approach, however, you have to remember three important things: (1) you need to select capable master teachers. Second-rate instructors will only succeed in reproducing their mediocrity in others. (2) You need to have a definite plan of attack. You could develop a list of skills that your trainee needs to possess by the end of his apprenticeship program. Then, the lead teacher could check off each of these items as his understudy masters that particular area. (3) You have to encourage plenty of interaction between the trainer and trainee outside of the classroom. Each week the two teachers should get together to plan the lesson, discuss the teaching techniques involved, talk about the students, and evaluate what happened the previous week."

"Boy, that sure is a lot of work for the lead teacher!" said Jim.

"That's true," agreed Jill. "However, you and the trainee won't be the only ones who benefit from this type of a program. This arrangement also rewards the trainer. Toward the end of the program, he will get valuable help in his classroom. In addition, he has a chance to make a profound impact on his trainee, the church's educational life, and the students who will eventually be taught by the trainee."

Jim thought a moment about this approach, scribbled a few notes, and then suggested another idea.

"You know, instead of presenting isolated training workshops," he said, "I could establish entire training courses. For instance, my high school leaders could get together once a week (for three months) to study youth work. During that time, they could read books on the subject, listen to lectures and discuss the various aspects of their ministry. At the end, they could receive a diploma which would certify that they had completed the course."

"Our denomination has developed some wonderful materials that could help you out with that approach," suggested Jill. "Or, you might want to create your own training course and tailor it to fit the specific needs of your teachers. You could design an 'Excel Program' for teachers who want 'to be the best that they can be.' In this advanced course, you could require teachers to:

- Create a personal plan of improvement which would spell out how they intend to sharpen their teaching skills during the year.

- Study a certain number of training books, teaching tapes, and educational videos.

- Complete a prescribed number of study courses.

- Attend a specified number of workshops or training conferences.

- Observe and evaluate other Sunday School classes in action.

- Let the director of training observe and evaluate their teaching. This could be done at the start, middle, and end of the program.

- Take an exam which would test their knowledge of the Bible, teaching techniques, and the principles of learning.

- Reach a specified level of performance in each skill area that their job requires.

- Display the personality traits of a good teacher."

"You sure have given me a lot of ideas," said Jim with a smile of admiration. "If I implement just one-third of them, our church will have a training program unsurpassed by anyone else in this area. "It's really wonderful being married to such an intelligent woman."

"Well, when you've grown up in the church, your dad has been a pastor, and you've received straight A's in your Christian education courses at Highland Christian University, you're bound to learn something," said Jill with a smile.

TYPES OF TRAINING

At the next staff meeting, Jim proudly reported how the VBS workshop had gone and outlined his training plans for the new school year.

Pastor Grant responded to Jim's report with a back-handed compliment. "That's wonderful! It's about time that we start to provide adequate training for our workers. Jim, we're expecting a lot from you in this area.

"As you put your plans into action, though, make sure that you maintain a proper balance in the type of training that you offer. From what you've told us, you're going to emphasize in-service training.

"Now, don't misunderstand me. It's important to train your current teachers. Those who stay in the same job for a while need to be challenged, stretched, and reminded to strive for excellence. Teachers also need to stay abreast of the latest techniques and technology. There's a tremendous need for life-long learning on the part of all of our teachers.

"However, I hope you're also going to furnish pre-service training for raw recruits. When people step into new positions, they usually lack a lot of confidence. They're afraid of failing or of being left alone to sink or swim.

"These fears can be countered with a course of study that explains the basics of their teaching task. Elementary teachers, for example, need to know how to prepare lessons, tell stories, exercise loving discipline, use their curriculum materials properly, and help children with art activities.

"Even seasoned teachers need to know the specific policies and procedures of any new organization they join. So you or your leaders need to teach them how to keep attendance and offering records, order curriculum materials, find their way around the resource center, handle emergencies, obtain needed supplies, and contact substitute teachers.

"In addition to pre-service and in-service training, I think *we* should conduct a course for prospective teachers. New or uninvolved members need an opportunity to determine where God wants them to serve. So *we* should offer a class that deals with such topics as the importance of teaching, characteristics of a good teacher, teaching ministry of Jesus, teaching methods, principles of learning, a survey of our church's educational programs, and a survey of the various age-divisions within our church."

"You could also give them a chance to assess their gifts and interests," recommended Shirley. "In fact, you could even let them try their hand at teaching a particular age-group before they had to commit themselves to a specific teaching position."

PROMOTION OF TRAINING EVENTS

"Jim, you mentioned earlier that the Cody Lake Area Sunday School Convention is going to be held in October this year," said Pastor Grant. "Since you're the publicity chairman for that training conference, maybe you could fill us in on some of your plans to promote the event in our church."

"Gladly!" responded Jim. "First of all, we're going to use a lot of routine publicity methods. We're going to put up posters in the church foyer, put 'advertisements' in the church newsletter and church bulletin, make several pulpit announcements, and give each teacher a brochure about the conference.

"In these public announcements, we'll try to answer some of the basic questions that most people might have.

- What is the event?
- When will it be held?
- Where will it be held?
- What kind of topics will be discussed?
- Who will be speaking at the event?
- Who should attend?
- Why should they attend?
- How much will it cost?

- Will child-care be provided?
- Will lunch be provided?
- What is the conference's schedule?

"In addition to the public appeals, I'll be sending out printed invitations to every worker. Then, about a week after I mail these cards out, I'll try to contact each teacher and personally ask them to attend the convention. I've also asked some of our educational leaders like Mary Black and Kay Williams to 'touch base' with their workers and urge them to go.

"I'm also trying to think of some unusual ways to reach our teaching staff. We may ask our teachers, for example, to wear buttons which say: 'I'm going to CLASS! Are you?' Or, we may do some skits in the morning service, but I'll talk to you about that later.

"By the time we're finished, it's going to be impossible for anyone in the congregation to say that they haven't heard about the Sunday School convention."

"Just don't get too wild," warned Pastor Grant.

If Jim heard the comment, it barely slowed him down. He was too intent on sharing his plans.

"We're also trying to make the conference as easy as possible to attend," said Jim. "Someone in the congregation has already volunteered to pay registration fees for any church member who goes. For those with young children, we're going to provide child care. We're also trying to arrange for a bus or a fleet of vans to take our teaching staff to the conference together; this will not only reduce transportation problems but also promote a team spirit among our workers.

"As I've been preparing for the CLASS convention, I've also thought a little bit more about how we can tout our own training program. From now on, our teacher's covenant and our job descriptions will lovingly urge our workers to take advantage of the training opportunities that our church provides. We want our teachers to know that training is not an option; we expect them to attend.

"After people finish a training course, I'd like to honor them in the same way that our church recognizes our graduating seniors, complete with cap, gown, and diploma. This would praise people for their diligent efforts, and tell the congregation that exciting things are happening in our educational program."

Pastor Grant wasn't so sure that those theatrics were necessary; however, he didn't want to interrupt his associate's enthusiastic presentation. He made a mental note to talk to Jim about this at another time.

"At the conclusion of our VBS workshop," Jim went on, "I asked the participants to evaluate our time together. They came up with a lot of good suggestions, including some ideas for making our training programs more alluring. Let me read you some of the things that they said:

- 'Our teachers are busy people. So make sure that you announce any training dates far enough in advance so that everyone can arrange to attend. You might even consider establishing a regular workers' meeting.

- 'Please serve coffee and refreshments. I can't think without a cup of the brown stuff in my hand.

- 'Ask people to research some aspect of the workshop's theme and present their research during the training session. Having an assignment will encourage them to come.

- 'When promoting training opportunities, emphasize the importance of the subject rather than the duty of attending.

- 'Distribute curriculum materials, books, or teaching aids at the meetings. This will encourage people to come rather than make a special trip to see you about these supplies.

- 'Let absentees know, in a loving way, that they were missed and share with them some of the exciting things that happened at the training event.

- 'If it's okay with Pastor Grant, give people who have attended a training workshop an opportunity to tell what the experience meant to them. This could be done either on a Sunday or Wednesday evening.'"

Pastor Grant had only one comment to make. "Those are good suggestions, Jim, the desire to attend will ultimately stem not from gimmickry but from the quality of your workshops. You have to make it worthwhile for your teachers to come, by producing a superb product. You have to give them some 'take-home value.'"

SKILLS TRAINING

After the staff meeting, Jim went back to the church office with Shirley. She had asked him, the day before, to help her out with a new computer program that she was learning. Since he knew the program well, loved computers, and enjoyed training people, Jim had gladly agreed to become her tutor.

Jim had prepared for this meeting in the same way that he prepared for most workshops. He had written down a brief list of skills that he wanted Shirley to learn and determined what methods he wanted to use. Also, he had rehearsed the techniques that he would demonstrate and gathered all of the materials that he would need.

Because he was well-prepared, Jim was eager to begin his instruction. However, despite his enthusiasm, he didn't immediately launch into an explanation of the program. Instead, he took the following steps to get their training session off to a good start.

- He put Shirley at ease by complimenting her willingness to learn the new program and told her that she would really enjoy using it in her work.

- He emphasized the importance of the skills that she was going to learn.

- He found out what she already knew about the subject of computer graphics. He didn't want to be repetitive; neither did he want to be neglectful.

- He gave her an overview of what they would be discussing.

Once Jim had laid this foundation, he began to teach Shirley the major tasks that she needed to learn in order to use the graphics program effectively. As he did, he went through a simple, six-step process.

First, Jim explained the task point by point. For example, in describing how to move a picture around the screen, he told Shirley: "When you use the computer mouse, click on the picture's frame. Then, continue to hold down the mouse button as you drag the picture to its new location. When the picture is properly positioned, release the mouse button."

During his explanation, Jim emphasized both the how and the why of each operation, as well as the key points that were essential to the performance of the task.

As Jim described the procedure, he also demonstrated it on the computer. When Shirley saw the operation with her eyes, it reinforced what she heard with her ears.

After Jim finished his explanation and demonstration, he paused to let Shirley respond to his instruction. She usually had questions about what he had done and the terminology that he had used. So Jim used this step to clarify any misunderstandings.

Then, Jim asked Shirley to try out the procedure for herself. Although Shirley was slightly embarrassed by her slow and awkward movements, Jim knew that she would learn more by practicing the process than by simply observing it. As usual, experience proved to be an excellent teacher.

Of course, watching Shirley at this stage meant that Jim had to be very patient. Moves that seemed so natural and automatic to him seemed quite difficult and cumbersome to her.

Quite often, Jim was tempted to jump in and do the task for Shirley. However, he knew that this kind of intrusion would only impede her progress. He consoled himself with the knowledge that, with time and practice, she would be just as proficient as he was.

At each step of the training process, Jim wanted to make sure that Shirley understood the instructions that he was giving her. So, in addition to having Shirley perform each task herself, Jim also asked her a number of questions.

From past experience, Jim had learned to avoid the question: "Do you understand?" People often answer this inquiry with a polite yes. However, a positive reply often shows people's reluctance to admit their ignorance rather than their true understanding of the concept. So Jim asked open-ended questions that were preceded with words like: 'Why?' 'What?' 'How?' and 'What if?'"

After Shirley had performed a task, Jim evaluated and corrected her performance. If she made a mistake, he told her not only what had gone wrong and why it had gone wrong but also how she could perform the task correctly next time.

As Jim made constructive suggestions, he tried to be as positive, patient, soft-spoken, gentle, and reassuring as he could. After all, he was a trainer, not a faultfinder. To ease Shirley's nervousness, Jim made it clear to her that an error on her part indicated not so much her failure to learn as his failure to teach the concept correctly.

Once Jim had discussed with Shirley how she could improve her performance, Jim asked her to repeat the task once again. With each repetition, Shirley's speed, accuracy, and confidence improved.

Finally, when Shirley performed the task to the satisfaction of both of them, Jim moved on to the next concept. *Again, Jim went through his six-step process of explanation, demonstration, reaction, application, evaluation, and repetition.*

After several hours of training, Shirley felt fairly comfortable with the fundamentals of the new computer program. Jim decided to let her put her new knowledge to work. He asked her to design a preschool brochure. This exercise definitely required her to use all of the techniques that she had been taught up to that point.

Within an hour, Shirley was able to produce an attractive flyer. Of course, while she was composing this piece of publicity, Jim was on hand to answer her questions, review concepts, give her suggestions, and demonstrate several new techniques that she needed to complete her task.

Since Shirley had done such a good job on the brochure, Jim felt confident that she could now use the program without his help. However, he didn't want to abandon her. So he urged her to come to him in the future with any questions that she might have. He also left her with a thick handbook which would help her as she continued to develop her skills.

From that point on, Jim checked in periodically with Shirley to find out how she was doing with the program. At first these check-ups were quite frequent. However, as Shirley became accustomed to the program, Jim gradually tapered off his coaching sessions.

With Shirley's successful training experience behind him, Jim began to think of other times and places where he could use his six-step training procedure. To his amazement, he concluded that he could use this process whenever a skill was involved. With it, he could train leaders to set goals, plan special events, and recruit people. He could also use it when he trained teachers to tell stories, exercise discipline, and make overhead transparencies.

TRAINING FOLLOW-UP

Unfortunately, not all of Jim's training programs were uniformly successful. Several weeks after Jim had conducted his VBS training workshop, he was wandering through the church's educational wing to see how his teachers were doing. As he did, he was a bit discouraged by what he saw. Some teachers were reading, instead of telling, their Bible stories. Other teachers were ridiculing their students as they disciplined them. Still others were teaching their children to memorize Bible verses through "vain repetition."

After making his rounds, Jim returned to his office in disgust. "Why are teachers falling back into their old ruts, violating the principles that I taught them, and failing to use the exciting, creative methods that I introduced to them?" he asked.

As Jim mulled over this question, a number of possibilities occurred to him.

- "Maybe my teachers are just waiting for VBS to start. Then, they'll try out my suggestions."

- "Maybe they don't like my ideas. When I was training them, I just assumed (because they smiled, participated in the training exercises, and never objected) that they thought I was teaching them some wonderful principles and methods. Perhaps that assumption was wrong."

- "Maybe they agree with me. However, they've found that it takes too much time and effort to implement my ideas."

- "Maybe, in the heat of the moment, they've reverted to their old ways because their new-found skills aren't firmly established."

The more Jim thought about the problem, the more upset he became. *I know it's unrealistic to expect all of my teachers to accept and employ all of my suggestions,* he thought. *I have to do something, however, to make my training more effective.*

"Next time, I'll do a few things differently.

- I'll follow up my training efforts more quickly to see if and how my teachers are using their new skills. If they don't use my suggestions in the first few weeks after the workshop, they'll probably never use them. In fact, even if they try out my ideas, it's natural to slip back into comfortable, old habits as time passes.

- I'll never assume again that workshop attendance equals life application.

- I'll show people, by my attention and questions, that I'm interested in what they've learned at training events and expect them to employ that learning in the classroom.

- I'll avoid information overload. People are unlikely to practice everything they learn if they're deluged with too much information at once.

- I'll seek people's reaction to a training session personally and privately. Maybe our conversation will uncover some hidden objections that I can overcome.

- I'll be open to suggestions. Maybe my ideas don't work as well as I think they do—in the 'real world.' If they don't, perhaps I can learn something from their failures.

- I'll ask the teachers, who try my suggestions and succeed, to spread the good news of their successes. Peer pressure can often encourage people to experiment with something at least once.

- I'll ask people to 'overlearn' new skills so that they won't be as likely to follow their old, well-worn routines.

- I'll reward and praise application rather than attendance.

- I'll offer my teachers the personal coaching and resources that they need to overcome any difficulties that they might have in implementing my ideas."

As Jim thought about the training process, the fog covering his usually buoyant spirit began to lift. He was pleased with his newly devised strategies. He also had to admit that there were quite a few teachers who were following his advice and employing the new techniques that he had taught them.

Jim was confident that, in time, he could build an outstanding training program. When that happened, everybody would benefit. Experienced teachers would be more effective; new teachers would be more confident; students would be more Christ-like; educational leaders would have less problems; and Pastor Grant would be pleased!

POINTS TO PONDER

1. Why do people who need training the most seldom seek it?

2. Why is it important to keep good training records? What kind of information should be included on each record?

3. What do you think Pastor Grant meant by the phrase "take-home value?"

4. Why do some churches provide so little training for their workers? How can leaders overcome these training obstacles?

5. How can a leader encourage his workers to use the things that they have been taught at training events?

PRACTICAL PROJECTS

1. Develop a church training calendar that starts in September and ends in June. Include, with this calendar, a one-page outline of each training event or a one-page description of each approach (book, tapes, etc.) that is used.

2. Design a survey sheet that you could use to discover the training needs of either your preschool teachers or youth workers.

3. Plan a three-hour training workshop using the following form for each session within that period of time.

Session #1

- Background Information (students, setting):
- Topic:
- Length:
- Needed Equipment, Materials and Supplies:
- Goal(s):
- Brief Outline (content, timetable, and methods):
- Bibliography:

4. List and define twenty different teaching methods that could be used in a training session.

5. Make a list of the skills, information, and attitudes that you would want a new children's teacher to possess at the end of an apprenticeship program.

8

One for All
and All for One

(BUILDING TEAM RELATIONSHIPS)

Jim leaned back in his chair and clasped his hands behind his head. *Who*, he wondered, *can I get to head up the church's fall retreat at Mt. Willow?*

His mind went blank for a moment or two. Then, without fanfare, Bill Chamberlin's name burst into Jim's consciousness.

Yes, of course. Why didn't I think of him before? thought Jim. *Bill would be perfect for the position. Ever since he accepted Christ at a marriage retreat, he has enjoyed Christian camping. He's organized, and he works hard. He's also familiar with the program since he's already attended the church's annual outing a couple of times.*

Jim flipped though the church directory until he came to Bill's name and work number. Then, with a few quick taps on his telephone, Jim sent his electronic knock through the wires to Bill's office. When Bill answered, the usual sparkle from his jovial voice was missing. However, Jim was too preoccupied to notice. He wanted to get right down to business. So, after a little habitual banter, Jim popped the important question.

"Bill, I was wondering if you would be willing to coordinate the church's fall retreat."

It seemed like an entire baseball season could have been played in the pause that ensued. When Bill didn't immediately reply, Jim rushed in to fill the uneasy moment of silence.

"I know you're still there," laughed Jim. "I can hear you breathing."

Then Jim heard what he thought were quiet sobs. After another long pause, Bill finally responded.

"Jim, I'd love to do that sometime, but right now it's impossible."

Jim finally realized that something was terribly wrong. Bill didn't sound like himself.

"You see, my brother's cancer has taken a turn for the worse," explained Bill. "So I'm flying out to see him and to help my sister-in-law with some of Craig's business affairs. In fact, I'm going to be leaving tomorrow for Iowa."

Jim was stunned. He thought he knew Bill. But evidently that wasn't the case. Although Jim and Bill had worked together on the computer committee and frequently talked with each other at church, they had never discussed his brother. In fact, Jim didn't even know that Bill had a brother, let alone that he was dying of cancer.

At first, Jim was tempted to excuse his lack of knowledge. After all, he was still rather new to the church and couldn't possibly know all of its members and their problems. However, despite his attempts to soothe his conscience, he still felt upset by this unexpected revelation.

Jim talked with Bill for a few more minutes. Then he ended the awkward conversation with some perfunctory words that he had heard so many other Christians use: "Well, Bill, if there's anything I can do, let me know. We'll be praying for you."

How trite, well-worn, and utterly hollow those words seemed to be. However, that was all Jim could utter at the moment.

CULTIVATING TEAM RELATIONSHIPS

After Jim hung up the phone, he asked himself: *How well do I really know my educational workers?*

Then he answered his own question with the words: *Well, I guess there's one way to find out. I'm going to give myself a pop quiz.*

Jim quickly jotted down the names of all of the church's educational staff—or, at least the ones that he could remember. Then, for each name that he had listed, he asked himself four questions:

"What do I know about this person's immediate family?"

"What does my co-worker do for a living?"

"What does he or she like to do in his or her spare time?"

"How does he or she feel about Jesus Christ?"

Jim was amazed by his ignorance. At Broadmore College, he had known everyone on his basketball team and known them well. He could tell you about their personal tastes, their family members, the status of their dating life, and the classes they were passing or failing. However, at Bethel Church, there were tremendous gaps in Jim's knowledge. His dedicated leaders sometimes seemed like distant strangers.

Of course, there was a good reason for this. At Broadmore College, his team practiced together; they played together; they ate together; and they studied together. They did everything together.

Jim knew that he couldn't duplicate that kind of togetherness among his coworkers at church. However, he still felt that it was possible to develop a strong, loving team spirit. He wanted to instill a sense of camaraderie so that people would be eager to work together, desirous to know one another and willing to support each other.[1] His goal was to emulate the body-life model portrayed in the Bible.[2]

Jim asked himself, *How can I promote an atmosphere where a 'one-for-all and all-for-one' attitude prevails?*

PRAYING FOR EACH OTHER

When Jim entered the church office a short time later, Shirley sensed his burdened disposition.

"Is something wrong?" Shirley probed.

"Did you know that Bill Chamberlin's brother was dying of cancer?" asked Jim.

"No, he's never mentioned it," said Shirley.

"I just found out a moment ago when I called him about another matter," said Jim. "I just can't believe that I didn't know!"

Shirley tried to comfort him. "Don't be so hard on yourself. Bill's very quiet and seldom talks about himself or his problems."

"That may be true," said Jim, nodding his head in agreement. "However, I still think that I should have known about Bill's brother.

"And, this specific experience has pointed out an even larger problem. Our educational staff isn't very cohesive. We don't know each other like we should. I want to develop a plan to draw our teaching and support staff closer together. Have any ideas?"

Shirley was happy to offer a few suggestions.

"When you first came on staff," she said, "didn't you promise to pray weekly for each member of your educational team?"

Jim was embarrassed. He remembered making that pledge, then being overwhelmed by the frustration that followed. During the first month, he had tried to keep that vow. However, there were just too many people for whom to pray.

Eventually, he decided to modify his goal so that he prayed for each of his workers once a month. However, even that proved to be difficult. Too many demands were screaming for his attention.

After all, he wasn't being paid to pray for people. He was being paid to achieve results and run programs. At least that's how most church members would evaluate his performance.

As Jim and Shirley talked, the church's secretary encouraged him to fuel his prayer furnace once again. Jim was willing to try. After all, if busy people like Paul,[3] Moses[4] and Jesus[5] could find time to pray for others, he could too.

Jim really longed to be a leader like Paul, who was firmly committed to intercessory prayer. He wanted to emulate this enthusiastic apostle who constantly prayed for his fellow believers[6] and repeatedly asked that they pray for him.[7]

In order to pray for everyone, of course, Jim needed an up-to-date list of his entire educational staff. However, because of his recent pop quiz, he realized that he didn't even know everybody that was serving in the church's education program.

When he voiced his dilemma, Shirley volunteered to call his leaders and compile the necessary registry. Jim protested. He wanted to do that himself. However, Shirley finally convinced him that he could use his time more wisely by pursuing other tasks.

As Jim walked back to his office, he remembered his first feeble attempts to pray for his coworkers. He tried to clothe each worker in a general, one-size-fits-all prayer. However, that approach hadn't proved very satisfying.

This time, Jim wanted to take a different tact. He wanted to see if he could tailor his petitions and pray specifically for each worker's individual needs.

When Jim arrived back at his office, he immediately set out to discover his team member's concerns. Within a few seconds, his nimble fingers had dialed June Johnson's home telephone number.

"Hi, June. This is Jim Stafford."

"Don't tell me you've got another job for me already," groaned June. "We've just barely finished Vacation Bible School."

Jim realized, from June's comment, that he usually called people only when he wanted to ask them for a favor or discuss some church business. Hopefully, his intercessory prayer project would show his workers that he was concerned about them and their well-being instead of just what they could do for him.

Jim reassured her that he wasn't calling to recruit her for some task. He told her about his renewed commitment to pray for his educational workers and asked if she had any special prayer concerns.

"Well, not for myself," she replied, "but I'm worried about one of my students—Rick Williams. His father has just lost his job and his family is barely scraping by on his mother's secretarial salary. They really need someone to go over there and encourage them. Maybe even give them some financial assistance."

As Jim listened, he realized that praying for others often requires more than simply talking to God. It sometimes demands that the petitioner get involved in other people's lives and help them with their problems.[8]

This discovery made Jim anxious. He was afraid that he was once again climbing a mountain that was too high for him to reach.

After they had talked for a few minutes, Jim told June about Bill's situation.

"I'm glad you told me," June said. "I'll be sure to pray for Bill and for Craig's family this week.

"Can I huddle our teaching team so that we can bring this matter to God corporately?[9] I'd be willing to both round up the people and lead the meeting."

Jim was torn by June's suggestion. He thought that it was a good idea. However, it would be just one more activity begging for his time and attention. Of course, if he wanted to promote team unity, this seemed like a good way to begin. So, Jim gave June the green light and asked her to call him back with further information about the meeting's time and place.

By the time Jim had made ten more phone calls, he had come to two conclusions. Many people were reluctant to share their deep hurts and festering ills. This was especially true if they didn't know Jim very well. Some people seemed hesitant because they didn't trust Jim to keep their secrets.[10] Others seemed ashamed to admit that they or their families had problems. If people conceded that they had difficulties, their confessions made them feel like spiritual failures or heightened their fear of rejection and condemnation.

Jim also realized that most of his workers had asked him to pray for sick and unsaved people.[11] However, he felt that he needed to extend those borders and pray for other issues as well.

So, as Jim knelt in his office, he consciously asked God not only to remove the negatives from, but also to produce some positives in, people's lives. He prayed for his workers' spiritual growth, and he thanked God for the partnership he had with them in the gospel ministry—just like Paul had done for his fellow believers.[12]

After ten minutes of intense prayer, a gentle knock on Jim's door brought him back to earth. Shirley's quiet voice announced, "It's time for our staff meeting."

APPRECIATING AND ENCOURAGING EACH OTHER

Most of the staff meetings at Bethel were routine. First, Shirley, Pastor Grant, and Jim discussed a passage from the Bible. Next, each of them reported on their past and future activities. Then, they concluded their meeting with a short period of prayer.

The meetings were usually OK, as far as they went. However, they lacked a certain amount of warmth and exuberance for the church's mission and ministry.

This time, Jim was hoping that the ambiance would be different. He wanted to ignite a spark of appreciation for the church's hard-working laity. So, when it was his turn to speak, Jim started with a somewhat critical observation.

"Pastor Grant, I feel that we're taking our teachers for granted. They simply aren't receiving enough recognition for the time and effort that they put into their jobs.

"I think that we, as paid staff, need to change that situation. We can do that by embarking upon a program that will highlight the teaching ministry of the church. Such a focus would help us to recruit more teachers, to involve more people in our educational activities and to fulfill the Bible's admonition to honor one another."[13]

"What did you have in mind?" asked Pastor Grant. His question was wrapped in guarded apprehension. Inwardly, this seasoned veteran was wondering: "What kind of new-fangled idea does my associate have this time?"

Jim presented his proposal with all of the excitement of a father announcing the birth of his first child. "Well, I've thought of several ways that we, as a church, can show our appreciation.

"On September 15 we're planning to start our fall Sunday School season. On that day, we could plan the entire morning worship hour around an educational theme and use that time to dedicate our teaching staff.

"We could also devote ten to fifteen minutes of the morning worship service, once a quarter, to promote one of the church's educational ministries. For example, at Thanksgiving time, we could have our children bring food baskets for the needy up to the front of the sanctuary and then sing a few Sunday School songs.

"Another way that we could recognize the importance of the teaching arm of the church is to hold an appreciation banquet for our educational workers next spring. This would provide an opportunity for our team to relax, eat together, hear some good music, and enjoy a challenging speaker. It would also be an excellent time to make some presentations and give out some awards."

Riding Jim's wave of enthusiasm, Shirley added: "If we do that, I'm sure that we could get Dan and Kelly Rivers to liven up the festivities by creating some fun decorations and arranging a few humorous skits."

"That's a great idea!" said Jim.

"Maybe we could even designate the complete month of May as 'Appreciation Month.' During that time, we could ask our members to do something different each week to say 'thank you' to their educational workers. For example, on the first week of the month, we could encourage them to pray for their teachers. During the second week, we could ask them to write notes of appreciation. The following week, we could urge them to telephone their workers. And, during the final week, we could suggest that they invite their workers out for coffee and cake.

"Like I said, we could encourage our congregation to write notes to their teachers one week in May. However, we don't need to wait until then. We could make some 'appreciation cards' and place them in our pew racks almost immediately.

"On the outside of these cards, we could print a nice graphic along with Hebrews 10:24-25 which says: 'Let us consider how we may spur one another on toward love and good deeds. Let us not give up meeting together, as some are in the habit of doing, but let us encourage one another—and all the more as you see the Day approaching.'

"On the inside, we could provide a couple of lines on which people could write their words of encouragement. They could drop these cards into the offering plates and I would see that they are passed along to the appropriate people."

Pastor Grant mulled over Jim's ideas for a moment. Then he said, "Well, Jim, you have a lot of good ideas there.

"I fully want to support our teachers. However, I don't want to do things during our morning worship service that would distract from the reverent atmosphere that we're trying to cultivate.

"Frankly, I've had some bad experiences with 'educational promotions.' In my first church, the Sunday School director convinced me to let a preschool class sing a couple of songs during the worship hour. It was a disaster! The children held up their dresses, stuck their fingers in their noses, waved to their parents, and generally made a mess of things. It was extremely difficult to draw people's attention back to God while they were still snickering and thinking about the shoddy performance that they had just witnessed.

"If any church group wants to promote their ministry, they're going to have convince me that they can do it in a way that contributes to, rather than distracts from, our worship efforts."

While Pastor Grant was expounding his beliefs, Jim tried to rein in his look of astonishment. He was stunned by Pastor Grant's cool response. Jim never would have suspected that his pastor held such strong views on the subject.

"Another thing," said Pastor Grant. "If I let you push your programs, I'm going to get all kinds of requests from other organizations to do the same thing. If that's the case, these rival presentations could end up dividing rather than uniting our church. Comparisons and competition can be deadly."[14]

The fire in Jim's spirit flickered and almost vanished. He thought to himself, *Well, the promotional door isn't locked yet but it certainly seems tightly closed.*

Pastor Grant continued his discourse. "Jim, I also have another concern. I don't want to encourage our people to serve for the wrong reasons—that is, to satisfy their hunger for recognition. That's just not biblical.[15]

"Stroking people's egos also encourages timid workers to give up when difficulties come their way or when praise isn't forthcoming.

"Most of the time, I receive more flack than praise. However, I continue to do my job anyway. That's because I'm trying to please God rather than people."[16]

If Pastor Grant was implying that Christians should never praise one another, Jim strongly disagreed. Both Jesus[17] and Paul[18] were generous with their praise when it was deserved.

Jim was sorry that Pastor Grant didn't receive much encouragement. Maybe Jim needed to start his appreciation campaign with his own colleague. Now that he thought about it, Jim couldn't remember the last time that he had praised Pastor Grant for his tireless efforts.

As Jim started to think of ways to remedy this oversight, Pastor Grant turned his attention to another one of Jim's suggestions.

"Jim, I like your idea about the appreciation banquet. However, we're going to run into a few problems with that, too. We may not have enough money to handle that event well and I don't want to do a second-rate job. Right now, we're really struggling financially. I know your banquet wouldn't be held until next year. However, if our cash flow doesn't improve, we may have to cut rather than add programs."

Shirley rushed to save a remnant of Jim's proposal. "Maybe we could start with a dessert get-together. If that goes well, then we could try a banquet the following year."

"That's a possibility," agreed Pastor Grant. "I think that approach would work much better than a full-scale banquet.

"Lastly, if you can work out the details with Shirley and our head usher, I'm willing to try your idea about the appreciation cards for a couple of months and see how it works."

Jim left Pastor Grant's office somewhat discouraged. He wished the three of them could have voted on his suggestions because it seemed like Shirley was on his side. However, Pastor Grant didn't exactly believe in leadership by majority rule.

Of course, Jim knew that trying to ramrod his ideas into existence wouldn't have worked anyway. Jim needed the willing, enthusiastic support of his pastor in order to properly promote the church's educational program.

Hopefully, Jim had sown some thoughts that would take root and ripen as time passed. *Maybe I should have presented the need and asked for input from the pastor before suggesting my own ideas*, thought Jim as he rehashed the meeting in his mind.

In the meantime, he'd have to work with what he'd been given. He'd try to implement the appreciation card project and the teacher's appreciation dessert so well that he would earn Pastor Grant's respect. Once Jim had a proven track record, maybe he could try some other approaches as well.

Of course, there were some things that Jim could do that didn't require Pastor Grant's blessing. For example, he could verbally pat people on the back with his positive comments. And he could also pass along the accolades that other people voiced about his teaching staff.

As Jim passed out compliments, he wanted to adhere to several principles. So he wrote these guidelines down in the big yellow pad in front of him.

I, the undersigned, do hereby resolve:

1. To make my compliments specific, sincere, and appropriate to the size of the achievement.

2. To praise people as soon after their outstanding performance as possible.

3. To give out rewards that are creative, varied, and meaningful to the receiver.

4. To compliment people not only for their results but also for their efforts.

5. To praise team accomplishments as well as individual ones.

Jim Stafford

While Jim was thinking about each of these points, Shirley softly tapped on his door and then entered his office. "Jim, don't be too discouraged by Pastor Grant's fire-hosing. He seems to be in a pretty gloomy mood today."

Jim certainly agreed with that observation.

"I've been thinking about what you said in our staff meeting," said Shirley, "and I think you're on the right track. Would you be interested in another idea for your appreciation campaign?"

Jim was open to suggestions and encouraged her to share her thoughts.

When Shirley saw Jim's willingness to hear her out, she responded immediately. "Why don't we select a different 'Teacher of the Week' each Sunday and feature that person on the bulletin board across from our second grade classroom? We could post pictures of these teachers along with some information about their families, jobs, and conversion experiences. We could also let the congregation know something about their favorite foods, trips, hymns, and Bible verses.

"What an excellent idea!" replied Jim. "Would you be willing to post that information each week?"

"I don't have enough time to do that," said Shirley, "but I'll bet Delores Wright would be glad to help us out. She's a retired teacher whose health doesn't permit her to teach children any more. But she cares for teachers, loves to chat on the telephone, and has good typing skills."

"Thanks for the idea," said Jim. "I'll give Mrs. Wright a call tomorrow.

"You know, Shirley. I really feel fortunate to work with a secretary like you. You come up with so many wonderful ideas like this 'Teacher of the Week' concept. In addition to that, you know our church people so well that you can even suggest some possible recruits. Thanks."

SHOWING INTEREST IN EACH OTHER

Jim was glad that Shirley had stopped by the office. Before he went into the staff meeting, he was convinced that the church needed to do a better job of acknowledging the accomplishments of its workers. However, during his encounter with Pastor Grant, he began to doubt his stance on the issue. So, he desperately needed her affirmation.

As he savored her words of encouragement, his thoughts traveled back to the telephone calls that he had made earlier that day. Over and over, he had found out that people were surprised but gratified to hear that he wanted to pray specifically for them. Many of them had remarked: "It's refreshing to hear that somebody's interested in us and what we're doing."

These memories and Shirley's positive comments nudged Jim's efforts forward. Despite Pastor Grant's resistance, Jim renewed his commitment to praise people and show them that they and their efforts were being noticed.

Initiating a "Teacher of the Week" program was one way of achieving that objective. Making sure that his workers were supplied with all of the tools that they needed, in terms of curriculum materials, equipment, and classroom supplies, was another way.

Jim also planned to revive a practice that was effective in the dawning days of his ministry. When Jim started his work at Bethel, he had made a habit of roaming the church's hallways to find out what was happening. Although he had discontinued that routine after the first couple of months, Jim decided to return to it once again.

As he popped into classes, he made positive comments about what he saw, asked questions about what the class was doing, and took the time to listen to people's answers.

When Jim was on his walk-about's, he didn't just talk about church matters. He also made a point to ask about the teacher's job, family, and special interests.

After chatting with an educational worker, he'd write down what he had learned about the person. Later on, he transferred this information to a card file system that Shirley had prepared for him.

Every once in a while, Jim would refer to a comment that a teacher had made several weeks before. When he did so, the worker was usually amazed at Jim's phenomenal memory. What was his secret?

Although Jim hated to admit it, he had usually reviewed his personnel files just before making those astonishing references.

Pleased by the usefulness of his growing personnel files, Jim started to ask all of his incoming teachers to fill out a questionnaire. The profile sheet that each of them completed contained questions about their conversion experience, Christian walk, training, family, interests, abilities, and background.

Jim used this information to expand his records, to aid him in his recruitment, and to supply Mrs. Wright with the data that she needed to carry out her "Teacher of the Week" program.

Sending birthday and anniversary cards was another way that Jim showed interest in his educational staff. Shirley printed these cards with the help of a special computer program that Jim had bought for her. Then, while Jim watched television in the evening, he wrote brief notes in each card to its recipient. In the morning, Shirley would take Jim's greetings and send them on their way.

Every once in a while, Jim added something extra to his cards. He found that including a cartoon, a picture drawn by a child, a joke, or a poem was always welcome.

The birthdays and anniversaries of his team members kept Jim quite busy. However, he realized that sometime in the future he might want to expand his repertoire and send other types of cards as well. He knew that card shops would supply him with materials expressing a variety of sentiments including: "Congratulations," "Best Wishes in Your New Life Together," "Thank You," "Bon Voyage," "We Missed You," "Welcome Back," and "Happy Easter."

SPENDING TIME TOGETHER

Before Jim initiated his team-building efforts, he had always thought of visitation as a job for the pastor or the outreach team. However, it began to dawn on him that visiting people in their homes could pay big dividends.

For one thing, it provided Jim with a wonderful learning lab. When he stopped by to chat, he could see how his teachers related to their family members. The decor of the homes often revealed tantalizing hints about the church member's spiritual standing, interests, and abilities. Jim marveled at people's willingness to drop their facades, bare their needs, and share their opinions in the familiar surroundings of their home.

Jim also realized that people didn't have to be sick, new, dying, or unsaved to appreciate a visit from a pastor or a staff member. His co-workers enjoyed just sitting down and talking about common, every day activities. He could always count on an interesting conversation when he asked people about their children, their jobs, their homes, their vacations, or current events.

There was just one big problem with home visitation. Families often felt compelled to serve desserts when Jim came by to see them. If he visited people too often, he would never meet his goal of weighing 180 pounds by the end of the year.

In addition to his visits, Jim wanted to invite people over to his house. However, since both Jill and he worked, it was hard to find time to make the necessary arrangements.

After some discussion, Jill and Jim devised what they thought would be a workable plan. They decided to have a big open house once a year for all of the educational workers.

During the rest of the year, they tried to keep their entertaining simple. Instead of having people over to the house for big meals, they invited people over for coffee and cake after church. When they could afford it, they took single people and couples out to local restaurants. This approach minimized the house-keeping chores and kept get-togethers within a manageable time frame.

Accommodating large families was more difficult. However, Jim and Jill found that parents, as well as children, appreciated hot-dog and hamburger barbecues or old-fashioned picnics in the park.

Mindful of Jill's activity-packed schedule, Jim also tried to do some entertaining on his own. He found that taking businessmen or students out for lunch was a quick, painless way to get to know people. As Jim looked for opportunities to get together with his colleagues, he found that people were eager to golf, hunt, bowl, or hike together. Whenever Jim and Jill attended a concert, play, or sporting event, Jim would also try to get others to come along with them.

****

Late one afternoon, as Jim was writing a few notes of encouragement to his coworkers, Bob Sparkman called. With pride, Jim talked with his mentor and explained how his team-building efforts were going.

"It sounds as if you're getting to know your team members rather well," replied Bob. "But, are your teammates getting to know each other just as well?"

Jim thought for a moment and then confessed reluctantly, "Not really. I've been very successful in developing relationships with individuals. However, my staff members still haven't formed close friendships with their coworkers."

"You can take several steps to correct that," advised Bob. "You've established a good role model. That's great. Now, urge your troops to follow your lead.

"They need to support, encourage, and praise each other's actions, just like athletes do in the middle of an exciting football game. In a successful team effort, the coach isn't the only one that dispenses the commendations.

"Secondly, employ a trickle-down approach to your team relationships."

"What do you mean by that?" queried Jim.

"Jim, tell me the truth. Don't you feel frustrated by all of the time that this team-building takes?"

"Well, as a matter of fact, I do," admitted Jim. "And, so does Jill."

After a slight pause, Jim quickly added: "But it's sure worth it. Isn't it?"

"You can save yourself a lot of frustration," noted Bob, "and be just as effective if you narrow your focus. Begin to concentrate on building relationships with those who report directly to you—people like your Sunday School director, your children's church coordinator, the director of your midweek club, your preschool director, and other organizational heads.

"Then let these leaders emulate your example and develop close ties with their immediate workers. Urge your teachers to use the techniques that you and your leaders have been employing to disciple each of their students.

"Thirdly, at your regular meetings and training events, emphasize the social component just as much as you do the work component.

"Use any excuse that you can to get your workers together as a group. Plan a retreat. Get Doug Saxby to host a pool party out at his ranch. Celebrate someone's birthday or holiday together. Throw a big bash after your team completes a difficult project."

"I probably should have done that after VBS was over," interjected Jim.

"Fourthly, change your speech patterns," continued Bob. "Stop talking in terms of 'I,' 'you,' or 'they.' Instead, sprinkle your conversation generously with 'we.' For example, when a group puts a new plan in place, say: 'We' expect great things from this new endeavor' rather than 'They' expect great things from this new endeavor.'"

Eager to show Bob that he was not only listening but also applying his instructor's advice, Jim spoke up. "You know, Bob, I'm already unconsciously doing that."

Bob affirmed his disciple's progress. "Good. These small changes in your speech patterns may seem minor. However, they both reveal and spark a much deeper change in attitude.

"Here's something else you might want to try. When you refer to your educational organizations, start using the word 'team' frequently and enthusiastically. Instead of talking about your 'Board of Christian Education' or 'preschool committee,' refer to these groups as your educational *team* or your preschool *team*.

TEAM SYMBOLS

"Another way to promote team spirit is to devise common team symbols," Bob said.

"Remember how your college basketball team used to have team uniforms, a team mascot, a school song, and school cheers? These devices were used to elicit unity and team spirit.

"Well, you can use a similar approach with your educational organizations. Take group pictures. Wear team buttons. Select a team slogan or Bible verse. I'll bet that you could even convince your youth workers to wear a really radical t-shirt with some catchy slogan on the front."

"It's interesting that you should mention that," commented Jim. "My children's choir has been pushing me to do something like that for them. Right now, we're in the middle of a contest to select a name for the choir. So, by the end of August, we hope to have some t-shirts printed up with the choir's name and logo on it."

"Wonderful!" exclaimed Bob. "I'll look forward to seeing them 'in uniform' when they present their choir concert at our church next spring."

HELPING ONE ANOTHER

Jim really had enjoyed his refreshing talk with Bob. It was nice to have a mentor boost his batteries and give him new insights.

However, Jim didn't have time to digest all of Bob's suggestions. It was already fifteen minutes past five, and he had told Jill that he would try to be home by five o'clock.

Just as Jim was locking up his office, the church's telephone began to bellow. Jim quickly opened his door, walked over to his desk, and scooped up the receiver on the third ring. If he had let the telephone ring once more, the church's answering machine would have automatically recorded the call.

However, Jim gambled that Jill was calling and he wanted to explain to her why he was running late. As soon as he recognized Martha Kraft's anxious voice on the other end, Jim realized that he had lost his wager. His spirit sagged with regret. He knew that he should have gone straight home.

"Boy, am I glad I caught you," wept Martha. "Could you come over and visit us tomorrow night? Walter and I can't seem to agree on anything anymore. I'm afraid we're on the verge of a divorce."

Intellectully, Jim knew that God blesses those who try to be peacemakers.[19] However, in this case, he would have happily foregone such a blessing.

Jim could identify with the priest and the Levite in the parable of the good Samaritan.[20] Hundreds of good reasons for by-passing this "opportunity" raced through his mind. *Tomorrow, Jill and I were planning to spend a quiet day at home—the first chance to do so in over a month. Tomorrow evening, my favorite baseball team is playing on television. Counseling isn't my forte. Can't you wait until Pastor Grant gets back from his evangelism conference?*

Despite these unvoiced objections, Jim couldn't convince himself that he had a right to refuse Martha's plea for help. *After all,* he thought, *the Bible says that Christians are supposed to be more than practitioners of religious ritual[21] and proclaimers of sweet-sounding words.[22] Doesn't it?*

As Jim wrestled with himself, he remembered the sacrifices that the good Samaritan had to make. This gracious man had exposed himself to danger, given of his time, overcome his racial prejudice, provided ointments and bandages, become involved with messy procedures, walked on foot while his donkey carried the beaten traveller, paid for this person's bills at the inn . . .

If the good Samaritan could do that for a stranger, Jim asked himself, *shouldn't I, as a church staff member, be willing to help out one of my flock?*

Spurred by these motivations, Jim made an appointment to visit the Krafts at eight o'clock the following evening. As he did so, he thought: *How am I going to break the good news to Jill? She must already be upset with me because I'm not home like I promised to be.*

****

The next evening, Jim dutifully went to fulfill his commitment to the Krafts. He tried to meet their short-term needs by facilitating a communicative process that had atrophied over the years. His therapy consisted of asking questions, listening, sharing pertinent Bible verses, and encouraging the combatants to see things from the other person's point-of-view.

How much had he accomplished? Jim wasn't sure. He felt like he had applied some very dainty bandages to some very deep wounds. Perhaps they would hold long enough for the Krafts to seek out a specialist.

Since the Kraft's ailment had developed over five years, it certainly wouldn't be cured in one short counseling session. That's why Jim, like the good Samaritan, also tried to provide for his patients' long-term needs.

Jim recommended a two-part prescription to promote healing. He asked Walter and Martha to read Will Moister's book on communication and conflict. To make sure that they followed his suggested remedy, he also arranged to see them again in two weeks so that they could discuss the book together.

Secondly, he persuaded them to make an appointment with a family counselor. This hurting couple needed more than Jim had to offer. Fortunately, for all of them, the church encouraged families in difficulty to seek out help. It paid for the first four visits that church members made to an approved Christian psychologist.

Whether or not the Krafts would heed his advice was largely up to them. At least, they admitted the severity of their problem, recognized their need for help, and were willing to change—three essential ingredients in a recipe for recovery. Now, Jim would just have to wait and see.

In the meantime, the rest of Jim's 'people campaign' started to bear fruit. People came up to him in the church hallways and thanked him for the birthday cards that he was sending. They also told him how they were beginning to feel like team members instead of isolated individuals working by themselves.

Jim's educational workers weren't the only ones who were touched by the new team spirit. Before starting his emphasis on team-building, Jim had been a hard-driving, task-oriented person who was sometimes more interested in results than in people.

As Jim talked and socialized with his workers, he found that God had given him a new desire. Now, Jim wanted to be a minister to people rather than a pusher of programs.

POINTS TO PONDER

1. What are some methods, not mentioned in the chapter, that a leader might use to build a team spirit among his or her team members?

2. How can leaders encourage workers to pray for each other?

3. The world is full of people who are crying for assistance. How do Christians decide whom they will and will not help?

4. Why is it easier to build relationships with some people than others?

PRACTICAL PROJECTS

1. Write out a detailed plan for an appreciation banquet.

2. Write five thank-you notes to people this week.

3. Keep a diary of your intercessory prayer life for a week. List some of the problems and blessings that you encountered while praying for others.

4. Compliment at least ten people face-to-face this week. Then list the different reactions that you received.

9

Speak Up!

(THE ART OF SPEAKING)

"**W**hy do I get myself in these predicaments?" mumbled Jim as he hung up the telephone.

"What's wrong?" asked Jill as she came into the living room with a nursing journal in her hand.

"That was Bob Sparkman. He wants me to speak at a single's conference at Calaway Church next month. He was originally scheduled to talk. However, his father has just had a small stroke. So Bob's flying back to Montana next week to visit his parents and help his mom with some financial matters while his dad is recovering."

"I'm sorry to hear about Bob's father," Jill responded, "but this speaking engagement is a great opportunity for you. It'll give you a chance to expand your network of friends. You'll also be able to influence a lot of people in their Christian walk."

"That's easy for you to say," retorted Jim. "You don't have to give the speech. If I thought I was such a great orator, I would have become a preacher."

"Oh, don't worry so much," Jill said as she rubbed Jim's tense shoulders. "You just have a case of the Moses' Miseries."

"The what?"

"The Moses' Miseries," Jill chuckled as she saw the bewildered look on Jim's face. "When God called Moses to deliver his people from Egypt, Moses felt the same way that you do—miserable. He was distressed because he didn't think that he was an eloquent speaker.[1]

"So, like several other reluctant prophets,[2] Moses started to recite all of the reasons why he wasn't the right man for the job. He pointed out that there were others who were better qualified. He protested that he didn't know enough. And, he was afraid that his people wouldn't listen to him.

"After listing his inadequacies, Moses thought that God would exempt him from his assignment. But the Lord didn't accept any of Moses' excuses. Instead He transformed 'Moses the Meek' into 'Moses the Mighty'. That's why Stephen could describe him as a man who was powerful in both *speech* and action."[3]

"Well, even Moses had Aaron to help him out," said Jim. "Do you think you could give me a few tips on how to prepare this talk? After all, you were a speech major before you decided to become a nurse, weren't you?"

"Wait a minute," Jill protested. "I'm not the preacher in the family. You are. And they asked you to speak, not me."

Despite her feeble protests, Jill knew that she would finally break down and help Jim with his talk. After all, she wanted him to do well. In addition, she couldn't stand to see the pained "help-me-out" expression on his face.

"Okay. I'll help you get started" she said reluctantly. "But," she added, "remember this is your speech, not mine."

"Agreed," replied Jim eagerly. He was relieved that his wife had agreed to his plea for help.

PRELIMINARY DECISIONS

Jill began, "When and where does the single's group want you to speak? How long do they want you to speak? Who is your contact person? Will they be sending you a map so that you can find your way to the church? How much will they be paying you?"

Jim shook his head in embarrassment. He sheepishly admitted that he hadn't thought of asking all of those questions. It was evident that he would have to call Bob again. *Better yet*, Jim thought, *I'll contact Calaway Church directly to get more information.*

Jim decided that a follow-up letter would be the best way of doing that. In it, he could both request the information that he needed and confirm some of the details that he already knew—like the time and place.

After Jim wrote a note to himself about this confirmation letter, Jill continued. "Next, you have to decide what your topic is going to be. That will depend on several things like: the occasion, your audience, your interests, and your resources.

"Did the group ask Bob to talk about anything in particular or mention the theme of their conference?"

"Bob didn't suggest any specific subject," responded Jim. "However, he did say that the group called their get-together a 'care and compassion conference.'"

"Good. That gives us a start. You know the general thrust of the conference but you still have a lot of latitude in choosing your topic. "Of course, sometimes that can be a problem. When you have so many topics from which to choose, it's hard to make a decision.

"Another thing we need to do is to analyze your audience. This analysis will help you not only select your topic but also tailor your illustrations and suggestions to fit your listeners.

"What can you tell me about the group's age, sex, occupations, interests, spiritual standing, attitudes, and educational level?"

"Well, not much," answered Jim, "But I'll check that out when I write my confirmation letter."

"Okay. In the meantime, let's turn our attention to your own interests," said Jill. By this time, she was somewhat exasperated because Jim had accepted the engagement without asking some crucial questions.

"What topics really excite you? On what kind of topics can you speak with authority?"

"That's easy," said Jim. "I believe in the power of prayer. That's why I'm trying so hard to recruit a group of people who will pray for our teachers every week."

"Prayer is a pretty broad subject," cautioned Jill. "You can't possibly cover that topic in twenty minutes. What particular area of prayer do you want to emphasize?"

"Well, I suppose I could talk about intercessory prayer—like Paul's prayer in Philippians 1. It fits the theme of the conference, dovetails with my interests, and would be applicable to singles."

"Has the group at Calaway heard anyone speak on that topic recently?" asked Jill.

"I don't know."

"But I'll check that out in my confirmation letter," said Jill in unison with Jim. Then they laughed together. Jim's letter was going to be quite long.

"Do you have enough resources to prepare a speech on that topic?" asked Jill.

"Sure. I have a number of commentaries on Philippians, a terrific little booklet called *Caring Leaders Pray*, and a series of tapes on "Passionate Prayer" by my favorite evangelist, Ken Daylight. I can even supplement my outline with some classroom notes that I took while I was attending college."

"Great!" shouted Jill. "It sounds like you have plenty of materials with which to work. You're on your way."

"Well, not quite," protested Jim. He didn't want to release his personal coach too soon.

"The single's group at Calaway wants me to send them the title of my talk as soon as possible so that they can include it in their conference brochure," explained Jim. "So I need to come up with a catchy phrase that will spark interest in my speech. Have any ideas?"

"Let me think," said Jill as she paused momentarily to ponder Jim's dilemma. "You can dramatize your title with powerful words and call it 'The Dynamics of a Revolutionary Prayer Life.' Or, you might want to use numbers to arouse curiosity and entitle your talk: 'Six Ways to Energize Your Prayer Life.' Maybe, you can use alliteration and give your speech the nomenclature: 'The Path to Powerful, Personal Prayer.'"

"No, I don't think so," said Jim. "All of those sound overly dramatic."

Jill thought a few more minutes and then suggested two further ideas. "You could pose a question like: 'Is Prayer Really Necessary?' Or, you could state your title in the form of a simple request like: 'Pray for Me.'

"I like that," said Jim, nodding his head in approval. "It's both simple and descriptive."

"Good. Anything else?"

"No. I guess I'm set for now."

"Good. The next step is to research your topic. That you'll have to do yourself."

Jill was delighted that she could help Jim launch his speaking career. She was convinced that he would turn out to be an excellent Christian speaker.

RESEARCHING A TALK

During the next few days, Jim attacked his research assignment. He explored his commentaries, listened to his tapes, and read books and magazine articles on intercessory prayer. Jim wasn't totally satisfied with these traditional research methods and he took several other steps to lasso fresher and more practical ideas than they had to offer.

Before prospecting for other people's opinions, Jim wrote down his own thoughts on the subject. He called up a few of his educational workers and interviewed them about their prayer life. When he spoke with them, he asked them such questions as "For whom do you pray?" "For what do you pray?" and "What kind of results have you experienced in praying for others?"

Observation also played an important role in his research. As he prepared his talk, Jim carefully noted how people prayed in church and in small groups. Watching children petition God was especially fun. For example, Jim was really impressed by the simple and fervent faith of his own two daughters.

Some of Jim's insights came from his own experiences which he faithfully recorded in a daily prayer journal. In this log, he noted several things: when he prayed, for whom he prayed, for what he prayed, how he prayed, the results of his prayer efforts and the barriers that kept him from praying for others.

By the time Jim had completed his research phase, he had discovered a great deal not only about his subject but also about himself and his congregation.

Furthermore, Jim had gained a new respect for his senior pastor. He wondered: *How can Pastor Grant deliver two to three sermons a week in addition to all of his other tasks? If I were a senior pastor and had to put this much work into each of my sermons, I could only preach a couple of times each month.*

ORGANIZING A TALK

With notes in hand, Jim started to arrange his materials into a clear and coherent outline. This framework, he knew, would enable his audience to follow his train-of-thought and remember his major points.

As he assembled the basic structure for his speech, Jim considered several ways to organize his information. He could arrange it in a chronological, geographical, psychological, deductive, or inductive order. He could also sequence his thoughts according to their difficulty (simple to complex) or their importance (most significant to least significant). And, if he really wanted to get fancy, he could use one of four approaches that his speech instructor in college had given him in the following handout.

Label	Description	Example
Alliteration	Each element of the outline begins with the same letter or sound.	Effective leaders are: positive practical predictable productive progressive prudent
Repetition	Each element of the outline begins or ends with the same word.	Pray constantly Pray righteously Pray expectantly Pray thankfully Pray submissively A Humble Prayer A Passionate Prayer A Persistent Prayer A Submissive Prayer
Acrostic	Each element of the outline begins with a letter that spells out the speaker's theme.	**L** ove your people **E** quip your workers **A** nimate your followers **D** eclare your intentions
Rhyme	Each element of the outline ends with the same sound.	Evaluation Preparation Implementation

Jim finally decided to combine two of these patterns into a six-point outline. The main points of his speech would be:

1. The Privilege of Prayer

2. The Practice of Prayer

3. The People of Prayer

4. The Purpose of Prayer

5. The Persistance of Prayer

6. The Power of Prayer

INTRODUCTIONS

Since Jim was speaking at a luncheon, he knew that it would be hard to capture his audience's attention. Their thoughts would be focused on other things like the food and the people around them. So, after making a transitional reference to the conference, the meal or the person who had introduced him, Jim wanted to begin with a power-packed introduction.

At first, Jim wasn't sure what kind of opening he would use. However, he did know what type he wanted to avoid. He wanted to steer clear of long-winded explanations which would chloroform his listeners, irrelevant openings which wouldn't fit into the rest of his speech, and stupefying jokes that would leave his audience yawning. He also wanted to shun apologies and negative comments which would belittle his stature, his message, the situation, or other people.

As he thought about his prelude, Jim knew that he had a wide-range of options. He could start with a quotation, a startling statistic, a provocative question, an audio-visual aid, a story, a relevant joke, a touching poem, a testimonial, a demonstration, or a skit.

After Jim carefully considered these alternatives, he decided to open his speech with a three-pronged offensive. First, he would give his audience a test. His little exercise would help people evaluate their present prayer life, involve them in the presentation and, hopefully, create a desire to improve their prayer efforts.

After this, Jim planned to direct his listeners' hearts toward God by offering a short prayer. His prayer would serve as a model others could imitate.

Finally, he wanted to tell his audience a story about the time when he promised to pray for a friend's family but promptly forgot that pledge. It was an illustration with which many people could identify; it would get people emotionally involved with what he had to say; and, it would lead naturally into his first point.

CONCLUSIONS

Once Jim had selected his introduction, he moved on to his next step: the planning of his conclusion. At this juncture, he voiced a crucial question. "What do I want my audience to know, understand, feel, or do at the end of my presentation?"

Jim had noticed, with some dismay, how church members usually greeted Pastor Grant at the close of the Sunday morning service. Most of the time, they thanked him and praised his speaking ability.

While these heart-warming comments stroked the pastor's ego, they seldom translated into life-changing results.[4]

Could Jim make a more profound impact upon the lives of his audience? He didn't know. But he was going to try.

Jim decided that, at the end of his speech, he was going to supply each person with a piece of paper and ask each one to jot down two things: one step that they would take, during the week, to improve their intercessory prayer life and the names of five people for whom they would promise to pray.

Then, to encourage his audience to fulfill their personal commitments, Jim would ask the participants to enclose their pledges inside envelopes (which he would provide), address these envelopes to themselves, and hand the envelopes to ushers who would collect them for Jim.

At the end of the week, Jim planned to mail the letters back to the conferees. He was hoping this approach would remind his listeners of the commitment that they had made and motivate them to develop a more effective prayer life.

Jim realized that this approach was going to cost him a little money. However, he wanted to see if this technique would have a significant impact upon people's lives.

SUPPORTIVE MATERIALS

Now that he had a framework on which to build, Jim began to flesh out his outline with supportive material. As he did this, he used the same building blocks that he had considered for his introduction: illustrations, quotations, facts, jokes, poems, analogies, audiovisual aids, demonstrations, and skits.

Jim felt that the key to his presentation would be his illustrations. They would make his speech memorable, keep his talk practical, and stir his listeners' emotions.

Because Jim was young, he could have complained that he didn't have a large reservoir of illustrations upon which to draw. However, his preparation had largely mitigated that. He felt that his own experiences, the experiences of others, his research, current events, and biblical stories would provide him with more than an ample amount of material.

Of course, not just any old stories would do. Jim wanted them to be fresh, relevant, concise, interesting, and geared toward his audience.

Jim's anecdotes also had to meet one other requirement. Jill had made it clear to him that he would have to get her permission before telling any stories about her or the girls.

Another key element that would make Jim's presentation come alive would be his audio-visuals. They would play a crucial role in capturing his audience's attention, maintaining their interest, explaining abstract concepts, and reinforcing his ideas. *Maybe that's why they're mentioned so frequently in the Bible*, thought Jim.[5]

As Jim considered what kind of devices he would use, he knew that he had quite a number from which to choose. Blackboards, flip charts, slides, maps, cassette tapes, and videos were among his many options.

Jim finally decided that his weapon of choice would be an overhead projector. It was simple and economical to use. This versatile instrument would also allow Jim to maintain eye contact with his audience, to easily edit the sequence of his visuals, and to develop the visuals himself. With the aid of a computer graphics program and a photo-copy machine, even amateurs like him could produce professional-looking materials.

As Jim was preparing his visual aids, Shirley reminded him to keep one thing in mind. She said, "Make sure your group can see the information on your overhead transparencies. Write in large letters, limit the amount of information on each transparency; and focus your audience's attention with arrows, bullets, and color. I know that sounds elementary but you'd be surprised how many presenters violate this principle of visibility.

"Oh, and by the way, if you're going to use audio aids, make sure that your group can hear them clearly."

PRACTICING THE TALK

Once he had outlined his speech on 4 x 6 cards and prepared his audio-visual aids, Jim began to practice his speech. At first, his talk didn't flow very well; Jim stopped, stumbled, and stammered. However, the more he practiced it, the smoother it became.

As Jim rehearsed his talk, he realized that he had too much material. He hated to deprive anyone of his wide-ranging knowledge of the subject. However, he decided that it was better to drive home a few important points than to deluge his audience with superfluous information. As Voltaire had once said, "The secret of being a bore is to tell everything."[6]

So Jim edited his speech ruthlessly, keeping only the best and most relevant data. His goal was to adhere to the KISS formula (Keep It Short and Simple).

DELIVERING THE TALK

After practicing and revising his speech several times, Jim decided that he was finally ready for his best and toughest critic—his wife. He corralled Jill one evening, and treated her to what he thought was a dynamic presentation. After he finished, he asked: "Well, what do you think?"

His question begged for applause. However, what he received was an honest evaluation.

"Overall, your talk was very good," said Jill. "I can see that you've put a lot of time and effort into preparing your speech. "However, if you want to improve your talk even more, you need to do at least four things.

> First, use your body more effectively. This means that you'll have to look up from your notes more often and do a better job of maintaining eye-contact with your audience.

"It also means that you'll have to smile more. Jim, I know you're discussing a serious subject, but your audience will have more fun if they know you're having fun."

"I think I'll be too nervous to enjoy my speech but I'll try," said Jim. "Any other ways to use my body more effectively?"

"Just one. Right now, your gestures look a bit stilted. But you can cure that problem easily if you'll just relax and act naturally. Remember, you're not an evangelist who is preaching before a crowd of ten thousand people.

> Secondly, "You need to eliminate what I call 'annoyance factors.' For example, meaningless fillers like 'ummm,' 'ah,' or 'well' make your speech sound unpolished. Distracting mannerisms like putting your hands in your pockets or fidgeting with your glasses divert the audience's attention away from your message. And, rambling through 'tangent town' with off-beat quotes or irrelevant illustrations sidetracks your listeners.

> Thirdly, "use your voice more effectively. Jim, there are speakers, orators, and talkers. I think you'd be better off if you cultivated a natural, conversational tone and become a talker. You can do this by getting out from behind the

podium, pretending you're talking with your brother, and thinking of yourself as a teacher rather than a preacher.

"When you speak, talk slowly enough to be understood but quickly enough to keep your audience's interest. And, as you speak, vary your tempo. Pause occasionally when you want to emphasize a point, create suspense, or recapture your audience's attention.

"Variety in your speaking volume will also make your talks more interesting. Just remember to speak loud enough so that your grandmother could hear you if she was seated in the last row.

"Fourthly, you need to maintain a winsome attitude. I enjoy speakers who are positive rather than critical, enthusiastic rather than lifeless, humble rather than proud, and sincere rather than sanctimonious.

"So inspire me, encourage me, challenge me. Talk 'we' instead of 'you' and 'I.' Touch my emotional buttons rather than drowning me with factual information. "Then I'll respond to your message"

"You've mapped out a pretty difficult road to success!" lamented Jim.

"Maybe. But striving for excellence seldom takes you down an easy path," said Jill. "Of course, the more you speak, the easier it will get."

"I hope so. Preparing this talk has taken plenty of my time," said Jim.

"That's why you should start developing some more speeches immediately after you're finished with this one," cautioned Jill. "This early preparation will save you a great deal of time in compiling your next talk.

"One other thing. Don't forget to save your notes from this speech," Jill advised. "You may want to use them again—with a few suitable revisions to fit your new audience and situation."

"Good idea," concurred Jim. "I wouldn't want to waste all of this hard work. But I'd better label my speech so that I don't give it to the same group twice. That would be embarrassing!"

PRESENTING THE TALK

Finally, D day came. Jim felt like a soon-to-be mother at the end of a long, hard pregnancy.

He arrived at Calaway Church thirty minutes before the beginning of the banquet. His early arrival gave him just enough time to find his contact person, practice with the auditorium's equipment, and look over the situation. This extra time also acted as a buffer just in case he ran into a problem—like a flat tire—along the way.

As Jim looked around Calaway's social hall, he was glad that he was there ahead of time. At the last minute, he had decided to bring along a tape recorder so that he could play an excerpt from Ken Daylight's sermon on prayer. When he noticed that the room's electrical outlets were too far away from the podium and that there was no place to set his recorder, he had a short panic attack.

Fortunately, Jim came prepared for this situation. A short walk to his car provided him with the small folding table and the two long extension cords that he needed.

One item that Jim hadn't brought along was an extra bulb for the church's overhead projector. He was dismayed when he saw that it didn't have a spare one attached. However, when he talked with Pat Miller, his contact person, she reassured him there was an emergency bulb in the church's resource center.

Pat helped Jim test the microphone and open a few windows so that the social hall wouldn't be too stuffy during Jim's presentation.

While Jim made these last-minute preparations, he felt the adrenaline racing through his veins. He knew that it was natural to be nervous but, on this occasion, he wished that he wasn't so normal.

Being well-prepared helped Jim keep his nervousness under control. However, to net a few more butterflies, he walked around the church, did some breathing exercises, and mentally relaxed each part of his body.

When it was his turn to speak, Jim didn't focus on the situation. Instead, he channeled his excess energy and excitement into his talk and concentrated on his topic and its value for his listener's lives. After all, he had something important to say!

THE IMPROVEMENT OF SPEAKING SKILLS

When Jim returned from the conference, Jill was waiting in the living room with great anticipation. "How did the speech go?" she asked as Jim walked through the front door.

"Not bad. Several people came up to me after the luncheon, complimented me on my talk, and discussed several problems that they were having with their prayer life. Frankly, I think my speech turned out rather well.

"Of course, one good speech doesn't exactly qualify me for a 'Toastmaster of the Year' award."

"I'm sure you did a terrific job," said Jill as she gave him a Texas-size hug.

"Of course, if you really want to become an even better speaker, you can take several steps to improve your skills," she suggested "You can:

- Analyze radio and television sermons. As you do this, ask yourself what makes them good or bad.

- Give more speeches. Volunteer to speak in the church's worship services and at other organizational meetings.

- Evaluate your own speeches. Record your talks on a video or cassette recorder. Then, as you listen to your talks, ask questions like: "Did I accomplish my goals?" "What were my talk's strong points and weak points?" "What changes would I make if I were to give that talk again?"

- Read books and articles on public speaking.

- Attend preaching seminars."

That was good advice and Jim planned to act on it as soon as possible. His first speaking experience had been a good one and, at least while the adrenaline was still flowing, he felt that he could really make a difference in people's lives.

POINTS TO PONDER

1. What techniques can a speaker use to produce life-changing results in the lives of his audience?

2. What are the characteristics of an interesting illustration?

3. How can pastors save time in preparing sermons?

4. What is the difference between a speaker, an orator, and a talker?

5. Think of three speakers that you admire. What do you like or dislike about their speaking style?

PRACTICAL PROJECTS

1. Prepare a short story that you could use as an introduction to a speech.

2. Prepare seven or eight overhead transparencies that you could use to illustrate a speech.

3. Prepare an outline for a twenty-minute speech.

10

What Did You Say?

(COMMUNICATION)

Taking a stroll around the neighborhood was one of Jim and Jill's favorite pastimes. These jaunts provided them with a relaxing reprieve from the normal whirlwind of church activities. However, this particular evening, their respite didn't last very long.

As soon as Jim and Jill returned to their house, the telephone began to ring. It was Mike Todd, one of Jim's adult Sunday School teachers. From the sound of Mike's voice, Jim deduced that his co-worker was quite upset.

"I'm just calling to find out what's happening with my Sunday School room," said Mike. "Tonight, when I stopped by the church, I found my classroom in complete disarray. There were sleeping bags scattered everywhere; and all of my chairs and tables had been removed."

After Jim took a long, deep breath, he tried to explain the situation. "A youth choir from San Diego called Pastor Grant on Tuesday and asked if they could sing at our church. They evidently had an unexpected cancellation in their tour's schedule.

"Since Pastor Grant knows their choir director quite well, he invited the group to sleep at our church tonight and sing in tomorrow's worship service.

"Since your classroom is the largest in the church, I thought that some of the choir members could sleep in it and use it as a changing room tomorrow. Mary Black and I were planning to move your class to room #203."

"Thanks for letting me know," said Mike sarcastically. "Tomorrow, I was planning to divide my Sunday School class into three discussion groups. However, if we're going to meet in room #203, we won't have enough space to do that."

Jim couldn't believe what he was hearing. Mike always lectured. *Why did he have to pick this Sunday to change his teaching habits?* thought Jim.

"And, what are you going to do with Mrs. Perth?" asked Mike. "She has trouble climbing stairs."

"I'm sorry, Mike," said Jim. "I talked to Mary about the situation on Wednesday and she approved the classroom switch. I guess we didn't realize that it would cause you such a hardship. I also assumed that she would tell you about our plans."

Jim and Mike debated the issue for another five minutes. Finally, Jim yielded to Mike's pressure and promised that he could use his regular room the next day. However, Jim wasn't quite sure how he was going to keep everybody happy. *Maybe a talk with the youth's choir director would help,* thought Jim as he considered his options.

From the way that her husband slumped into the living room chair, Jill could tell that the telephone call had not brought good news.

"What's wrong?" she asked.

Jim was evasive. "Oh, just a little misunderstanding with Mike Todd.

"Lately, I seem to have a burgeoning Babel [1] on my hands. Phrases like 'that's not what you said,' 'I never knew that,' and 'I'm always the last to know' keep cropping up—just like those dastardly little dandelions on our front lawn."

COMMUNICATION GUIDELINES

"Jill, you're the communication expert around here," said Jim. "How can I improve my communication skills?"

"Well, I think you've already taken the first step. Through this experience, you've realized the importance of keeping everybody informed.

"I know quite a few leaders who have never come to that realization. They hoard information because it gives them a certain amount of power or because they're just insensitive to other people's needs. Their actions also create resentment, conflict, and confusion. Their lack of communication hurts relationships, encourages failure, hinders the coordination of a group's efforts, and fosters rumors.

"Recognizing the importance of communication, however, isn't enough. You have to go one step further. When you communicate with your co-workers, you have to do it well. That means that the information that you share with your team should possess at least a dozen characteristics. It should be clear, complete, concise, considerate, consistent, accurate, relevant, simple, desired, interesting, organized, and timely."

"I think you missed one," said Jim.

"Oh?"

"Messages should also be tactfully delivered."

"That was definitely an oversight on my part," giggled Jill. "My apologies."

"Anything else?"

"Just one more thing. When you communicate, you also have to watch out for impediments that can muddle your messages. These communication barriers include: noise, prejudice, overload, vocabulary, distrust, stress, haste, exhaustion, preoccupations, anxiety, distance, distractions, and large amounts of information."

Jim took a moment to ponder Jill's litany of lists. Then, he stood up resolutely and announced to Jill, "I need to go back to church."

"Not again!" complained Jill.

"Yes, again. I need to practice some of those communication tips that you gave me, do some problem solving, and keep everybody on my team informed. Otherwise, I'm going to be in deep trouble with Mike Todd, Mary Black, Pastor Grant, and forty college students."

THE ART OF WRITING

Jim's communication problems were still on his mind when he arrived at the church office on Monday morning.

"Shirley, I've been thinking about developing a newsletter called 'Teaching Tips,'" announced Jim. "It'd be designed specifically to inform, inspire, and train our educational staff. Maybe it would even foster a little team spirit around here."

Shirley could feel the breeze of work blowing her way. So she quickly moved to squash Jim's idea.

"I think that's a great idea and I'd love to help," said Shirley. "But I already have so much to do. That's why Margaret Hanson puts together our church's newsletter."

"That's okay," chuckled Jim. He could see that Shirley had jumped to a false conclusion—just as he had done with Mary Black and Mike Todd. "I was thinking about compiling the newsletter my-self," said Jim.

"That's a lot of work," warned Shirley, as she thought about all of the other ways that Jim could be using his time. "Are you certain you want to do that?"

"Sure," said Jim quite confidently. "I don't think it'll be that hard. And, it'll give me an excuse to stay in touch with my teaching staff. However, I was wondering if you could do me a small favor. You have a wonderful way of expressing your thoughts. Could you jot down some tips on how to write a good article? I'd like to give these guidelines to the people who want to contribute to the newsletter."

"Sure, I'd be glad to do that," said Shirley, now breathing more easily.

The next day, when Jim came back from lunch, a neatly typed handout entitled "Shirley's Suggestions for Effective Writing" was waiting in his in-box. It explained:

If you want to write an interesting article for "Teaching Tips," here are some hints that you should follow.

✓ Preparation

- Decide what your purpose is.
- Outline your main points.
- Make sure you have something worthwhile to say.

✓ Consider their knowledge, experience, concerns and questions.

- Your Audience
- Tailor your writing to fit your readers.
- Choose topics that are interesting to both you and them.
- Use illustrations which are meaningful and interesting to them.

✓ Structure

- Capture your reader's attention in your first paragraph.
- Arrange your material so that the most important information is mentioned first.
- Organize your material and plan your transitions so that your writing flows easily from one idea to the next.
- Stick to your subject.
- Confine each paragraph to a single idea.
- Delete unnecessary words and information.

- Use parallel constructions. For example, use sentences like: "He prepared frequently, practiced diligently, and played enthusiastically."
- Keep introductions and conclusions short.
- End with a strong conclusion that will make your reader think or act.

✓ Words

- Avoid slang, technical terms, religious jargon, and abbreviations. However, if you must use terms that are unfamiliar to your readers, define them first.
- Use simple and clear terms: for example, "do" instead of "implement."
- Avoid trite, overworked expressions.
- Use strong, colorful verbs: for example, "the team trounced their opponents" rather than "the team won."
- Use descriptive adjectives such as "gruff" and "awkward" but avoid long, poetic descriptions.
- Use such dynamic adjectives as "fresh," "new," and "challenging." However, don't exaggerate.
- Vary your word usage to make your communiqué interesting.
- Avoid using the same words too often, especially in the same paragraph. Use synonyms for reoccurring concepts and pronouns for reoccurring nouns.
- Be specific. Use words which describe the names of people, places and things or precise quantities: for example, "Forty teachers attended the banquet" instead of "The banquet was well-attended."
- Avoid long words with several syllables.
- Avoid tentative words, such as "generally," "rather," "perhaps," "maybe," or "largely."

✓ Style

- Use the active voice. For example, say: "He completed the report" instead of "The report was completed by him."
- Use examples, quotes, facts, and graphics to illustrate your points.
- Use only top-quality pictures, graphs, and diagrams.
- Use short sentences and paragraphs.

- Vary your sentence structure and length to make your writing interesting.
- Use fresh and creative expressions.
- Create vivid word pictures.
- Use proper grammar, spelling, and punctuation.
- Stir the heart as well as the mind.
- Avoid sexual and racial bias.
- Use the present tense as much as possible.

✓ Tone

- Be positive.[2]
- Be tactful and pleasant; otherwise, your words may come back to haunt you.
- Be enthusiastic.
- Use a conversational style. Imagine that you are talking with your reader.
- Use contractions to make your writing more readable.
- Don't patronize the reader.
- Don't try to be cute.
- Personalize your message so that your readers know exactly how the article applies to them or how they can get involved.

✓ Additional Guidelines

- Answer six important questions: Who? What? Why? When? Where? and How?
- Use action and direct quotes to spark interest.
- Ask questions to involve your reader but use them sparingly.
- Be practical.
- Choose subjects that can be covered adequately in the space that you have.
- Evaluate your article by reading it out loud.
- Let someone else proofread your article before submitting it. They may catch errors that you have overlooked or they may offer a few suggestions which will improve the article.
- Make sure that your submission is typed with a fresh ribbon, and free from mistakes and smudges.

Attached to this handout was a one-page addendum which said, "Jim, Here are a few additional tips that you should keep in mind as you edit your newsletter."

- Use underlining, color, bullets, numbers, graphics, headings, boxes, and other visual devices to highlight important information. However, remember that over-using a device will reduce its impact.

- Use our church's clip art books and desk-top publishing program when designing your newsletter. Both of these aids offer great graphics. Someday, I hope we'll be able to afford a scanner. That way, we can copy pictures and photographs directly into our word processor.

- Don't use too many different fonts or type sizes in the same newsletter. This can be very distracting.

- Leave plenty of white space around your articles so that your newsletter won't look too cramped and cluttered.

- Experiment with your newsletter's layout. With our computer, that will be easy.

- Collect sample newsletters from other churches. They can give you a lot of ideas that will improve your newsletter's design.

- Make your headlines or headings short, interesting, and related to the story.

- Select only those articles that will suit your purposes and interest your readers.

- Proofread your publication carefully before printing it.

THE ART OF LISTENING

For months, Jim had wrestled with his decision to start a singles group. He knew that there was a tremendous need for this type of ministry; however, he didn't feel that he had enough expertise to approach the project with confidence.

Bob Sparkman had suggested that Klaus Schuller, an international student from Berlin, could be a splendid source of innovative and practical ideas. His work with students who attended Fremont University had been remarkable. According to Bob, Klaus had transformed First Church's bland, meat-and-potatoes singles ministry into a gourmet's delight.

When Klaus appeared at Jim's office, though, Jim began to doubt Bob's assessment. Klaus's puny physique, haphazard dress, and shy demeanor didn't square with Jim's picture of a dynamic leader. He tried to remind himself that the contents of a package can't always be judged by its wrapping paper.[3]

From the outset, Jim tried to put Klaus at ease. He offered him a cup of coffee and a comfortable chair, talked about Fremont's football team, and complimented him on his work at First Church.

"Thanks for coming over, Klaus. I've really looked forward to meeting you. Bob tells me that you've done a remarkable job of transforming the singles ministry at his church. Tell me, why do you think your singles group has been so successful?"

At first, Klaus was reluctant to talk about his achievements. However, Jim was intent on learning all that he could from this humble servant of God. So, to encourage Klaus to talk, Jim did several things.

He sprinkled their discussion with phrases like:

"Uh-huh," "That's interesting," "Tell me more," and "Really?"

He maintained good eye contact.

He leaned forward in his chair and assumed an open position with arms and legs uncrossed.

He nodded his head whenever he agreed with Klaus's statements.

And, he asked a myriad of open-ended questions.

Then, once Jim had opened the door to a particular topic, he heeded Polonius' advice to "give every man thine ear, but few thy voice."[4]

Of course, Jim didn't remain totally silent. That might have indicated indifference. So he interacted with Klaus just enough to display his interest and draw Klaus out.

Jim also avoided any behavior that would have indicated that he was bored. Interruptions, negative comments, pencil tapping, folded arms, restless movement, and clock watching were definitely on Jim's list of no-nos.

Abiding by that list wasn't always easy. Klaus' accent was thick and his pace was glacial.

Because Jim was able to think faster than Klaus could speak, he was tempted to rush Klaus or finish Klaus' sentences. Jim also found himself formulating his responses while he should have been listening to his guest.

To counteract these tendencies, Jim took several steps to keep himself involved in the conversation. He started to take notes. He looked for specific information that would be useful to him. He paid close attention to Klaus' demeanor and body language. And, he used his 'spare processing time' to evaluate Klaus' ideas.

Fortunately, Jim was interested in what Klaus had to say.

It was also fortunate that Bob had forewarned Jim that it might be difficult to understand Klaus. Jim had taken the precaution of making his office as listener-friendly as possible. To minimize distractions, he had closed his door and window, turned off his radio, and asked Shirley to hold all of his calls.

As Klaus began to warm up to Jim and Jim became accustomed to Klaus' accent, their conversation became more lively and interesting. As they talked, Klaus even shared some of the struggles and the failures that he had faced in his ministry.

As he did, Jim was aware of the trust that Klaus had put in him. So he reassured Klaus that he would keep his confidences.[5]

By the end of the conversation, some of Jim's earlier impressions had melted away. Jim had developed a liking for this tall, slender foreigner. He was smart, interesting and compassionate. And, Jim appreciated his willingness to help Bethel Baptist launch its new singles ministry.

THE ART OF TELEPHONING

The next day, Jim presented Shirley with a box of Swiss chocolates and thanked her for the writing guidelines which she had provided. She, in turn, thanked Jim for the candy and offered another piece of helpful information.

"Since you're so communication conscious this week," said Shirley, "you might be interested in a little article that I recently clipped from 'The Savvy Secretary.' Although it's business-oriented, it has a lot of tips about telephone etiquette that I try to use here at the church."

"I'd love to have a copy," said Jim. He collected training handouts like a philatelist collects stamps.

As Jim read the article, he noted that it made the following suggestions.

✓ When the telephone rings,

- Answer it promptly.
- Greet the caller with a pleasant phrase.
- Identify yourself and your organization properly.
- Treat every call as an important call.
- Ask people how you can help them.

✓ When making a call,

- Place your own calls.
- Call at a time when you're most likely to reach the other person.

- Call people at a reasonable hour. Be mindful of the differences in time zones.
- Make a list of the topics that you want to discuss or the questions that you want to ask before dialing.
- Be prepared with all of the necessary information and materials that you need before dialing.
- Make sure that you have the correct name, number, and extension of the person whom you're trying to contact before dialing.
- Give the person sufficient time to answer the telephone.
- Greet the person in a friendly way. Then identify yourself and your organization.

✓ When you leave a message for someone, let them know:

- Who you are and what company you represent.
- When you called (date and time).
- When and where you can be reached (include your telephone number even if they can find it in a directory).
- What information you need or why you want them to return your phone call.

✓ When you leave a message on an answering machine,

- Speak distinctly.
- Spell your name or the name of your organization if it is difficult to spell or to understand.
- Speak slowly and pause strategically when leaving important information like phone numbers, addresses, or statistics.

✓ If somebody is copying down the message that you're leaving,

- Ask the person to read it back to you so that you can check it for accuracy.
- Don't wait for the intended recipient to call you. They may not receive your message or the correct information.

✓ When speaking to a person on the phone,

- Let callers know that you're glad that they called—if that's the case—with phrases like "It's good to hear from you."

- Begin your conversation with a *short* period of "small-talk." Then get quickly to the point.
- Speak naturally.
- Smile as you talk.
- Picture the person with whom you're talking.
- Speak directly into the telephone.
- Speak distinctly.
- Give the other person your full attention.
- Listen carefully.
- Be positive.
- Use good grammar.
- Maintain a relaxed and easy-going attitude.
- Lead the conversation if you initiated the call.
- Speak slowly enough to be understood but quickly enough to avoid boredom. Talk more slowly if you have a noticeable accent.
- Strike a balance between a loud and a soft voice.
- Call from a quiet setting—one without a lot of background noise.
- Ask for verbal feedback since you can't obtain visual feedback.
- Use vivid word pictures since you can't display visuals.
- Take notes. This is especially important if vital statistics, names, street addresses, telephone numbers, legal matters, or long lists of information/instructions are discussed.
- Pause frequently enough so that the other person has a chance to talk or ask questions. Also, pause for emphasis.
- Be courteous. Use phrases like "please" "thank you" or "you're welcome." Exercise the "Golden Rule."

✓ If the caller is phoning you at a bad time,

- Let him or her know that you appreciate the call.
- Explain that you are busy at the moment.
- Arrange to call back at a later time.
- Record your promised callback in your calendar.
- Call the person back at the promised time and place.

✓ When closing your call,

- Ask for the best time to reach the person again—if you need to call the person back.

- Say "good-bye" pleasantly.
- Leave the caller feeling good.
- Let the other person hang up first.
- Replace the receiver gently in its cradle.

✓ After making the call,

- Follow through with the promises that you've made.
- If any agreements were reached, write a confirmation letter.
- File away the information that you received if the phone call requires follow-up or contains important information that you'll need to refer to in the future.
- Call people back at the time and place promised.

✓ When taking a message for another person,

- Write the message down immediately.
- Include the caller's name and the name of his organization, your name, the date, the time, the telephone number where the caller can be reached, the information or request that was made, and any impressions that you had about the caller.
- Record the message accurately.
- Leave the message where your colleague will find it quickly.

✓ When a person can't be reached,

- Don't offer any information which would reflect badly on that person. For example, don't say:
- "He stepped out for coffee," "He hasn't come in yet," or "He never tells me where he is."
- Instead, tell the caller that the person can't be reached immediately. Then, offer to take a message or let the caller know when the person can be reached.

✓ When putting a caller on hold,

- Ask the caller "Would you mind waiting or shall I call you back?" and wait for their reply.
- Deal with people in the order that they called.
- Return to the line every thirty seconds and assure the caller that they haven't been forgotten. Give them a chance to leave a message.
- Express your appreciation for the caller's patience with phrases like "Thank you for waiting."

✓ When you need to transfer a call,

- Explain why you need to transfer the call.
- Tell the caller where they're being transferred.
- Tell the person to whom you're transferring the call: who is calling, why they're calling, and any other pertinent information that they may need.
- Don't "cut people off."

✓ When you're put on hold for a long time,

- Hang up.
- Call the office back and explain the need to reach the person quickly.
   Leave a message or time and place where you can be reached.
   Or, find out when is the best time to reach the person.

✓ To make the telephoning process go smoothly,

- Give prompt attention to your telephone messages when you receive them.
- Tell your secretary when you leave the office.
- Record your voice on a tape recorder so that you can evaluate and improve it.
- Provide message pads for your secretary.

MEETINGS

"Thanks for dropping by the office," said Jim as he stood to shake Phil Tagger's hand. The vigor with which this athletic young man gripped Jim's hand was indicative of his tremendous enthusiasm and outgoing spirit.

"It's my pleasure," responded Phil. "I'm really excited about launching our church's new singles ministry. It'll be a blessing to our church and to those who attend."

"I like your optimistic attitude!" said Jim. "And, if you put as much energy into this project as you do into your handshakes, we ought to do well."

Phil laughed heartily. "Well, I'm ready. Where do we begin?"

As Jim and Phil both sat down, Jim tried to answer his friend's question: "Well, as I mentioned to you on the phone, I think the first thing that we need to do is to call an organizational meeting.

Then, we should try to get everybody who's interested in starting a singles group to attend."

"Can anything good come from a meeting?" quipped Phil.

"I can understand your skepticism," responded Jim. "Many people feel that meetings and committees are a waste of time.

"In fact, I never call a meeting without first asking myself: 'Is this meeting really necessary?'

"Frequently the answer to that question is 'no.' My team members and I don't have enough things to discuss. The items on our agenda aren't urgent. Or, we're just planning to have a meeting because tradition demands it.

"When that's the case, I try to achieve my goals by other means. Many times a telephone call, a face-to-face conversation with an individual or a written message will do just as well and save a lot of time.

"However, in our case, I think a meeting is imperative. We need to get together with other people and tap their collective experiences, needs, interests, and viewpoints. They can provide us with a lot of valuable ideas.

"A meeting will also help us in several other ways. It'll improve our communication and coordination. It'll generate enthusiasm for our singles ministry. It'll quell false rumors. And, it'll save us a great deal of time in collecting and disseminating ideas.

"The next question that we need to address is: 'What do we want to achieve during our get-together?'

"Meetings are conducted for a variety of reasons: to solve problems, to inform, to socialize, to build things, to pray, to praise, to teach, and to reconcile conflicts.

"In our case, I think our primary purpose is to discover how much interest there is in starting a singles ministry. In addition, we also want to plan activities, generate creative ideas, make decisions, and get as many people as possible involved in developing this program.

"We also need to ask: 'When and where should the meeting be held?'"

"I've already talked with several of our students about that," said Phil, "and they feel that we should hold our meeting on a Friday evening after a potluck supper.

"We could meet in Mike Todd's classroom. It's big enough to accommodate everybody. It also has proper ventilation, good temperature controls, comfortable chairs, and adequate lighting. And, if we arrange the chairs in a semi-circle, we'll be able to elicit a lot of participation."

"That sounds like a good idea," said Jim.

"Next we need to decide whom we want to invite. Most of the time, the membership of our church committees is decided by the church's constitution. In our case, however, we can invite whomever we'd like."

"Except, of course, we don't want to invite people who have no reason for attending," said Phil. "This would only be a waste of their time."

"Right," agreed Jim.

"In our case, I think we need to invite two types of people—university students and potential sponsors."

"We should also invite Pastor Grant," said Phil. "If he has a chance to see what we're planning, I think he'll be more supportive. His presence will also let the singles know that the church is behind this program. We could even have Pastor Grant bring an opening challenge."

Jim was a little offended that his support didn't seem to be enough. However, he acquiesced to Phil's suggestion.

"OK, let's do that. Make sure that Pastor Grant knows the time limit for his talk," warned Jim.

"We should also invite Klaus Schuller. He's experienced, and he has a lot of ideas about how churches should minister to university students."

"OK. But's let's not invite too many people," said Phil. "If the group is too large, only a handful will participate."

"Agreed," nodded Jim.

"Next, we need an agenda. It'll give our meeting a clear focus and direction. It'll show the participants that we're prepared and organized. And, if we include the agenda with our invitation, it'll let everybody know what to expect and give them a chance to prepare for the meeting."

In ten minutes, Jim and Phil hammered out a letter to all potential participants which included the following agenda.

6:00	Potluck dinner (Those with last names beginning with A-E should bring salads or vegetables, those with last names beginning with F-K should bring desserts, those with last names beginning with L-Z should bring a main course.)
6:40	Welcome and Opening Prayer
6:45	Opening Remarks: "The Importance of a Singles Ministry"

6:50	Establishment of Fall Calendar of Events
7:20	Organization of Single's Ministry
	President
	Vice-President
	Secretary
	Publicity Coordinator
	Social Committee
	Outreach Coordinator
	Sunday School Teacher
	Assistant Sunday School Teacher
7:40	Selection of Sunday School Curriculum
8:00	Closing Prayer
	Note: The next planning meeting will be Sunday, September 30.

"Along with this agenda," said Phil, "I think we should send everyone a survey sheet which would ask people what kind of activities they want to participate in. These questionnaires should be turned into the church office the week before our meeting."

"Good idea," encouraged Jim. "One more thing that I almost forgot. We're going to need a secretary for our meeting."

"I think John Rogers will be willing to help us there," volunteered Phil.

"Good. Would you ask him if he'd accept that position?" inquired Jim.

"Sure. But, when he asks me what his responsibilities are, what should I tell him?"

"Well, for our purposes, I think his job is four-fold. He should: (1) type the meeting's invitation, agenda and activity survey, (2) notify potential attendees about the meeting, (3) record the meeting's proceedings and decisions, and (4) distribute the minutes of our meeting.

"If he'd be willing to serve as our group's permanent secretary, I'd also ask him to do three other things: (1) prepare and distribute any materials that will be used in our meetings, (2) keep the group's records, and (3) assist the group's president in taking care of the group's correspondence."

"Will you lead the meeting?" Phil asked Jim hopefully.

"No. I'd like you to chair our little get-together," said Jim.

Phil thought for a while and then responded: "I'm willing to do that. However, I've never led a meeting before. What am I supposed to do?"

"Well, before the meeting, you'll need to talk to John, Mike, Pastor Grant, and Klaus so that everybody knows what's expected of them. You'll also need to arrange for any special materials and equipment that we will need. Klaus, for example, may want to show some slides or display some brochures, curriculum materials, and activity calendars.

"Then, on Friday, you'll need to arrive early. This will give you a chance to make sure that the facilities are in order and that the temperature is adjusted properly.

"Next, I think it'd be a good idea if you and I stand near the doors and welcome people as they come into the room.

"During the actual meeting, you'll need to:

- Begin and end on time.

- Open the meeting with a welcome, prayer, and an interesting introduction.

- Create an atmosphere that is friendly but businesslike.

- Guide the participants through the agenda.

- Introduce special speakers as necessary.

- Keep the group focused on each topic that is discussed.

- Ask stimulating questions.

- Listen to people's input.

- Encourage discussion.

- Seek clarification of issues.

- Summarize the discussion periodically.

- Encourage the group to reach satisfying decisions.

- Handle conflict, if it arises.

- Focus the group's attention on issues rather than personalities.

- Make assignments as necessary.

- And, at the end of the meeting, thank the participants for their involvement."

"Boy, that sounds like a big job," exclaimed Phil.

"Don't worry," said Jim, "I'll be there to help you.

"Any questions?"

"Two!" said Phil. "Can I state my opinion and take sides in our discussions?"

"Personally, I don't think that's wise," said Jim. "If you're not an honest broker of ideas, you're likely to upset the participants.

"What's your other question?"

"How did I get myself into this?" asked Phil.

Two weeks later, Jim and Phil got together to discuss the first meeting of the singles group. Jim thought it had gone rather well. Before saying anything, however, he wanted to get Phil's opinion. "Well, what did you think of our little get-together yesterday?" he asked.

"It was great!" said Phil. "I was surprised but glad to see that so many people are interested in starting this new ministry."

"It was exciting, wasn't it?" said Jim. "Of course, even though our organizational meeting is over, our work isn't. In fact, we've just begun."

As the group's newly elected president, Phil knew that the task that lay ahead of him would be a challenging one. However, he was looking forward to the experience. He was convinced that this new venture would have a tremendous impact upon people's lives.

"You'll need to talk to John and have him send out the minutes of the meeting," said Jim. "They should go to three groups of people: (1) those who attended, (2) those who are interested but couldn't attend, and (3) those who are in a position to influence our ministry—people like the church moderator and the members of our Christian Education Board. In fact, we might want to summarize the gist of our decisions in the first issue of 'Teaching Tips'—our new newsletter for teachers.

"When you talk with John, let him know that you'd like the minutes sent out immediately. In addition, remind him that the minutes should be typed, accurate, clear, complete, concise, and unbiased. They should also mention the date of the meeting, the people who were present, the major issues that we discussed, the decisions that we made, and the assignments that we made.

"If the minutes need to be revised, we can do that at our next meeting. Also, make sure that he retains a copy of the minutes for our official records.

"Oh, and don't forget. In the minutes that are sent out, we should also remind people of the date, time, and place of our next meeting."

"Whoa. Slow down," said Phil, as he furiously tried to scribble all of Jim's suggestions in his notebook.

Jim waited until Phil had finished capturing his recommendations. Then, he began with renewed vigor.

"You'll need to follow up on the assignments that were made during the meeting so that they're properly carried out.

"As with all of the meetings that you lead, you should also spend some time asking the following questions.

- What was accomplished? Did we meet our goals?

- What went well? Why?

- What went poorly? Why?

- Who participated? Why?

- Next time, what can we do differently?

"The answers to these questions can help you to improve your future meetings.

"One last thing. As the president of the singles group, you'll be expected to represent your organization at a variety of church functions. For example, I'll want you to attend the monthly meeting of our Christian Education Board. I'd also like you to give a short report about the start of our singles group at our next church council meeting."

"Oh no," groaned Phil. "More meetings?!"

"Afraid so," smiled Jim. "Christ has given each of us a cross to bear."

POINTS TO PONDER

1. How would you define the word "communication?"

2. What elements are involved in the communication process?

3. What are the advantages and disadvantages of writing, telephoning, face-to-face conversations, and audio-visual materials?

4. What is "body language"? What role does it play in the communication process? Share some examples of how you could convey a message without even using words.

5. How would you handle the following personalities at a committee meeting?

   a. Tangent Tanya

   b. Domineering Dan

    c. Quiet Quincy

    d. Argumentative Alice

6. How should committee chairmen deal with conflict in their meetings?

7. How should leaders respond to rumors?

PRACTICAL PROJECTS

1   Using the guidelines given in this chapter, design a brochure that will promote your church's adult, youth, preschool, choir, or children's ministry.

2. Write a sample one-page agenda for a Christian Education Board meeting, a meeting of youth sponsors, or a choir team meeting.

3. Attend and critique a church committee meeting.

11

We're Facing an
Energy Crisis

(MOTIVATION)

"**W**hat's wrong, Jim? You sound discouraged," said Bob Sparkman as he chatted with his distressed friend on the phone.

"Well, I'm facing a bit of an energy crisis," said Jim.

"Having trouble with your electricity?"

"Not exactly," responded Jim. "People seem to be afflicted with a dreadful case of the apathies."

"There seems to be a lot of that going around," kibitzed Bob.

"Maybe. But I don't have to like it or accept it," said Jim in a decidedly solemn tone. "Outside the church, millions of people are dying without a saving knowledge of Christ. Inside the church, our members are biblically illiterate. And, yet, our people don't seem to care.

"Yesterday, for example, one of my teachers told me an appalling story. Evidently he had spent five, sixteen-hour days working on a big sales contract. After the deal was completed, he went to the beach and celebrated the whole day.

"Because of all these activities, he put off preparing his Sunday School lesson until late Saturday night. Then, he said, 'the Holy Spirit' gave him a sudden flash of inspiration. He bragged that, with this instant insight, he was able to build an entire lesson in less than ten minutes.

"Well, I just couldn't believe how proud he was of his delinquent behavior. There was absolutely no sign of remorse for his misguided priorities.

"If he were the only one who displayed that kind of lackadaisical attitude, I wouldn't be so concerned. But we seem to be plagued with lukewarm members. My teachers seem more interested in attending tennis matches and playing computer games than winning the world for Christ.

"What's worse, I don't know what to do about it. Unlike bosses in the businessworld, I don't have the carrot of money nor the stick of job security to urge people forward.

"Do you have any words of wisdom for me?" pleaded Jim.

"Well, 'motivation' is a pretty broad subject, and I really don't have time to discuss it right now. I have some people coming in for pre-marital counseling in a few minutes," explained Bob. "Maybe we could talk about this more on Thursday."

"I suppose," muttered Jim. He was reluctant to wait that long but it seemed like he had no other choice.

"In the meantime," said Bob, "why don't you visit the library and see if they have any books on motivation."

MOTIVATIONAL THEORIES

As Jim hung up the receiver, he felt like a drowning man who had just been hit by a tidal wave. This was the first time that his friend had let him down.

That afternoon, Jim dutifully heeded his mentor's advice and went to Cody's Memorial Library. He found three books on motivation nestled away in its stacks. Jim hoped that they would supply him with the answers that he so strongly craved.

Abraham Maslow's Hierarchy of Needs

As he leafed through the literature on the subject, Jim noticed that several men were mentioned over and over again. One of these psychologists was a man by the name of Abraham Maslow. According to this theorist, people's needs fall into the following categories:

1. *Physiological needs* include a person's demand for oxygen, food and water, rest and exercise, sleep, sex, and elimination.

2. *Security needs* include a person's yearning for physical safety, shelter, economic security, emotional security, structure, and stability.

3. *Social needs* include a person's hunger for belonging, group acceptance, affection, mutual trust, friendship, intimacy, and love.

4. *Esteem needs* include a person's longing for respect, status, prestige, adequacy, recognition, approval, and self-worth.

5. *Self-actualization needs* include a person's craving for self-expression, creativity, growth, and self-realization.

Maslow contended that people move up this *hierarchy of needs* only when their desires at lower levels have been predominantly met. In other words, people aren't motivated to start a new, creative project if they've just been told that they have three weeks to live.

Frederick Herzberg's Hygiene Theory of Motivation

During the course of his research, Jim also came across Frederick Herzberg's *hygiene theory of motivation*. This behavioral scientist discovered that removing obstacles that frustrate people doesn't necessarily make those people happy.

For example, if people don't have adequate job security, a good salary, or a pleasant environment in which to work, they're going to be dissatisfied. However, even if an employer provides all of these elements, his workers still won't automatically become more productive. He'll only have succeeded in keeping them from being unhappy. To motivate his workers, a leader must provide recognition, enlarged responsibilities, chances for people to grow and advance, and opportunities for people to succeed.

Douglas Mcgregor's Theory X and Theory Y

A third researcher, Douglas McGregor, suggests that leaders function with one of two assumptions in mind. A leader who believes in *Theory X* assumes that people hate work, lack ambition, and shirk responsibility. Therefore, they need close supervision and frequent prodding.[1] Otherwise, they'll never become a productive group member.

A leaders who accepts *Theory Y* assumes that people are willing to accept responsibility, are capable of directing their own efforts toward a goal, and are interested in doing a good job. Therefore, a leader who acts on this assumption will give subordinates a freer reign than a leader who believes in Theory X.

B. F. Skinner's Behavior Modification

The last man whom Jim studied was B. F. Skinner, a Harvard psychologist who became known as the father of behavior modification. Although Skinner worked primarily with laboratory animals, he and his disciples came to the conclusion that people do things either to obtain pleasure or to avoid punishment. In other words, a person's behavior is determined by the consequences of his or her actions.

Therefore, management theorists who accept Skinner's conclusions feel that leaders can shape the conduct of their workers by applying the correct reward or punishment—in the correct dose and at the correct time. To achieve this goal, four basic approaches are used.

1. Positive reinforcement is used to increase the occurrence of a desired behavior. For example, compliments and awards encourage good performance.

2. Punishment is used to decrease the occurrence of an undesirable behavior. For example, reprimands discourage poor work habits.

3. Avoidance of punishment is used to strengthen the occurrence of a desired behavior. For example, the knowledge that one will be reprimanded for tardiness encourages people to be punctual.

4. Removal of positive reinforcements is used to eliminate the occurrence of an undesired behavior. For example, ignoring a person's accomplishments will diminish the quality of his or her work.

MOTIVATIONAL TECHNIQUES

Although Jim's research had netted him a number of stimulating ideas, he still wasn't totally satisfied with what he had found. He could think of many cases in the Bible where people had given up their basic needs for security and belonging in order to endure persecution for God's sake. He also thought that the theories were, at times, a little too simplistic or even irrelevant for his type of work. Furthermore, he wasn't sure how to put these generalities into practice.

Because of this disenchantment with his research, Jim decided to bring up the issue of motivation during the next meeting of the Christian Education Board. He wanted to see what suggestions its members had to offer him.

****

The Christian Education Board's meeting had gone well. Its pace had been crisp. Its decisions had been both solid and courageous. Its atmosphere and exchange of ideas had been warm and friendly.

Since the Board had completed most of its business, Jim decided that it was time to turn the group's attention toward the training portion of the meeting. He stood, applauded their efforts, and announced: "This week I've really been struggling with the issue of motivation. I've been asking myself: 'How can we inspire our people to do their very best?'

"I thought one way to find out the answer to that question was to come here and ask you: 'What motivates you? What gets you excited about your ministry?'"

Alice Anderson was the first one to respond. "For me, that's easy. I'm a youth sponsor for the high school group because I believe in what I'm doing. I'm convinced that I'm making a difference in the lives of our young people and that my influence will be felt far into their future.

"Last night, for example, one of our young ladies came over to my apartment and talked to me for three hours about her father's drinking problem. She's really finding it difficult to cope with him and his verbal abuse. By the end of the evening, she had made several important decisions—including one to accept Christ as her Lord and Savior."

"Praise the Lord!" came the cry of several board members.

"That's great!" echoed Jim. He didn't want to pass over that victory too quickly. So he paused for a moment before summarizing Alice's comments. *"Championing a worthwhile, life-changing cause is one way to motivate people."*

"It sure is," responded Alice with glee. "Some work to save the environment. Others try to renew the inner cities. I'm working for the cause of Christ in an effort to bring about spiritual change.

"Of course, I wasn't always so enthusiastic about the church's youth program. I hate to admit it, Jim, but just before you came, I complained at one of the business meetings that we were spending too much money on youth activities. Since I've become involved with the young people and I've seen the tremendous needs that they have, my attitude has changed completely. Now, I feel that the church isn't spending enough money on them."

"*Involvement motivates*," said Jim. "The more you participate in a ministry, the more excited you're likely to become."

"That's true," agreed Alice. "But, remember, my involvement didn't appear suddenly in full bloom. It came gradually.

"At first, you asked me to drive a few kids to a concert to hear 'Ben and His Brassy Band.' Since I thought we could save the church some money by taking cars rather than renting a bus, I agreed to your request.

"Then, a couple of weeks later, you asked me to lead a devotional at a youth retreat. Now, four months later, here I am—fully immersed in the group's activities."

"In other words, Jim used an old political ploy," said Kay Williams, the preschool coordinator. *First, you get your foot in the door. Then you keep asking people for more and more.*

"I've used that trick myself from time to time. However, in the long run, it doesn't work very well. I've found that some people agree to do an increasing amount of work until, suddenly, they drop out of the program entirely. I guess they quit because they feel like they're being sucked into a bottomless pit, with no chance of escape."

"Well, I'm not advocating trickery and treachery to motivate people," protested Alice. "I'm just saying that once a person feels comfortable with one aspect of a ministry, they're more likely to try another aspect of the same ministry."

Jim jumped into the conversation to keep it on track. He said, "I want to talk more about motivation versus manipulation a little later. For now, though, let's concentrate on the positive factors that motivate people."

Sam Lark dashed to Jim's rescue. He said, "*I think reciprocity is a great motivator.*"

"What do you mean?" asked Kay.

"Well, when you do something for someone else because they've done something for you, you're reciprocating," explained Sam. "That's how I became involved in the children's church program. Chad Blue really helped me when I was out of work. So, when he asked me to accept my present position, I was more than willing to lend him a helping hand.

"I also accepted my position for another reason. It posed a big challenge. When I took over the children's church program, it was really faltering. Attendance had dropped from forty children down to ten. And the children who came didn't learn much. Up to that point, the church viewed the program as a baby-sitting service for lazy parents who wanted to attend the worship service in peace and quiet.

"Well, successful, business-as-usual enterprises bore me. I think Chad knew that. He didn't minimize the problems or tell me how easy it would be to revive the program. Instead, he compared the job to tuning an old, neglected piano. When I was through, he said, everyone would be able to notice the difference.

"Well, I responded to Chad's *challenge* the way an expert climber salivates at the thought of tackling Mt. Everest. To me, Chad's list of problems was only an opportunity in disguise.

"Ever since then, Jim has followed in Chad's wake. He constantly challenges me to evaluate, change, and improve the program. That's good! Because, as soon as the program becomes routine, I'll be out looking for a new mountain to climb."

"It sounds like you take after Caleb in the Old Testament,"[2] said Jim. "He was an overcomer, too. Despite the fact that he would have to face fierce warriors and strong fortifications, he begged for a chance to conquer the territory around Hebron. The hearts of younger men would have melted if they were assigned such a formidable task. However, Caleb volunteered for the job at the ripe old age of eighty-five!"

"You know, even if we don't inherit a struggling organization like you did, Sam," said Mary Black. "We can create our own mountains. That is, *we can set goals for ourselves that will require our very best.* Setting an attendance goal of 300 in Sunday School has certainly motivated my staff to do things than they never would have done without such a demanding target."

After a slight break in the conversation, Jim simply asked: "Any more ideas?"

Fran Cooper, the church's librarian, responded with an astute observation. "Did you notice how excited Alice and Sam became when they talked about their groups?" she asked. "You could hear the devotion that they have for their ministries in their voices and see it on their faces.

"That kind of enthusiasm is contagious. We all would do a better job of 'turning on' people if we had some electricity in our own souls."

"You're plum right, ma'am," drawled Sam in his best Southern accent. "As my mama used to say, 'You can't light a fire with a wet match.'"

"And, if anyone should be enthusiastic, it ought to be Christians," continued Fran, as she prepared to catalog her ideas. "The word 'enthusiasm' comes from two Greek words which mean 'God within.' Effective leaders in the Bible always had a passion for their people[3] and their mission.[4] Also, the Bible commands us to be enthusiastic and diligent in our work.[5] And, we have so much about which to be passionate."

"Well, I don't know about the rest of you; but I'm not about to become a boisterous, back-slapping kind of a person. It's not my nature," objected Kay Williams.

"We don't have to display that kind of exuberance," suggested Sam. "If we'll just focus on the importance of our ministries and the tremendous impact that we can have in people's lives, a quiet enthusiasm will begin to emerge. Before we know it, we'll all have a sparkle in our eye, a smile on our face, a bounce in our walk, and an effervescence in our voice."

"Jim, you're great in modeling that kind of enthusiasm for us," asserted Kelly Rivers. "When you see the improvements in our resource center, you'll rant and rave. It makes us feel like we've really done something special.

"But that's not the only thing that you model for us. When you ask us to work hard, you put in long hours, too. When you ask us to strive for excellence, you show us the way by producing quality brochures, quality training workshops, and quality Bible studies."

"That's important," agreed Fran. "*'Practicing what you preach' is a powerful motivator.*"[6]

"And, it's biblical," chimed Mary. "Paul, for instance, was a real proponent of leading by example. On several occasions, he told his people to imitate his behavior.[7] More importantly, he asked his readers to pattern their lives after his because he was following Christ's example.[8]

"Now, the Pharisees were just the opposite. They engaged in a sanctimonious life-style which was unworthy of imitation.[9] No wonder Jesus condemned them for being 'hypocrites'[10] and 'blind guides.'[11] They were like salespeople who promote their company's product while using their competitor's brand."

"Boy, that puts a lot of pressure on us as leaders, doesn't it?" remarked Jim.

"Well, I guess I'd better stop shouting at my children: 'Don't *yell* in the classroom,'" said Mary, barely managing to keep her smile under wraps.

"Good idea!" whispered Alice.

After everybody had a chance to snicker their approval of Mary's comment, Holly Smith offered her contribution to the discussion. *"Another motivator is people's expectations.* Rightly or wrongly, I perform only as well as other people think I will.

"When Jim recruited me, I tried to repel him with every excuse that I knew because I didn't think I could succeed.

"Jim patiently countered each objection with phrases like: 'I know you'll do a good job,' and 'With you at the helm, this Sunday School picnic will the best one ever.'"

Fran stifled her urge to react. She remembered how she had coordinated the church's picnic several years before. It had gone rather well, and Holly would have a tough time trying to top it.

Unaware of Fran's reaction, Holly continued to tell her story. "Look at me now. Here I am—having the time of my life and continually trying to live up to Jim's expectations."

"I think, in educational circles, they even have a name for what you've been describing," said Mary. "It's called: 'The Pygmalion Effect.'"

"In fact, I heard about one teacher who was able to get her students to do extraordinarily well in school. When the school's principal asked her for the secret to her success, she replied: 'They're all brilliant students. So I just expected them to live up to their potential.'

"The principal asked why she thought her students were exceptionally bright. Puzzled by his question, she showed him a piece of paper and said: 'Here's the list of my pupil's I.Q. scores that you gave me at the beginning of the year.'

"'Those aren't their I.Q. scores,' he chuckled. 'Those are the student's locker numbers!'"

Again, the meeting room echoed with laughter. Mary always had a way of getting her point across with a story. Once the giggles had subsided, Kelly provided the group with the scriptural framework for their discussion.

"As 1 Corinthians 13:7 points out, telling your people that you believe in them is very biblical," she asserted.

"Certainly, Paul was a practitioner of this principle. For example, when he wrote Philemon on Onesimus' behalf, he said that he fully expected his friend to heed his wishes and do even more than he asked.[12]

"On another occasion, when Paul was collecting money for the believers in Jerusalem, he told the Corinthians that he had complete confidence in their ability and in their desire to make a large contribution."[13]

"We just finished studying 2 Corinthians in our Sunday School class," said Sam. "I believe that Paul used a few other techniques, in that passage, to motivate his readers.

"For one thing, he told the Corinthians that the Macedonian churches had already given generously and he wanted them to do the same.[14] That sounds to me like he was encouraging a little competition."

Mary thought that Sam's inference was imprudent and unscriptural. So she jumped in and tried to derail the direction of the discussion. She didn't want the group to reach a false conclusion.

"Wait just a minute!" she demanded. "Competition between athletic teams may be fun and exciting. But when you pit church members against each other, you're dancing with danger.

"Look at the lives of David and Saul,[15] and the relationship between Joseph and his brothers.[16] Their stories demonstrate that people who try to play one-upmanship with their rivals will experience nothing but heartbreak.

"In a church that I used to attend a few years ago, we ran a contest to boost our Sunday School attendance. To motivate our children to bring their friends, we gave out prizes to those who brought the most visitors.

"As an outreach tool, it worked splendidly. We filled all of our classes to the brim. The competition also created a lot of bad feelings—especially when friends and siblings tried to 'recruit' the same person. Pretty soon harsh words and even fights broke out.

"The children were doing the right thing when they brought their friends to hear about Jesus. However, they were doing it for the wrong reason.

"That distinction is important! Paul points out, in 2 Corinthians 8:12 and 9:7, *that our motives are just as important as our actions.*"

Jim agreed. He told his educational team, "Jesus also emphasized the importance of pure motives. Our Lord made it clear to the Pharisees that religious practices devoid of holy intentions were an affront to God. That's why these supposedly holy men had solicited God's wrath with their hypocrisy.[17]

"In the Old Testament, God expressed a similar concern through his prophets. He said that he hated outward religious routines that weren't accompanied with the inward attitudes of love, compassion and mercy."[18]

Sam took advantage of another pause in the conversation to shift the discussion once more.

"*'Nothing succeeds like success'*—as one sage put it," said Sam. "When I achieve a goal, even a small goal, it gives me the confidence needed to mount an assault on a larger task. That's why I think it's important for us as leaders to plan for small wins at the beginning of new projects or new ministries.

"I remember how one of my former pastors started his ministry. He didn't try to hit a home run the first time he was up to bat. Instead, he looked around for small doable projects that he could accomplish in a relatively short period of time. Once he had built an impressive track record by successfully completing these tasks, he began to grapple with much more difficult issues."

As the meeting went into extra innings, its pace began to accelerate and the length of the member's replies shortened considerably.

"You've all heard that *need* is the mother of invention," said Alice. "Well, it's also the mother of motivation. If I need to quote the Bible so that I can witness to my neighbors, I'll start to memorize scripture verses like never before."

"*Peer pressure* is another motivator," added Alice. "Just ask the teenagers in our youth group or marketing experts that urge us to jump on a particular bandwagon."

"*Relationships*, in general, motivate," said Fran. "I'll do things for my friends and family that I won't do for strangers."

"I feel fulfilled when I get *a chance to use my gifts*, interests, training, and experience," noted Clint Wagner. "That's why I decided to help out in the children's choir."

"I like it when people give me *the authority and freedom* that I need to carry out my tasks," said Fran. "If my boss is always looking over my shoulder, I'll tell her to leave me alone or do the job herself."

"Jim, when you started this discussion, you sounded quite discouraged," said Holly. "Well, don't let a few apathetic individuals bog you down. I think you've already discovered many of the elements of effective motivation. Ever since you decided to develop our team spirit,

- You've given us a sense of belonging.

- You've thanked us for our efforts.

- You've showered us with attention.

- You've taken interest in our personal lives.

- You've praised, recognized, and rewarded our achievements.

- You've been careful not to criticize too much.

- You've remained loyal to us in defeat as well as in victory.

- You've encouraged us.

- You've expanded our responsibilities.

- You've displayed a positive, optimistic attitude.

- You've kept us informed about the church's affairs.

- You've urged us to strive for excellence in all that we do.

- You've appealed to people's emotions as well as their logic.

- You've helped us to remove obstacles and deal with problems that get in our way.

- You've supported us by providing the tools, training, and money that we need to do our jobs.

"I think you've done rather well so far."

Jim was glad to hear that his efforts had not been made in vain. Maybe the situation was not as bleak as he had first thought. Or, maybe, Holly was just prejudiced.

EXTRINSIC VERSUS INTRINSIC MOTIVATION

Frank Barns, the coordinator of the church's midweek clubs, had remained silent during the entire meeting. When he finally spoke, however, his loud, booming voice commanded everyone's attention.

"During this entire discussion, we've left out one vital element," observed Frank. "Not once have we mentioned the *convicting power of the Holy Spirit*.[19] If we want revival and renewal in people's lives, we better ask the Lord to stir people's hearts.

"Remember Nehemiah? He asked God to convince King Artaxerxes to supply him with all of the materials that he needed to rebuild Jerusalem;[20] and God answered his prayer. We would do well to follow the example of that dynamic leader."

"Another thing," continued Frank. "I think we've spent far too much time concentrating on external factors. In the final analysis, we as leaders can't really motivate anyone. All we can do is *tap our workers' intrinsic motivations*."

"I disagree," objected Clint. "Leaders can make a profound difference in their group's performance. Look at the coaches who have taken dismal, dispirited teams and transformed them into vibrant contenders.

"I agree, however, that we need to capitalize on our workers' inner desires. If we don't, people will continually depend on us for their motivation. And, frankly, I can't afford that kind of drain on my time and emotional energy."

"If we want to tap our worker's intrinsic motivation, as you say we should," said Sam, "that means that we have to know our people well. We need to know what drives them and then we need to show them how their job can satisfy those desires."

"What are we supposed to do?" said Kay Williams. "Walk up and ask them how we can push their motivational buttons?"

"I think we can be a little more subtle than that!" said Frank.

"We need to be keen observers of human nature. Remember Fran's comment about Alice's enthusiasm? When Alice spoke about the youth group, passion poured out of her eyes, her pace accelerated, and her volume increased. She was telling us, through her body language, that she was excited about her ministry. If we watch our workers carefully, we can pick up similar clues.

"We need to ask our workers about their families, jobs, training, and leisure activities. That doesn't mean that we should interrogate them with probing and penetrating questions. All we have to do is express our sincere interest in them, during casual conversations, and then listen to their answers. I'll bet that if you discover where Alice invests her spare time, money, and efforts, you'll find a warehouse of hints about what motivates her."

MANIPULATION VERSUS MOTIVATION

The Board's discussion had been stimulating and had provided Jim with more ideas than he expected to receive. He decided to conclude the group's session with one last question.

"In our remaining five minutes," said Jim, "I'd like to return to a question that Kay and Alice raised at the beginning of our discussion. What's the difference between manipulation and motivation?"

Clint was quick to offer his answer to that question. "Motivation is stimulating. Manipulation is destructive. Motivators want the best for their people and for their group. Manipulators use people for their own selfish ends.

"I'm sorry to say that, in the early days of my business career, I pushed people's buttons, twisted arms, and played games with people's guilt until I received the kind of support that I needed for a project. That worked fine for a while. However, if we hit a snag, my support melted away. I was left 'holding the bag' because my workers had never really owned the project in the first place."

"Manipulative tactics don't work very well," said Frank.

"No. They sure don't," said Clint. "Herod tried them and they backfired.[21] Daniel's enemies used them and later paid with their lives.[22] David employed them and he reaped God's wrath.[23]

"Once people realize that you're trying to manipulate them, they'll react in a way that will destroy the cohesiveness of your group. Your co-workers or family members will distrust your suggestions. They'll grow to resent your deception (after all, nobody likes to be treated like a pawn in a chess game). They'll be afraid to take risks. And, they'll learn to retaliate with similar, subversive tactics."

After discussing this subject for four or five more minutes, Jim finally concluded the meeting with prayer. Then he and his teammates left the church, content that their time together had been well spent. Now, Jim was eager to see if applying the techniques that they had talked about would make a difference in people's responsiveness.

MOTIVATIONAL PRINCIPLES

By the time Jim came home, Jill was already in bed. As he slipped into his pajamas, she noted that it was almost eleven o'clock and pleaded with him to get some sleep. However, he was restless and needed some time to unwind. So he gave his wife a peck on the cheek, told her to go to sleep without him, and explained: "Before going to bed, I want to jot down some of the lessons that I've learned today about motivation."

As he exited the bedroom, Jill grumbled to herself: "Evidently, I could use some lessons in 'practical persuasiveness' myself."

Oblivious to Jill's murmurings, Jim headed for the living room where he found his leadership diary. He had been writing his thoughts and observations in it ever since he had come to Bethel. In it, he made the following notations.

1. God expects us to be fervent in our devotion to Him.[24]

2. All behavior is caused.

3. Leaders can make a difference in people's motivational levels.

4. Leaders may try to stimulate people with extrinsic motivational techniques or tap their intrinsic motivations. However, in the final analysis, leaders cannot be responsible for people's lack of motivation. Unless people are having prob-

lems with their health, the absence of fervency is usually a result of a decision that they have made for themselves and for which they will be held accountable to God.

5. People are the targets and focus of our ministries. They are not means to an end.

6. God knows our motives.[25]

7. Our motives are just as important to God as our actions.[26]

8. People respond differently to the same stimulus.[27]

9. Motivations vary in type and intensity from day to day and from year to year. For example, adults are usually driven by different urges than children are.

10. There is no ideal incentive which will motivate everybody to produce their maximum effort all of the time.

11. Leaders, even charismatic ones, will never be able to motivate some people. For example, even though Jesus urged people to take up their cross and follow Him, some rejected His call for action.[28]

12. People's motivations are complex.

13. One's motivation has a natural tendency to decrease rather than increase over time.

14. We should endeavor to please God rather than man.[29]

Now that Jim had unburdened himself of these thoughts, he was ready for bed. It had been an Olympic gold day.

LEADERSHIP STYLES

Jim had barely sat down in Tony's Spaghetti Parlor when Bob Sparkman walked through the restaurant's door. Bob was right on time, as usual, for their regular mentoring meeting.

As Bob strolled up to Jim's table, he said, "Well, my scholar, how's your research going?"

It was just like Bob to get right to the point. Despite Bob's jovial mood, however, Jim didn't feel very congenial. He was still upset over their last conversation. Asking him to research the subject of motivation at the local library hadn't endeared Bob to him. Of course, Jim had to admit that Bob had probably done him a favor. He had been forced to develop some ideas on his own instead of relying on Bob for all of his answers.

Jim decided to bury his resentment and offered a mildly enthusiastic, "Pretty well, thank you." As he and his colleague talked, Jim's spirit warmed even more. Except for a couple of brief interruptions by the waiter, Jim talked non-stop for fifteen minutes about the results of his research and his Board's round-table discussion.

"I'm glad to hear that you've netted so many ideas," Bob said. "When you called me last week, I could sense how frustrated you were by your inability to stir people to action. If it's any consolation, I've felt that way myself. There have been times that I wished I had more power and authority so that I could whip my people into shape.

"However, that kind of authoritarian rule is dying a slow death around the world. It doesn't work in business. It doesn't work in government. And, it certainly doesn't work well in churches. Barking out orders to compliant underlings may appeal to our sinful nature and our desire to wield power.[30] However, in the long run, an autocratic leadership style spells T-R-O-U-B-L-E.

"It demolishes people's initiative. It tramples over people's feelings and ideas which, in turn, fosters rebellion. It slows down the decision-making process because everything has to be funneled through the leader. It leaves people undeveloped. It assumes the leader has all of the answers. It invites corruption. It limits a group's vision. It fans the leader's arrogance. And, it provides no mechanism for curbing abusive behavior.

"If people disagree with dictatorial rule, they're left with only three options: blindly obey, challenge their leader's authority, or go somewhere else. The problem is, most of the people who leave are usually capable self-starters with creative ideas. Direct or indirect challenges of a leader's authority tears groups and churches apart. And, I've already mentioned the deadly consequences of blind obedience.

"More importantly, the Bible condemns an autocratic approach. When the disciples were vying for positions in his kingdom, Jesus made it clear that their model of leadership was flawed. He said:

You know that the rulers of the Gentiles lord it over them, and their high officials exercise authority over them. Not so with you. Instead, whoever wants to become great among you must be your servant.[31]

"The Bible repeats this admonition in 1 Peter where it says:

> Be shepherds of God's flock that is under your care, serving as overseers—not because you must, but because you are willing, as God

wants you to be; not greedy for money, but eager to serve; not lording it over those entrusted to you, but being examples to the flock.[32]

"So, Jim, you have to make up your mind. In light of these biblical teachings, do you want to rule or do you want to lead?"

Although Bob had brought up some good points, Jim wasn't totally convinced. He said, "Bob, I still think that there are times when strong, assertive leadership is required.

"Take my church, for example. Its members hired me to run the Christian education program because they have neither the time, training, or inclination to make every little decision. And, because of their limited involvement, they can't possibly grasp the big picture like I can.

"That's why I enjoy chairing the Christian Education Board meetings at my church. I've seen some educational boards where the staff member is merely a non-voting member. Even though the board consists of the team with which he works every week and deals with issues that constantly confront him, the pastor is relegated to the sidelines while someone else chairs the meeting and the committee makes the decisions. Often, he doesn't even agree with the decisions that he's asked to implement. It's ridiculous!

"Look at people like Nehemiah,[33] Moses,[34] Peter,[35] and Jesus.[36] They certainly were aggressive leaders who sometimes made harsh, unilateral decisions.

"In addition, the Bible has a lot to say about God's chain-of-command and how leaders should direct the efforts of others.[37] For example, doesn't Hebrews say: "Obey your leaders and submit to their authority. They keep watch over you as men who must give an account. Obey them so that their work will be a joy, not a burden, for that would be of no advantage to you."[38]

"Sure it does," agreed Bob. "But I don't think that that passage is sanctioning autocratic rule. New Testament writers always tempered their comments about God's chain-of-command with reminders of love."[39]

"So what should I do?" Jim asked. "Just let people do whatever they want?"

"No, I wouldn't do that either," cautioned Bob. "To me, a free-rein approach isn't leadership. It's abdication. But, Jim, there's a lot of leeway between the extreme approaches of autocratic leadership and laissez-faire leadership. For example,

- A leader may make a decision and expect his people to implement it with only slight modifications.

- A leader may explain a problem or situation and then ask for input; after discussing the matter, however, the leader is the one who makes the decision.

- A leader may explain several options and let people choose from these limited alternatives.

- A leader may allow his people to make their own decisions within certain parameters.

- A leader may recommend and try to sell a particular course of action. However, he may still allow people to make their own decision. This often means that his proposal, if heeded, is usually modified in the process.

- A leader may describe the problem without making any recommendations and then allow his people to make up their own minds on which course of action to take.

Jim considered this wide range of options and then asked his friend pointedly, "Tell me, Bob, which style do you think is the best?"

"Well, I don't know if there's one, absolutely correct leadership style," hedged Bob. "I think that the leadership style you choose should depend on several factors.

It should be governed by your situation. In a fire, a military operation or a crisis, leaders are expected to be more directive.

"It should governed by the type of people with whom you work. Experienced, gifted, motivated, well-trained people need less direction, than those who are doing a job for the first time. And, some workers just plain like more guidance than others.

"It should be governed by what the Bible says. We've already talked about this a little. But, let me share with you two important models that the Scriptures give leaders.

"One is the shepherd paradigm. As you read the Bible, this model brings to mind words like provision,[40] guidance,[41] sacrifice,[42] commitment,[43] intimacy,[44] rest,[45] exemplary living,[46] protection,[47] and rescue.[48]

"Another is the servant paradigm. This model is described in a passage that I quoted earlier. For reinforcement, let me just quote it again. Jesus said to His disciples:

> You know that the rulers of the Gentiles lord it over them, and their high officials exercise authority over them. Not so with you. Instead, whoever wants to become great among you must be your servant, and whoever wants to be first must be your slave—just as the Son of Man

did not come to be served, but to serve, and to give his life as a ransom for many.[49]

"As the last part of that passage indicates, Jesus was a wonderful example of the servanthood approach. I think Paul summarized Christ's leadership style pretty well in the second chapter of Philippians where he said:

> Do nothing out of selfish ambition or vain conceit, but in humility consider others better than yourselves. Each of you should look not only to your own interests, but also to the interests of others. Your attitude should be the same as that of Christ Jesus: Who, being in very nature God, did not consider equality with God something to be grasped, but made himself nothing, taking the very nature of a servant, being made in human likeness. And being found in appearance as a man, he humbled himself and became obedient to death—even death on a cross.[50]

"While He was here on earth, Jesus demonstrated the servanthood approach quite poignantly when He washed the feet of His disciples and then told them to follow His example."[51]

Jim thought for a moment and then said, "That doesn't exactly square with the can-do attitude and take-charge models that I've read about in management books."

"I guess not, Jim. But God commands us to be different—in our thinking, speech, and behavior—from those around us.[52] We're His special people with a special mission and a very special way of looking at things."[53]

POINTS TO PONDER

1. How can leaders motivate themselves?

2. Do you agree with the observations that Jim made in his leadership diary? What other principles would you add to his list?

3. What kind of things can stifle a person's motivation?

4. Jim's Board of Christian Education concentrated on the positive factors that motivate people. What kind of evil or negative motivations can drive people? What does the Bible say about these motivations?

5. Do you agree with the statement: "In the final analysis, leaders really can't motivate anyone. Motivation has to come from within." Why or why not?

6. How does the leadership style of a pastor in a small church differ from one who works in a large church?

PRACTICAL PROJECTS

1. List all of the motivational techniques that Paul uses in 2 Corinthians 8:1–9:15 and the Book of Philemon.

2. Explain how you would motivate:

    *   A nonChristian teenager to stop drinking while attending a church youth retreat

    *   A teacher to spend more time in lesson preparation

    *   A Sunday School coordinator who is a month late in delivering on her pledge to renovate the church's audio-visual/resource center

    *   A teacher, who is notorious for his tardiness, to show up each Sunday fifteen minutes before his class session begins

12

Family Feuds

(HANDLING CONFLICT)

The church council's retreat had sailed smoothly through a number of difficult issues until a budgeting session brought an unexpected surprise. In the middle of a discussion about purchasing a new sound system, Maria Shavez erupted in disgust.

"I don't understand why the music program always gets first priority," she said. "We would be better off if we gave this money to missions or used it to fix up the church's kitchen."

"Listen, Maria, you've been a pebble-in-the-shoe irritant ever since you've joined the church council," spewed Sid Simms. "Just because you're the president of the women's group, you think you have to control everything. Well, let me tell you something. Our church shouldn't give your squabble-and-squawk group one tiny peso. It brings down more ministries than it builds up."

"Oh yeah! Well, if you ask me, your washed-up warblers need a good tune up," retaliated Maria. "Maybe it would help if we had a new choir director."

The members of the church council stared in astonishment as the attacks and counter-attacks of these two church leaders continued.

When the room was ripe with tension, Jim stepped in and said (to everyone's surprise), "Thank you Maria and Sid for that riveting skit. You've captured our attention and started our workshop on 'Conquering Conflict' with a bang."

Henry Anderson, the church's moderator, watched the council members' reactions with a mixture of glee and concern. When he had agreed to let Jim exercise his creativity and introduce his workshop in the middle of another session, Henry knew that he was taking a chance. However, the group seemed relieved and amused by the incident. Even Pastor Grant laughed as he made the comment, "Boy, you had me worried. I've seen less commotion at a demolition derby."

THE PREVALENCE OF CONFLICT

As Jim made his way to the front of the room, he said: "The Bible tells us that one day the lamb will lie down with the lion.[1] However, since that day hasn't arrived, we'd better be prepared to handle conflict when it assails us.

"Let's face it. Conflict is inevitable. Ever since Cain killed Abel, people have had trouble getting along with each other. Our newspapers and magazines are saturated with stories about wars, muggings, disputes, thefts, and physical abuse. They're also filled with critical comments about our leaders, workers, and society in general.

"I wish that we could say that God has exempted us from the punishing process of conflict, but he hasn't. Abraham, Joseph, Jacob, Moses, and David felt the strain of conflict in their lives. So did Jesus, Nehemiah, the prophets, and the apostles. Even Paul tangled with such notable Christians as Barnabas and Peter.

"This really shouldn't surprise us. We all have sinful natures. We have different backgrounds, goals, interests, and viewpoints. And, we often compete for the same limited resources."

THE RESOLUTION OF DISPUTES

Jim paused for a moment to make sure that he had everyone's attention and then continued. "Last year, I applied for a job as a summer youth worker at my home church. In my initial interview with the church council, one of the deacons asked me: 'How do you handle conflict?'

"Before I could state my position, another deacon who was trying to be helpful answered the ticklish probe for me. He said, 'I'll bet you subscribe to the procedure outlined in Matthew 18:15-20, don't you?'

"My curt answer was 'I sure do.' However, as I've continued to study the Scriptures, I've discovered that that's not the only way to handle conflict. For example, I wouldn't bring my daughter, Brenda, before the church just because she refused to eat her vegetables.

"So, the question that I want us to explore today is: '*How do we* and *how should we* deal with conflict when it comes our way?'"

Immediate Responses

Vicki Cummings, the church clerk, was eager to share her opinion. "In the past, when somebody disagreed with me or hurt me in some way, I usually became angry,[3] frustrated, and defensive—just like Sid and Maria did. I was also tempted to lash out, either verbally [4] or physically.[5] After all, that's what my television 'heroes' do, at least most of the time.

"When I reacted that way, however, I found out that I only made matters worse.[6] My actions fueled the fires of discord that had been ignited.[7] They also blocked the channels of communication that were needed to resolve the problem."[8]

"So now, when an explosive situation develops, I take a different tact. I pause, pray, count to ten, take a few deep breaths, and then air my viewpoint calmly, softly, and slowly. I've also learned to ask open-ended, non-threatening questions and listen patiently to my adversaries. That usually calms them down and gives me a chance to understand their outlook.

"To avoid the snare of heated arguments, I've also done two other things. I've committed my emotional life to the Lord.[9] And, I've learned to stay away from argumentative people."[10]

"Wait a minute!" objected Ron Hogan, chairman of the deacons. "We're assuming that conflict is always bad, but that's not necessarily true. If all of us thought exactly alike, we wouldn't need so many on this council."

"I agree," said Mark Wallard, the church's missions coordinator. "We have to be able to express our different opinions. Otherwise, we can't explore issues fully or make decisions wisely.

"That's why Solomon said that critical comments from a friend are useful but compliant, manipulative comments from an enemy are dangerous.[11] He also said that, as iron sharpens iron, real friends can sharpen each other."[12]

"You make it sound like the more arguments we have, the better off we are," said Mary Black. "But that's not what the Bible says. It clearly condemns conflict and quarreling.[13] And, I think it does so for several good reasons. Conflict produces stress, causes confusion, and ruins relationships.[14] It also inhibits our progress, cripples our witness, and saps our strength.

"So the Scriptures urge us to strive for peace [15]and to live in harmony with others.[16] The psalmist puts it this way: 'How good and pleasant it is when brothers live together in unity!'"[17]

Passive Responses

"Genesis 13 gives us a wonderful story about a man who sought to achieve that objective,"[18] said Henry. "The servants of Abram and Lot disagreed because there wasn't enough pastureland for all of their sheep and cattle. When the dispute came to Abram's attention, he intervened, told Lot that they shouldn't argue about this problem, and suggested that they needed to go their separate ways.

"Abram didn't stubbornly stand up for his rights and demand the very best piece of property. Instead, he allowed Lot to decide where he wanted to settle. Then, and only then, did Abram chose from the land that remained.

"Jesus is another example of someone who was willing to give in or submit to His adversaries.[19] As the song says, 'He could have called ten thousand angels to destroy the world and set Him free.' But He didn't.[20] He died on the cross so that we could have eternal life."

"So submission is one way to maintain peace," said Jim.[21]

"Another way to reach that goal," said Maria, "is to simply overlook problems, insults, and irritating situations. As the book of Proverbs says, 'A fool shows his annoyance at once, but a prudent man overlooks an insult.'[22]

"This approach is especially appropriate when the problem is minor, unintentional, or temporary."

"It's also useful in marriage," said Katie, the church treasurer. "I once heard a counselor say: 'Before you get married, keep your eyes wide open. After you're married, keep them half shut.'"

"Overlooking an insult is also a wise course of action if your enemy is bigger than you or is holding a gun," chuckled Mary.

"So true," agreed Jim. "However, sometimes ignoring a problem can do more harm than good. If, for example, you have a worker or a family member with a drug problem, it's foolish to close your eyes or look the other way. In cases like that, you need to speak up, confront the person, and deal with the situation."

"That's not quite as easy as it sounds," said Katie. "I hate confronting people because:

- I don't want to make people mad or lose their love.

- I'm afraid my opponents will strike back, give me the 'silent treatment,' turn a deaf ear to my complaints, or complain to others about the way I've treated them.

- I don't want to hurt people or discourage them so much that they'll give up and quit.

- I don't want to admit that I've failed in raising my children or in training my workers.

- I hope the problem will simply go away on its own.

- I think the other person should already know how I feel, especially if I've expressed my frustration before.

- And, I've learned from pastors and teachers that the Bible condemns criticism."[23]

After a slight pause in the discussion, Sid cited another way to handle conflict. "Sometimes, if people can't ignore bad behavior," he said, "they try to run away from the situation. If they have trouble with their spouse, they get a divorce. If they run into a problem with their job, they quit. If they can't get along with church members, they go elsewhere."

"Sometimes, though, it's wise to make a strategic withdrawal,"[24] said Mary. "It allows people to regain their composure, to rethink their positions, to protect themselves, or to develop solutions to seemingly intractable problems."

"But, sometimes it's just plain cowardly," objected Mark. "There are times when you have to stand up for what you believe—regardless of the consequences.[25]

"We see an example of this principle in Acts 4. The Sanhedrin commanded Peter and John to stop witnessing, but these apostles refused to obey that directive. Instead, they boldly declared: 'Judge for yourselves whether it is right in God's sight to obey you rather than God. For we cannot help speaking about what we have seen and heard.'

"Once they were released, these disciples continued to tell people about Christ's death and resurrection. They decided that threats and warnings were not going to deter them from their course."

"It's wrong to use withdrawal in some other situations as well," said Susan White, the chairman of the trustee committee.

"You shouldn't retreat from a predicament if you're using that withdrawal as a weapon. It's also wrong to withdraw from a situation if people desperately need your help,[26] if you've already made a firm commitment to somebody, or if you don't seek reconciliation with your antagonists while you're separated from them.

"Furthermore, withdrawal is inappropriate if you use it constantly. I know some people who give up every time they experience even the slightest problem or the smallest bit of conflict."

"Speaking of cowardice," said Pastor Grant, "Sometimes, people try to avoid conflict and difficult situations altogether. To keep from being hurt, they build invisible walls around themselves. They shun social contact, try to please everybody, put up with irritating behavior, and steer clear of topics and behaviors that might kindle arguments.

"Although this approach may eliminate some stress in their lives, they're still left with an enormous problem. Fences always fence out more than they fence in."[27]

"I think the Bible clearly supports one other passive approach to conflict," said Jim. "It tells us that, when other people treat us poorly, we should exercise restraint rather than retaliation. Passages like Romans 12:17 say: 'Do not repay anyone evil for evil.'[28]

"This principle can be seen a number of times in the life of Christ. When James and John wanted to call down fire from heaven to destroy some Samaritans, Jesus stopped them.[29] When Peter cut off the ear of the high priest's servant while trying to defend his master, Jesus not only rebuked His eager disciple but also healed the servant whom Peter injured.[30] Furthermore, when Jesus was imprisoned, ridiculed, questioned, and finally crucified, He refused to lash out at His enemies."[31]

"So far, we've largely emphasized the positive side of reacting passively," said Ron. "However, there are a lot of drawbacks to this 'peace-at-any-price' approach. If we squelch our feelings and continually let other people have their way, we'll probably reap undesirable consequences such as:

- Communication may be hampered.

- Bitterness and resentment may fester.

- Problems may remain unresolved or grow worse.

- Relationships may become strained.

- New irritating behaviors may be encouraged.

- Old irritating behaviors may be allowed to continue.

- People may never learn how we feel or what we need.

- Pent-up feelings may lead to violent explosions of rage.

Aggressive Responses

"Ron's right," said Mark. "I don't think that responding passively is our only option. You just can't lie down and become a doormat for every bully that comes your way.

"As Vicki has already pointed out, lashing out verbally or physically doesn't honor God. There are times, however, when you have to act aggressively, when you have to defend yourself or exercise your authority.

"Every once in a while, for example, my children do something wrong. When they do, I discipline them.[32] If my employees step out of line, then I have to 'lay down the law' with them. In fact, I have a little sign in my office at work which says: 'Rule number one: The boss is always right. Rule number two: If the boss is wrong, refer to rule number one.'"

Jim winced as an uneasy laughter rumbled throughout the room. He saw a lot of Mark in himself—maybe too much.

"Sometimes, you don't even have to exercise your authority," said Ron. "All you have to do is threaten to retaliate or warn people of the impending danger of their actions."[33]

"If you're going to do that," said Sid, "just remember three things: you'd better be in the right, you'd better be sure that force is necessary, and you'd better be able to carry out your threat."

"Sometimes, we simply don't have the authority to act," said Katie. "In those cases, I think we need to enlist the help of others who do have the power to settle disputes. For example, if someone beats you up, you should call the police. If a fellow employee does something that displeases you, you should talk to the boss. If you're mistreated in school, you should go to the principal or to a teacher."

"Mark and Ron have made an important point," said Henry "There's a place for authority at home,[34] at church,[35] and at work, [36] and in our government.[37] However, the overuse or incorrect use of power and authority can easily lead to corruption and abuse.[38]

"Remember Queen Jezebel? She used her ruthless power and authority to kill Naboth. Why? Just so that her husband could obtain a piece of property that he wanted.[39] Remember King David? He killed Uriah in order to cover up his adulterous affair with Uriah's wife."[40]

Susan nodded in agreement and then added: "While you may have the right to exercise authority, it's not always wise to do so. Brandishing your dictatorial powers can:

- Squash your workers' confidence.

- Encourage your followers to please you rather than to tell you the truth.

- Rob your people of their enthusiasm.

- Prevent you from tapping other people's expertise because you're convinced that you 'know it all' and that you're always right.

- Lead to stubbornness and inflexibility on your part and on the part of your workers.

- Cause your friends, family members, and employees to act defensively because they want to protect their backs.

- Stifle people's initiative, creativity, and risk-taking.

- Keep people from suggesting alternative ways of doing things because they know that you always want to do it *your way*."

"There's another problem with exercising your authority," said Maria. "I know a lot of people who like to win confrontations at all costs. The interesting thing is, when they triumph, they think they've resolved the problem. Of course, that isn't always true. In fact, a dictatorial approach often leads to what I call, 'false victories.'

"I may insist that my son behave like a Christian or lose the privilege of using the family car. Outwardly, he complies. He attends church, he reads the Bible, memorizes Scripture verses, and prays when he's told to do those things. He listens quietly to our pastor's sermon, and he doesn't talk back to me or my husband.

"Inwardly, however, he may be seething with rebellion. If I'm unaware of his feelings and think I've been able to coerce him into God's kingdom, I'm going to be totally shocked when he leaves my sphere of influence. That's when he'll show me what he *really* thinks of my parenting skills and my religion.

"Have you ever heard the expression, 'you may win the battle but lose the war'? That saying, I think, pretty well summarizes the results of a heavy-handed, dogmatic approach to conflict."

"As our discussion has pointed out," said Pastor Grant, "there are a lot of drawbacks to dealing with disputes aggressively. I still think, however, that there's a valid place for confrontation in conflict. For example, numerous Scripture verses like Matthew 18:15-20 stress the importance of church discipline. In addition, Jesus,[41] Nehemiah,[42] Paul,[43] and the Old Testament prophets used confrontation throughout their ministries."

"I agree," said Jim. "In fact, you might be interested in a handout that Bob Sparkman gave me recently. It shows us how we can successfully confront difficult people and prickly situations."

As Jim distributed Bob's outline, he said: "Take a look at the following ideas and tell me what you think."

EFFECTIVE CONFRONTATION[44]

A. Deal with problems in a timely manner.
   1. Act to solve the problem as soon as possible (Eph. 4:26; Matt. 5:23-26).
   2. Don't let problems lead to bitterness (Eph. 4:31; Heb. 12:15).
   3. Give yourself enough time, though, to cool off (Eccl. 7:9; Jas. 1:19-20; Prov. 14:29; 15:18; 16:32; 29:11).
   4. Watch for an appropriate time to talk with the person; timing is important (Prov. 15:23; 25:11).
   5. Select a time which is convenient to both you and the other person, a time when both of you will feel relaxed and unhurried.
B. Before approaching the person, take the following steps:
   1. Make sure the criticism is necessary.
      a. It is easier to criticize than create.
      b. It is easier to criticize a person's actions after the game is over rather than make decisions while the game is still in progress.
      c. Ask yourself:
         (1) Will my criticism change the situation or the person?
         (2) Is the anticipated outcome worth the possible negative consequences?
         (3) How will the person react to criticism? Some people are devastated by criticism and quit. Others take it in stride and use it to good advantage. Still others despise it and become even more stubborn.
         (4) Was the other person's action intentional?
         (5) Was it a temporary lapse or routine habit?
      d. Don't make "a mountain out of a mole hill" (Prov. 12:16; 19:11; 29:11).

      e. Don't correct a person who loves to ridicule (Prov. 13:1).

  2. Do your homework (1 Sam. 1:9-17; 16:17; Prov. 3:30; 18:13).

      a. Know the issues involved.

      b. Get your facts straight. Don't base your confrontation on malicious gossip, vicious innuendoes, or unsubstantiated opinion (1 Tim. 5:19; Deut. 17:6; 19:15-20; Num. 35:30; Matt. 18:16; 2 Cor. 13:1).

      c. Document the problem's history.

      d. Be prepared to substantiate your charges with hard evidence.

  3. Consider your own failings.

      a. You may be guilty of the same offense (Matt. 7:1-5).

      b. You have your own weaknesses (Matt. 7:1-5; John 7:53-8:11).

      c. You are subject to the same pitfalls that other people are (Gal. 6:1).

      d. You will be judged in the same way that you judge others (Matt 7:1-2).

  4. Pray for the person (1 John 5:16; 1 Tim. 2:1; 1 Sam. 12:23; Matt. 18:15-20; Ex. 32:9-14,30-35; 34:8-9; Num. 11:1-2; 12:1-16; 14:10-25).

  5. Determine your approach.

      a. Pray about your approach (Neh. 2:4-5; Esth. 4:9-5:3; Dan. 2:14-28; Jas. 1:5).

      b. Analyze your aim. Is it to crush or correct?

          Is it to punish, foster self-discipline, or improve the situation for yourself and others?

      c. Go to the person because you want the best for him or her.[45]

C. Approach the person correctly.

  1. Make sure that you are talking to the right person.

      a. Don't blame a person for something he did not do.

      b. Don't talk to people who have no power to correct the situation.

      c. Don't reprimand an individual for a group failure.

2. Talk with the person privately, if possible (Matt. 18:15).

3. Talk with the person face-to-face (Matt. 18:15)—no anonymous letters or phone calls, please.

4. Talk with the person in a relaxed, quiet setting.

D. State your position.

1. Be specific.

2. Don't exaggerate.

3. Make sure that your attitude and tone-of-voice are correct (Eph. 4:15; Gal. 6:1; 1 Tim. 5:1-2; 2 Thess. 3:15; Jas. 1:19; Matt. 5:21-22; 7:12; 1 Cor. 13:4; Prov. 12:18; 14:6; 15:1; 29:11).

   a. Don't be condescending or sarcastic.

   b. Don't be shrill or irate.

   c. Air your viewpoint calmly, softly, and slowly.

   d. Be kind but firm.

   e. Use good manners and treat people graciously.

   f. Be tough on issues but gentle on people.

4. State your position positively. For example: Don't say: "You did a lousy job in recruiting people." Say: "We need to recruit more people."

5. Don't call the other person names.

6. Don't swear (Ex. 20:7).

7. Don't ridicule the person (Prov. 3:34; 11:12; 19:29; 24:9)

8. Avoid critical rhetorical questions like "Why can't you be a good father?"

9. Avoid comparing one person or organization with another.

10. Focus on the future rather than the past.

11. Use "I" messages instead of "you" messages. For example: Don't attack a person and say: "Hey, stupid, you sure are inconsiderate when you play your loud, raunchy music in the middle of the night." Say: "I don't like it when you play your music so loudly and so late at night. When you do that, I can't get to sleep."

12. Be constructive in your suggestions. For example: Don't say: "Your presentations sure are dull." Say:

"Your presentations would be even more interesting if you would add a few illustrations."

13. Don't sandwich criticism in between two layers of praise. After people know your approach, (1) the praise will seem insincere and manipulative and (2) they won't hear the praise anyway because they will be listening for the criticism that usually follows.

14. Tell them how you feel about their behavior.

15. Remind them how much you value them and care for them.

D. Discuss the matter.

   1. Keep your discussion on track.

     a. Don't bring up the past.

     b. Don't discuss peripheral issues.

     c. Don't attack the person about another matter in an attempt to put him on the defensive.

   2. Allow the other person to tell his side of the story.

   3. Listen carefully to the other person's point-of-view.

   4. Try to put yourself in the other person's shoes.

   5. Attack the problem rather than the person.

   6. Be willing to admit your contribution to the problem.

   7. Don't project your faults on others.

   8. Be sensitive to hidden issues, if there are any.

   9. Monitor your feelings and the feelings of others.

  10. Take a break if the discussion becomes too heated.

  11. Don't expect other people to read your mind. Communicate your feelings and opinions.

  12. Be sensitive to body language and remarks which point to deeper problems or unexpressed needs.

  13. Don't assume that you can read other people's minds. If you suspect that a person's body language and remarks are pointing to deeper problems or unexpressed needs, ask the person if your assumptions are correct.

E. Discipline the person, if appropriate.

   1. Treat people fairly and consistently (1 Tim. 5:19-22; Jas. 2:1-7).

2. Give the person another chance if it was his or her first offense.

3. Make the punishment fit the magnitude of the offense.

F. Work together to resolve the problem.

1. Provide counseling.

2. Provide the resources that are needed to do the job.

3. Train the person properly.

4. Remove the source of friction so that it won't happen again.

5. Ask for advice in solving the problem.

6. Agree to a specific time when you will check back with the person to see how the problem was resolved.

7. Aim for a mutually satisfying settlement that will last.

8. Maintain realistic expectations.

G. End the conversation on a positive note.

H. Follow up the discussion to see if the problem has been satisfactorily resolved.

1. Document your conversations, especially if the problem has legal implications.

2. Check back with the person at the time and in the manner that was agreed upon.

3. Monitor the situation to make sure the problem doesn't reoccur. It is easy to fall back into old habits.

4. Don't remind the person about this or other past failures once they have been resolved.

5. Institute disciplinary actions if the problem is not resolved satisfactorily.

Subversive Responses

After everyone had had a chance to review Bob Sparkman's suggestions, Henry spoke up. "This is a fine handout, Jim. And, I hope that all of us will apply its guidelines the next time that we have to confront someone.

"Unfortunately, some people don't deal with conflict quite so directly. Initially, they may give in or exercise restraint because they don't feel that they can win a confrontation. Later on, they do everything possible to get back at their enemies.[46] They manipulate people and events as if they were playing chess. They sabotage activities. They betray and try to entrap. They complain to third parties and ridicule their opponents' efforts. And, they arrange vindictive alliances. "Their motto is: 'Don't get mad; get even.'

"Of course, that approach is clearly wrong. Revenge is forbidden in the Scriptures,[47] and their time, energy, and creativity could be used in more positive and constructive ways. Vengeance just creates a vicious circle of retaliation that becomes harder to break the longer a feud continues."

Cooperative Responses

"There's one other type of response that we haven't considered yet," offered Katie. "We can cooperate with people to find mutually acceptable solutions.

"One way to do this is to develop an alternative which pleases both parties. For example, when this church began, we had two adult classes but only one overhead projector. This situation produced a lot of friction because both groups wanted to use this piece of equipment every Sunday. To solve the problem, both classes took up a collection to buy an extra projector and each class could have their own.

"Another way to cooperate is to compromise,"[48] suggested Vicki. "Each party in a conflict needs to give up something in order to please the other."

"There are times, of course, when that's appropriate," said Pastor Grant. "We may sing modern praise songs in the morning and older traditional hymns in the evening in order to appeal to the different musical tastes that exist in our congregation. When it comes to biblical principles, however, we need to stand firm!"[49]

That authoritative comment from the pastor brought a stop to the group's discussion. Eventually, however, a suggestion from Sid broke the silence. "Another cooperative way to settle disputes is to submit an issue to arbitration or mediation. In other words, sometimes we need to take our disagreements to an impartial third party."[50]

"Be careful, though, to follow the Bible's instructions when you do this," cautioned Mark. "Paul warns us that any differences that we might have with our fellow believers should be settled in the church rather than in the secular court system."[51]

"Another way to cooperate is to vote on an issue or seek a group consensus,"[52] said Ron.

"Of course, the majority isn't always right. It wasn't right when the Israelites refused to enter the Promised Land as God had commanded them to do. It wasn't right when the Israelites railed against

Samuel and demanded to have a king so that they could be like the nations around them. And, it wasn't right when the Israelites cried out for the release of Barabbas and the crucifixion of Christ."

Seeing that Jim's workshop had already taken up more than its allotted time, Henry jumped into the discussion so that he could bring it to a close.

"Let's face it," Henry said. "There are some subjects about which we will never agree. At those times, we may have to agree to disagree—just like Barnabas and Paul did when they argued about John Mark's faithfulness.[53] If you ever choose this path, just remember to 'disagree without being disagreeable.'

"And on that note, we're going to have to conclude our discussion. Thank you, Jim, for a very stimulating workshop.

"After lunch, we'll resume our budget discussions. Hopefully, we can deal with them more peacefully this time."

As the group headed for the dining room, Jim's thoughts raced back to an argument which he had had recently with Jill. Although the church council hadn't realized it, his preparations for this workshop had been more for his benefit than for their's.

During Jim's ministry at Bethel, Jill had become increasingly concerned about the time that her husband was spending with Holly. Jill had tried to display her displeasure through subtle hints, delicate comments, and indirect questions. When Jim ignored these storm warnings, she decided to become more direct.

One night, when Jim was late for supper and the girls were away at a friend's house, Jill pointedly asked him: "Where in the world have you been?"

When Jim nonchalantly explained that he had spent the entire afternoon talking to Holly about her responsibilities as the church's new athletic director, Jill exploded. She lambasted Jim for his insensitivity, accused him of being unfaithful, and threatened to leave him.

Jim, in turn, became angry and defensive. While he agreed that Holly and he were spending a lot of time together, he vehemently denied that Holly and he were having an affair. "Every time we get together," he protested, "we focus strictly on church business."

Despite his protests of innocence, Jim knew that he would have to act quickly and decisively if he was going to salvage his marriage. He immediately promised Jill that he would stop seeing Holly for any reason. He also agreed that Mary Black could oversee the church's new athletic program.

Jim hoped that his actions would allay Jill's fears.

Of course, Jim realized that his defensive moves wouldn't completely repair the rift which was threatening to destroy their marriage. He'd have to take some positive steps as well. He'd have to start spending as much time rebuilding his marriage as he had spent building his educational team.

Jim knew that that was going to be difficult to do. It's always easier to destroy trust than to restore it.

THE EXERCISE OF CHURCH DISCIPLINE

Just as Jim was trying to put several conflicts behind him, a new one loomed on his horizon. Alice Anderson came to him one morning and said, "Do you realize that Allen Wriggly might be arrested this week?"

"Arrested?" asked Jim. "For what?"

"For allegedly molesting two of our junior high girls," she explained.

Jim couldn't believe what he was hearing. Allen had worked with the church's youth group for nearly five years. And, as far as Jim knew, this dedicated worker was well respected by adults and young people alike.

After Alice left his office, Jim immediately called Pastor Grant at home and explained the situation to him.

Then Jim asked, "Do you suppose these accusations are true? And, if they are, what are we going to do? I don't have any experience in exercising church discipline."

"Neither do I," admitted Pastor Grant. "In fact, not one of my churches has ever formally and corporately corrected the behavior of one of its members. You see, churches are very reluctant to discipline people because:

- They don't know what the Scriptures have to say about the subject.

- They don't think it'll do any good.

- They've become insensitive to sin and its consequences.[54]

- They're afraid to cause divisions within the church.

- They're scared of the legal ramifications.

- They don't have any positive examples to follow.
  "Or, they feel that everybody should just 'mind their own business.' In fact, I think there are a lot of people in our con-

gregation who would say: 'Let's leave this matter to the courts and to the people who are directly involved.'

"The trouble is: the Bible doesn't give us that choice. It clearly tells us that God has given us the authority to discipline our members.[55] And, if we neglect our responsibilities in this area, then we'll pay the price for our inaction.[56]

- We'll lack God's blessing.[57]

- We'll be unable to maintain the spiritual purity that Christ demands.[58]

- We'll hurt our relationship with God.[59]

- We'll cease to grow.[60]

- We'll encourage people to sin.[61]

- And, we'll fail in one of our primary missions which is to call people to repentance.[62]

"In addition, we'll tarnish our witness in Cody. Can't you see the headlines now: 'Bethel Church Allows Sex Offender to Guide Its Young People.'"

"So what should we do?" asked Jim.

"First, we need to pray for God's guidance and ask Him to give us wisdom and an impartial spirit."[63]

"Secondly, Before we talk to Allen, we'd better double-check our facts.[64] I don't want anyone to be hurt by false rumors. Malicious gossip and vicious innuendoes have a way of racing ahead of the truth.

"Thirdly, if there's adequate and plausible evidence, we need to pray for Allen's restoration.[65]

"Fourthly, we (along with the girls who were molested) need to go to Allen and confront him privately with the charges that have been made."[66]

Jim mulled over Pastor Grant's approach for a few moments before trying to clarify a few issues for himself. "I'm trying to square our actions with the Bible's instructions. So I have two questions. According to Matthew 18, shouldn't the girls who were involved in this situation have come to us and asked for our help after they were molested? And according to 1 Corinthians 6, shouldn't we be settling this issue in the church instead of in the courts?"[67]

"Listen, my friend, we don't operate in an ideal world," said Pastor Grant. "I doubt that these girls know what the Bible has to say about church discipline. Young girls who are involved in this kind of a situation (with all of its trauma and stigma) aren't exactly eager to tell others about what they've experienced.

"Furthermore, state law requires us or anybody else who knows about this situation to notify the police. Then, it's out of our hands. It's up to the state attorney whether they want to prosecute or not."

"What if the girls are reluctant to confront Allen?" asked Jim. "Maybe their lawyers won't let them say anything before they take their case to court."

"I don't know," said Pastor Grant. "But let's hear what they have to say before constructing imaginary roadblocks."

Jim wasn't totally satisfied with Pastor Grant's answer. He didn't like venturing into difficult situations without being prepared. However, before he could pursue the matter further, his boss diverted his attention.

"By the way, Jim, we better review that sheet on confrontation that you gave us at the church council's retreat. If we have to reprimand Allen, I want to make sure that we do it correctly."

Jim's stomach tightened and his hands began to perspire. He hadn't anticipated using Bob Sparkman's handout quite so quickly.

"What are we going to say?" asked Jim.

"Well, I think we simply need to state the facts as we know them and present the evidence that we have," said Pastor Grant. "Then we'll need to give Allen plenty of time to respond.

"That last part is crucial. We may find out that his accusers are leveling false charges against him. If that's true, then we need to discipline them. Or, we may find out that the girls acted improperly. If that's correct, then we'll have to discipline both Allen and the girls."

"What if the accusations are true and Allen repents?"[68] asked Jim.

"I don't know what's going to happen legally," said Pastor Grant, but as far as the church is concerned, we'll need to forgive him, [69]love him,[70] celebrate his turnaround,[71] comfort him,[72] accept him back into the church's fellowship,[73] and refuse to remind him of his past."[74]

Jim doubted that everybody in the church would react that way, but he didn't voice his reservations to the pastor.

"It's very difficult," Pastor Grant continued, "for a sex offender to change his or her behavior. So, in addition to all of these things, we'll need to take two other steps. We'll need to establish a small group which will help Allen grow again in his spiritual life. And, we'll need to see that Allen receives in-depth counseling, the kind of counseling that I can't provide."

"Don't forget the girls," said Jim. "They'll need counseling too."

"You're absolutely right," said Pastor Grant. "Since Tom Brown is a high school counselor at Washington High, he might be able to help us out in this area. Maybe he could give us the names of some good family counselors who deal with sex offenders.

"In fact, it might be a good idea to take a Sunday evening and just sensitize our congregation toward this whole subject—without mentioning the specifics of this case."

"I hope that will help," said Jim with a somewhat skeptical tone-of-voice. "If what Alice told me is true, it's not going to be easy to forgive and forget what Allen has done!" said Jim.

"I know," said Pastor Grant sadly. "And, if *we* find it difficult to forgive him, just think of how hard this will be for the girls and their parents to do.

"But, Jim, if we're not able to forgive Allen, at least three things will happen. We'll violate God's clear command about this issue.[75] Satan will use this experience to destroy us.[76] And God will not treat us with compassion.[77]

"In light of Christ's death on the cross for our sins, we dare not show people less mercy than God has already shown to us."[78]

Pastor Grant paused briefly. "Since Allen is a church leader, we'll also have to take two other steps. Even if he repents, we'll still have to publicly acknowledge and condemn his actions[79]—maybe in an evening service or in a special church meeting. We'll need also to immediately remove him from his position."[80]

"Do you think he'll ever be a church leader again?" inquired Jim.

"It's possible," responded Pastor Grant. "However, we'll have to be extremely careful about putting him back into a position of leadership. The Bible commands us to choose godly leaders with a proven track record and with a good reputation. It also states that we should never select a church leader without carefully considering his qualifications for the job.[81]

"Before recommending Allen for another leadership post, I'd want to make sure that he had produced, as John the Baptist once put it, 'fruit in keeping with his repentance.'[82] In other words, if Allen is truly repentant, he'll confess his sins, show remorse for his deeds, make an 'about-face' in his mental outlook, and demonstrate to us that he is a changed person who really wants to serve and obey God.[83]

"One other thing. Even if Allen does become a church leader again, I don't think it would ever be wise to put him back into a position where he'll be tempted to molest girls."

"I hate to bring this up," said Jim. "But what if the accusations are true and he doesn't repent?"[84] asked Jim.

"Then the Bible says we should publicly condemn his actions,[85] 'hand him over to Satan,'[86] and avoid associating with him,"[87] said Pastor Grant.

"I suppose that some people will think, if it comes to this stage, that we're trying to persecute or crush him. That's not the case. What we're trying to do is bring him to a point where he'll realize the severity of his sin, repent, and agree to follow Christ obediently. If that happens, we'll gladly invite him back into our fellowship."[88]

"If we decide to excommunicate him," said Jim, "we'd better handle the matter carefully. Otherwise, we're going to get ourselves into deep legal trouble."

"Maybe we should contact the Christian Legal Society of Oak Park, Illinois," suggested Pastor Grant. "I understand that they help Christians or Christian organizations in resolving legal disputes. I also hear that J. Carl Laney has written a good book on church discipline.[89] We should see if Sweetwater's Christian Bookstore has a copy."

"Good idea!" agreed Jim.

"While I check into those two items," said Pastor Grant, "Why don't you talk some more with Alice and the junior high girls who are involved. We'll discuss the situation again after our staff meeting tomorrow."

THE TREATMENT OF ENEMIES

Although Doug had stopped by Jim's office to talk to him about the church's computer system, Jim sensed that his friend was preoccupied with other matters. After they concluded their business, Jim said: "Doug, you look unhappy. What's bothering you?"

Doug reluctantly explained his situation. "A couple of years ago, one of my business partners made some underhanded deals with our suppliers. His dishonesty cost me over ten thousand dollars and temporarily ruined my reputation.

"I know I should have been more careful in signing our contracts and more diligent in monitoring his activities, but I trusted him. Well, he used my faith in him to betray me.

"When I discovered what he had done, I dissolved our partnership and took him to court. What a waste of time! While my attorney became rich, I became mad, frustrated, and bitter.[90]

"And now, believe it or not, I've found out that I'll have to work with my old business partner again—this time in the state legislature. He was just appointed to fill the vacancy of Rod Witman who died of cancer a couple of weeks ago."

"Needless to say, I'm not looking forward to the experience. And, frankly, I feel like applying my own version of the golden rule: 'Do unto others as they have done it unto you.'"

"I don't think you'll find that verse in the Bible," laughed Jim.

"Yeah, I know," said Doug as his shoulders sagged. "And, my attitude probably isn't very Christian either.

"But tell me, Jim. How do you think I should treat somebody who has been so cruel to me?"

"Doug, I'm not going to answer your question," said Jim. "Instead, I'm going to let the Bible do that.

"I have to go down to the resource center, for a little while, to talk with Kelly about ordering some new curriculum materials. While I'm gone, I want you read the following scripture passages: Matthew 5:38-48, Luke 6:27-36, Romans 12:9-21, and 1 Peter 2:12-23; 3:8-17. When you find a principle that applies to your situation, write it down and then make a note of which Bible verses support that particular premise.

"When I get back, I'd like to discuss with you what you've discovered."

When Jim left, Doug felt a little like a child who had just been abandoned by his parents. He didn't like being left alone to fend for himself. He wanted some reassuring support and unambiguous advice from his pastor.

Nevertheless, he complied with Jim's instructions. By the time Jim returned to the office, Doug had compiled the following list of principles under the heading, "Facing Your Foes."

1. Don't retaliate (Matt. 5:38-39; Rom. 12:17,19; 1 Pet. 2:21-23; 3:9).

2. Do more than is expected or required.

   - Turn the other cheek (Matt. 5:39; Luke 6:29).

   - Give your enemy your tunic as well as your cloak or vice versa (Matt. 5:40; Luke 6:29; Ex. 22:26-27).

   - Go the extra mile (Matt. 5:41).

   - Lend your enemy money without expectation of return (Matt. 5:42; Luke 6:30,34-35).

3. Love your enemies (Matt. 5:43-44; Luke 6:27,32,35).

4. Pray for your enemies (Matt. 5:44; Luke 6:28; 23:34; Acts 7:59-60).

5. Treat your enemies better than they treat you (Matt. 5:44-47; Luke 6:32-35; Rom. 5:8).

6. Minister to your enemies' needs.

- Do good to your enemies (Luke 6:27,33,35; Rom. 12:21).

- If your enemy is hungry, feed him (Rom. 12:20; Prov. 25:21).

- If your enemy is thirsty, give him something to drink (Rom. 12:20; Prov. 25:21).

7. Bless your enemies (Luke 6:28; Rom. 12:14,21; 1 Pet. 3:9).

8. If a person takes what belongs to you, don't demand it back (Luke 6:30).

9. Treat others as you would like to be treated (Luke 6:31; Matt. 7:12).

10. Be merciful (Luke 6:36; Matt. 5:7; Jas. 2:13).

11. Don't rejoice when your enemies run into difficulties (Rom. 12:17; Prov. 24:17-18).

12. Trust God to take care of your enemies (Rom. 12:17-19; Ex. 14:5-31; Num. 12:1-16; 16:1-50; Isa. 36:1-37:38; 2 Chron. 20:20-30; Ps. 21:7-13; 27:1-3; 37:1-20).

13. Live such a good life that it will glorify God and shame your enemies (1 Pet. 2:12,15; 3:15-17; 4:14-16).

14. Honor and obey authority even when you are treated unjustly (1 Pet. 2:13-18; Rom. 13:1-7; Acts 5:29; Dan. 1:1-21; 3:1-30; 6:1-28).

15. Forgive your enemies (Matt. 18:21-35; Col. 3:12-15; Eph. 4:31-32; Luke 23:34; Acts 7:60).

16. Seek reconciliation (Matt. 5:23-26; Luke 15:11-21).

Jim examined his coworker's list with interest. "Doug, if I had told you to follow these principles, you probably would have ignored my advice. That's why I wanted you to see for yourself what the Bible has to say about this subject.

"When it comes to conflict, the world urges us to take the easy way out. It tells us to retaliate, manipulate, aggravate, and dominate.

"Christ, however, demands more from his followers. His approach to conflict isn't easy, natural or popular. In fact, it often involves sacrifice,[91] requires humility,[92] and entails pain.[93]

"You see, Christianity isn't for cowards.

"Now, I wish I could tell you that, if you followed all of the principles that you've outlined, everything would turn out just fine. Unfortunately, that's not always true. However, when we handle conflict well, several things usually happen.

- People and property are spared harm.

- Problems are solved.

- Tasks are completed.

- Evil is judged.[94]

- Christians are blessed.[95]

- Relationships are improved.

- Enemies become friends.[96]

- Enemies are shamed by their actions.[97]

- People are drawn to Christ.[98]

- People grow in their Christian walk.[99]

- New insights about specific people (and people in general) are gained.

"Now, like I said, we're not always going to reap these results. But I know two even more important things that will happen every time we deal with conflict correctly: God will be glorified and God's will will be done."

POINTS TO PONDER

1. What are the basic causes of conflict?

2. What is the difference between healthy and destructive conflicts?

3. This chapter has introduced a number of different ways to deal with conflict. How should leaders decide which method should be used in a given situation?

4. When a church disciplines one of its members, does the seri-
    ousness of the offense affect how the person who has sinned
    should be treated?

5. If someone who has suffered physical or verbal abuse comes
    to a leader for counseling, what are their legal obligations?

PRACTICAL PROJECTS

1. Write a short term paper which compares corporate disci-
    pline in the Old Testament with corporate discipline in the
    New Testament.

2. Record on a cassette or video tape a skit in which you pre-
    tend to mediate a dispute between two church leaders.

13

Troubled Waters

(PROBLEM SOLVING)

Jim came bounding into the church office, whistling a cheerful rendition of "How Great Thou Art." His mood quickly changed, however, when Shirley gave him some disturbing news.

"Jim, there's been a terrible accident" she said, barely able to keep the tears from her eyes. "Your daughter, Brenda, was hit by a car. Jill called an ambulance and rushed her to Woodlawn Memorial Hospital about an hour ago."

Jim stood stunned for a split second. Then he pivoted and dashed for the office door. As he left, he shouted: "Call the hospital and tell Jill that I'm on my way!"

FACING DIFFICULTIES

Once Jim arrived at Woodlawn, it took him only a few moments to track down his wife. She was sitting in the corner of one of the hospital's stark and sterile emergency rooms. Her limp body betrayed how exhausted she was.

As Jim entered the room, Jill quickly looked up to see who her visitor was. When she realized that her husband had finally arrived, relief washed the sadness from her face. She stood up to collect the strong hug and reassuring words that she so desperately needed.

However, before she could get her arms around Jim, he wanted to know: "What happened?"

Jill's somber response was muffled by a veil of tears.

"Brenda and I were playing 'catch' in the front yard. When Brenda missed one of my throws, she chased the ball into the street. I shouted, 'Don't cross the street!' But it was too late. A driver from Peter's Pizza Palace didn't see her and . . .

"Oh, Jim, it was so awful. I just pray that she'll be all right!"

"Where is she now?" inquired Jim as he surveyed the otherwise empty emergency room.

"They took her down to the X-ray department. Dr. Wilson suspects that she may have some broken bones and a concussion."

"Why in the world weren't you watching her more closely?" demanded Jim.

"Sure. Blame it on me!" responded Jill angrily. "I'm always at fault because I'm always the one who has to take care of the girls. You're never home anymore. If you're not attending a church meeting, you're working late at the office or visiting somebody in their home. I just can't take it anymore."

Jill paused slightly before she turned the tables and started to interrogate Jim.

"By the way, where were you this afternoon?" probed Jill. "Shirley and I tried to reach you for over an hour before you showed up at church. Were you *conferring* with Holly again?"

Jim winced at Jill's accusation. He knew that she was under a tremendous amount of stress. However, he felt that that was no reason to lash out at him.

"As I've told you before," snapped Jim, "Holly is working with Mary Black now—not me!"

The rest of the afternoon was tense and awkward for both Jill and Jim. They were skilled at comforting others. However, just when they needed each other's compassion, their caring skills seemed to abandon them.

After six straight hours at the hospital, the doctors finally told Jim and Jill to go home and get some rest. Brenda had suffered a broken arm, a broken leg, and a concussion. Despite these injuries, she was out of immediate danger, sedated, and resting comfortably. The doctors would know more about her condition once her swelling went down.

On Jim and Jill's trip home, there were long periods of uneasy silence, punctuated with bursts of anger. As they finally pulled into their driveway, Jill voiced a question that had been bothering both of them. She asked, "Jim, why is God doing this to us? Here we are, trying to faithfully serve Him and now this happens. We just don't deserve this."[1]

Jim wasn't quite sure how to respond to Jill's question. Intellectually, he knew some of the reasons why there was suffering in the world. People experience adversity in their lives because:

- They sin or do foolish things.[2] So God punishes them[3] or allows them to experience the natural consequences of their behavior.

- They are surrounded by people who are evil, cruel[4] or neglectful.[5]

- They are persecuted for their faith.[6]

- Satan wants to destroy them.[7]

- Their family members or leaders sin against God.[8]

- They try to live a righteous life.[9]

- God wants to refine them.[10]

- God wants to test their faith in Him.[11]

- God wants to display His glory.[12]

- God tries to warn them and prevent them from getting into deeper trouble.[13]

Knowing these reasons, however, did little to ease the tremendous pain that Jim felt. And, frankly, he didn't think that reciting these explanations for Jill would be very helpful. So he simply mumbled, "I'm not sure, Jill. I'm really not sure."

PROBLEM SOLVING

After a late and somber supper, Jim decided to return to the church office. It was Friday night and he still hadn't finished a devotional talk that he was expected to give at a men's breakfast on Sunday morning. Since he had an all-day outing with the youth group the next day, that evening was the only time that he had to finish his preparations. His busy schedule simply didn't allow for unexpected emergencies.

When Jim informed Jill of his decision, she protested vigorously. She urged him to "forget about that lousy talk." However, Jim's sense of duty was stronger than Jill's plea for companionship. He felt that working at the office would keep his mind off the day's events.

It would also give him an excuse to dodge the caustic remarks that Jill was certain to hurl at him—if he remained at home.

If Jim thought he could escape trouble by fleeing to the church, he was mistaken. Two troublesome documents were waiting for him on his desk. The first one was a note from Shirley. It said:

> *Mark Wallard called to complain about Helen Lademore. He said that she's never on time for her fourth-grade Sunday School class, let alone early enough to greet children as they arrive.*
>
> *If the problem isn't remedied, Mark may leave us and look for another church—one with a 'decent children's program.'*
>
> *I needn't remind you that Mark and Mildred's departure would be quite a blow to our church since they are very active, have lots of friends, and are big financial contributors.*

Jim was already aware of the problem. While some pastors set up elaborate early-warning systems of reports, records, and meetings to detect problems in their infancy,[14] Jim discovered most of his problems on his regular, Sunday morning "walk-abouts."

In fact, he had found out about Helen's tardiness in that way. One morning, as Jim was making his rounds, he heard a ruckus in Helen's class. When he entered the room, he had to break up a fight between two of her students. Helen was nowhere to be found even though her class should have started five minutes earlier.

Although Jim and Helen had briefly discussed the scuffle and her absence, it didn't seem to be a big problem. She apologized for her tardiness and treated it as a one-time, chance happening.

Jim hoped that their discussion had taken care of the situation. He just hated dealing with problems. He wished that he could deny their existence, ignore them until they would go away, give them to someone else, or just simply run away from them.

However, Jim knew that avoiding problems was virtually impossible. Troubles and trials were a natural, although painful, part of life.[15] In addition, wrestling with problems was an unspoken part of Jim's job description. In fact, he had once heard a speaker say that you can identify a leader by watching to whom people go with their problems.

After observing Helen's tardiness several weeks in a row and receiving a formal complaint from Mark, Jim decided that it was finally time to act. For the sake of the children, parents, and the church, he needed to sit down with Helen and have a heart-to-heart talk about the situation. And, the sooner that he dealt with the problem, the better it would be.[16]

So Jim quickly gave Helen a call and arranged to meet her at the church the following Tuesday.

As disturbing as Mark's note was, there was a letter on Jim's desk that was even more troubling. It was from Holly Smith. It said:

Dear Mr. Stafford,

> *Because of my busy schedule this fall, I will be unable to fulfill my duties as the church's new athletic director. Therefore, I am tendering my resignation which is effective immediately.*

Holly Smith

"How can she do this to me?" Jim screamed to his empty office. "We've put all of this time and effort into launching our new athletic/evangelistic program. Now, she childishly throws in the towel before the contest even begins. No warning. No personal call. Just this cold, impersonal note!"

Jim was certain that Holly's abrupt departure stemmed from the fact that he no longer paid as much attention to her as he once did. He was equally sure that her vindictive letter was designed to send their innovative ministry crashing to the ground.

Since their first big activity (an all-day basketball tournament) was only a week away, Jim was flush with panic. "What am I going to say?" and "What am I going to do?" he asked aloud.

Jim tried to reach Holly by telephone, but got only her answering machine. Although he left an urgent message, he didn't really expect her to respond. It looked as though he would have to make some quick decisions and revise his plans.

For the moment, though, Jim wanted to clear his mind of these distractions and focus on the preparation of his devotional. Although he tried diligently to redirect his thoughts, his efforts proved fruitless.

In fact, while Jim was editing his notes, he absent-mindedly hit a few wrong keys on his computer. In a split second, his careless actions erased six hours of arduous work from his hard disk. To make matters worse, Jim didn't have another copy of his devotional talk because he hadn't backed up his work properly.

Although Jim had tried to remain calm throughout the day's misfortunes, his dam of restraint finally broke.

"What's next, Lord?" shouted Jim as he slammed his fists on the desk. "My marriage is struggling. My ministry is falling apart. And, all I get for my dedication to You is more trouble."

Jim wept bitterly as he complained to God: "I just can't take all of this stress!"

Ten minutes later, Jim decided that it was useless to continue. Nothing more was going to be accomplished that evening. So he grabbed his jacket and headed for home.

Jim had criticized other people for coming to class unprepared. Now he knew what it was like to be in their shoes. Hopefully, his group would be understanding and the same Holy Spirit who seemed to provide instantaneous insights for others would give him the words that he needed on Sunday.

*****

Jim knew that confronting people about their delinquent behavior was a part of his job. Still, he dreaded talking to Helen about her persistent tardiness. *Hopefully, some good will come out of our meeting,* he thought as he waited for her to arrive.

When Helen finally entered his office (five minutes late), Jim tried to be as pleasant as possible. He could tell that she was just as apprehensive as he was about their get-together.

After some casual conversation, Jim stated his concerns in a calm and kind but firm tone. "Helen, I've noticed that you've been coming to your class at least five to ten minutes late the last few weeks. This is causing us some real problems. As you know, a couple of weeks ago, I broke up a scuffle between two of your students because you weren't there to supervise the class. This week, one of the parents complained about your tardiness. And, I can only assume that when visitors bring their children to your class, they leave with a bad impression because there's nobody there to care for them."

"I know. I know," she said softly. "I probably should resign but I love to work with children.

"You see, my husband is not a Christian. He lets me come to church, but he doesn't help me at all when I'm trying to get ready for Sunday School. He says that Sunday is the only day he has to sleep in and if I want to take the boys to church, that's my problem.

"Well, with two preschoolers, I really have a tough time feeding them, getting them dressed, and bringing them to Sunday School on time."

As Jim listened and discussed the problem with Helen, he tried to keep an open mind. He knew that it was important to understand a problem before offering solutions.

Once he had grasped the situation, however, he still didn't offer any prepackaged solutions. Instead, he worked with Helen to find an answer to her problem.

After discussing several options, they finally agreed on one that satisfied both of them. Helen volunteered to switch places with one of her friends, Bev Jordan, who worked in children's church. Since this group started an hour-and-a-half after Sunday School did, it would give Helen a chance to attend an adult class and still arrive in plenty of time to carry out her new responsibilities.

To successfully implement their decision, Helen and Jim also agreed on three other related matters.

- The switch would take place at the end of the month. This would give everybody ample time to prepare for the change.

- In the meantime, Jim would supervise Helen's class each Sunday until she arrived.

- Jim would monitor the situation for several months to make sure everything was going well.

After Helen left, Jim offered up a word of praise to God. The meeting had gone much better than he had expected.

Of course, Jim realized that not every problem that he faced would be solved so easily. Sometimes, as in the case of Brenda's accident and Holly's hasty departure, he would just have to make the best of a bad situation. At other times, he would have to accept the fact that some problems, like some diseases, are incurable. His lost devotional talk was a good example of that type of trouble.

While Jim's experience with Helen was still fresh in his mind, he wanted to record a few of his observations about the problem-solving process. So he took his leadership diary from the top drawer in his desk and jotted down the following suggestions to himself.

- Act promptly. Failing to deal with a problem quickly (because you hope it will go away by itself) is like postponing the treatment of a serious disease. Delay only encourages the problem to deteriorate further and makes the final remedy more drastic.

- Treat difficult situations as opportunities rather than problems. Talking with Helen has allowed me to reduce her stress level and improve the Sunday School program. Now that I am aware of Helen's plight, I'm also going to make a conscious effort to pray for and witness to her unsaved husband.

- Heed the old adage which says, "An ounce of prevention is better than a pound of cure." If I had known about Helen's situation, I could have urged her to become involved in a different ministry.

- Follow a seven-step process when tackling problems:

  1. Recognize the problem

  2. Decide who should deal with the problem

  3. Determine the cause of the problem

  4. Generate as many different alternative solutions as possible

  5. Select the best option available

  6. Implement the solution

  7. Follow up your decision to make sure that things are working out properly.

- Don't confuse a problem's symptoms with its root cause.

- Avoid implementing cures that are worse than the actual disease.

- Ask other people for their advice. They may have experienced similar problems and can offer potential solutions.

- Avoid the Grass-is-Greener Syndrome. Trying to escape difficult situations may create even more problems.

- Don't panic, act on impulse, or do something rash.

- Don't give up.

DEALING WITH CHANGE

In the early stages of Jim's ministry, Bob Sparkman had warned him to introduce new ideas slowly. However, Jim didn't always listen to his mentor's advice.

Church leaders and committees never moved fast enough for Jim. So twice, he had tried a tinge of subversion and coercion to bring about room and curriculum changes. These heavy-handed attempts to bypass the church's chain-of-command, however, brought him nothing but problems.

One night, after some of his innovative ideas had been rejected by the church council, Jim called Bob Sparkman to express his frustration.

"I get so upset, sometimes, with our church members," complained Jim. "They're so slow, stubborn, and inflexible.[17]

"I just don't understand why change is so threatening to them. It's not like I'm trying to alter their theology. I just want them to revamp their methods and procedures every decade or so.

"The trouble is, our church's decision-making process is absolutely glacial and our progress is measured in terms of inches rather than yards. At every turn, I seem to collide with the barrier of 'We've never done it that way before' or the impediments of 'It simply won't work' and 'Let's not rush into anything.'

"I don't think our members realize that the only thing in this world that is constant is change itself. And, unless we as a church are willing to change, we're not going to survive."

"Jim, you're absolutely right," agreed Bob. "The church needs to continually transform itself in order to remain vibrant and relevant. But remember two things: Change isn't always good or necessary. And, sometimes people oppose change, not because they don't like a new idea but because they don't like the way it's introduced.

"Jim, some friends of mine recently attended a symposium called 'Change and the Church.' You might be interested in what they learned at the meeting. I'll have one of them send you a copy of the group's proceedings."

A week later, Jim received a large envelop from Tri-City Church. In it was the outline that Bob had promised. As Jim glanced through the handout, he saw that it was divided into four sections.

1. Reasons People Resist Change

   - Change threatens to rob people of the stability and security that they crave in their lives.

   - Change implies that you dislike the way people are presently doing things and no one likes to be criticized.

   - Change often requires more time and effort than maintaining the status quo. The drag of inertia is difficult to overcome.

   - Change may interfere with people's social networks.

   - Change may threaten people's vested interests, power, and status.

   - People fear the unknown.

- People may have tried a similar idea in the past and it failed.

- People may be satisfied with their current habits.

2. Ways to Successfully Implement Change in the Church

   - Start small.

   - Go slowly and be patient.

   - Begin with areas where there's a crisis, where an obvious need exists, where people definitely want to change, or where you exercise a great deal of control.

   - Avoid attacking sacred traditions and interjecting frivolous change for change's sake.

   - Build up a credible track record before making any major proposals. This will give people a reason not only to believe in your recommendations but also in your ability to implement them successfully.

   - Assess your situation before voicing your ideas. Ask yourself questions like: "What changes need to be made?" "How urgent are they?" "Who will be effected by these changes?" "Who will favor or oppose these ideas?"

   - Plant ideas casually in the normal course of your conversations. Use phrases like "Maybe we could . . ." or "What if we . . ." to discover people's feelings. Use their objections and insights to revise your plans. Then let your suggestions simmer in people's minds before making formal proposals.

   - Anticipate objections and be ready to answer them.

   - Wait for the right time to introduce your new ideas.

   - Don't oversell your ideas. You may encourage unrealistic expectations and that will eventually lead to your plan's downfall.

   - Limit how much change is introduced at any one time.

   - Create a model or a picture of your idea for people to see, hear, or feel.

   - Think big but keep your plans simple and easy to understand.

- Don't spring ideas on people unexpectedly.

- Continue to ask people for their input. Use their suggestions to improve your plan. The more that people get involved in planning a change, the more likely they will accept that change and implement it successfully.

- Agree to a trial run in order to test the feasibility of your ideas. If your pilot project suggests that you should drop or revise your plans, be willing to do so.

- Prepare people for change by announcing your plans far in advance of their implementation.[18] Between the initial announcement and the actual execution of your plans, talk about them frequently—in newsletters, in casual conversations and in sermons.

- Explain to people the need for change. Show them how the change will benefit them or improve the situation. If you can, try to do this without criticizing the old approach or former leaders.

- Ask people to assist you in getting the idea off the ground. When you request their help, you appeal to their need to feel important.

- Don't insist on taking credit for your ideas and suggestions.

- Be specific about the changes that you want to make. Vague and ambiguous proposals lead to erroneous and anxiety-producing gossip.

- Be positive. Let your team members know that you believe in them and their ability to successfully implement the required change.

- Stay away from gimmicks, manipulating maneuvers, and high-pressure tactics. They will only increase resistance or drive it underground where it's hard to combat. Even if your 'arm-twisting' produces results, you may win the battle only to lose the war.

- Give people the training, information, resources, and help that they will need to bring about the change.

- Keep people informed about changes. Tell them what, why, when, where, and how the changes are to be made.

- Appeal to people's emotions as well as their minds.

- Make suggestions and ask questions rather than issuing commands.

- Seek the support of those who must approve your plan. You may not be able to please everybody but their help is essential.

- Enlist the help of influential people to promote your ideas.

- After initiating a change, publicize its success.

- Monitor the implementation of new ideas closely so that you can catch any problems early in the change process. Have a back-up plan in case your initial plan doesn't work out well.

3. Ways to Deal with Those Who Oppose Change

- Allow critics to fully voice their objections without interruptions.

- Listen to critics, try to understand their point-of-view, and, if possible incorporate some of their ideas into your plan.

- Be patient and even-tempered.

- Focus on ideas instead of personalities.

- Don't ridicule them or their ideas.

- Realize that your solution may not be the only or the best way to solve a problem.

- List the pros and cons of your idea. This will show them that you've given your proposal a lot of thought.

- Don't spend endless hours trying to win over determined opponents. Work with people who are receptive, try to change people who are unsure, and work around those who will never accept the change.

- Stay on good terms with your opponents—even if you can't agree with them on every idea.

- Make concessions when discussing unimportant matters.

- Know when to stop. Don't argue your position so strenuously and loudly that you make enemies.

As you try to utilize these principles, always keep one thing in mind: It's more important to change people than to change things.[19]

4. Ways to Maintain a Flexible Organization

- Encourage your team members to experiment and take risks.

- Reward those who are creative, flexible, and eager to change.

- Reward risktakers, even if all of their ideas don't succeed.

- Infuse your organization periodically with new people. Limit the terms of board members and ask group members to attend meetings in place of their group leaders.

- Ask your workers to read books and attend workshops to keep up with the latest trends.

- Attract independent, aggressive self-starters to your group.

- Challenge your group leaders to periodically review their activities and ask the question: "How can we improve our organization?"

- Ask questions to stimulate people's curiosity and make them aware of possible changes that they could make.

- Don't expect individuals or groups to act or think alike.

- Keep rules, policies, and procedures to a minimum and never incorporate them into the restrictive structure of a formal constitution.

COPING WITH ADVERSITY

Following Brenda's accident, the pressure and problems in Jim's life continued to mount. When he received an invitation from Bob Sparkman to go fishing, Jim quickly accepted his offer. It gave Jim a chance to get away from the difficulties that hounded him both at home and at the church. Since he hadn't taken a day off in three weeks, he decided that he deserved a little rest and relaxation.

On the way up to Kennsington Lake, Bob asked Jim how things were going. If he had been with a church member, Jim probably would have served up a superficial reply like "okay" or "just fine." However, with Bob, Jim found it easy to be himself and honestly share how he was feeling. So he openly admitted some of the problems he was having.

"Bob, the last couple of weeks have been horrendous. Brenda is gradually getting better but nurturing her back to health is going to take a lot of time, effort, and money. In addition to all of my regular duties at the church which keep me pretty busy, I've also been wrestling with some difficult situations. And, then there's Jill; I just can't seem to please her anymore.

"If problems were gold, I'd be a rich man.

"To make matters worse, some well-meaning people have tried to cheer me up with trite phrases like:

> 'Count your blessings.'

> 'Things could have been worse.'

> 'With every storm cloud comes a silver lining.'

> 'Well, when the going gets tough, the tough get going.'

> 'When life hands you lemons, you have to make lemonade.'

> 'We know that all things work together for good to them that love God, to them who are the called according to his purpose.'[20]

"While these statements may be true, they're not very helpful. What I really need are loving hugs, listening ears, and helpful actions.[21]

"Fortunately, most of our church members and friends have helped us out enormously. People have sent Brenda a lot of cards and gifts. They've prayed for Brenda's recovery;[22] they've brought meals over to the house; and, they've volunteered to take care of Barb whenever Jill and I need to run important errands."

"That's terrific!" said Bob. "I wish that all church members would be that generous with their fellow believers."

"It has been wonderful," agreed Jim. "Jill and I are very grateful for all of these expressions of love. However, at the same time, I'm torn by people's generosity. On the one hand, I feel a little embarrassed. I'm not used to receiving handouts. On the other hand, I worry about how long we'll be able to count on the support of our family, friends, and church members. I've seen some Christians swamped with gifts and offers of help during a crisis only to be abandoned after the initial emergency is over.

"And, I know that we're going to need a lot of help from people. Brenda is going to require a great deal of physical therapy to regain the full use of her leg. She's also going to need special tutoring to help her complete the school year."

Just then, Jim's discourse was cut short by their arrival at Kennsington Lake. However, after finding a good fishing spot, Bob once again steered the conversation back to the subject of adversity.

"Jim, I don't know if I ever told you this before, but Sharon and I had a daughter named Sarah who died when she was only two-years-old. One night, while we were attending a church banquet, she choked on a coin that I had left on top of our coffee table."

"I'm so sorry, Bob," said Jim. "That kind of experience would have devastated me. How were you able to deal with Sarah's death?"

"It took time—lots of time," said Bob in a low, soft tone.

"Although few people realized it, I was still filled with guilt and resentment years after Sarah died.[23] I was angry at God. I was angry at myself. I was angry at the baby-sitter who should have been watching Sarah more closely. I was angry at the church for keeping us so busy that we weren't with Sarah that night. I was angry at everybody!

"It took me nearly five years before I learned to deal with my anger properly."

"But surely, it took more than just the passage of time to heal your wounds," responded Jim.

"It sure did," said Bob. "Like you, Sharon and I received a lot of support from friends, family, and church members. That helped us immensely.

"In addition, I learned to focus on the future instead of dwelling on the past.

"I know that you said you don't like people coming up to you and telling you to count your blessings. But I've found that doing that can be very helpful. For me, it's healthier to focus on what I *do* have instead of what I don't have.[24]

"It's amazing how my attitude changed when I realized that not only could I not bring Sarah back but also that I did have a wife and two other children who needed my love and care.

"I was also encouraged by the way God had helped me through other difficulties in my life.[25] This wasn't the first crisis that I had faced, although it definitely was the worst. And, in every other dilemma God either delivered me from my problem[26] or He gave me the strength that I needed to weather its stormy blast.[27] In either case, I felt both God's comfort[28] and His presence[29] during the testing that I experienced.

"Surprisingly, I even saw some good things come out of our trag-edy.[30]

- It brought people in our church together.[31] Sharon and I realized that we had a lot of friends who would stick with us through the bad times as well as the good times.[32]

- It helped me in my ability to comfort others who were suffering.[33]

- It gave me numerous opportunities to witness to our friends, family, and congregation.[34]

- It sharpened my focus and helped me to establish my pri-orities.[35]

- It helped me cultivate a humble spirit.[36]

- It made me more dependent on God and actually pre-pared me for greater service.[37]

Bob paused to wipe the tears that were welling from his eyes. "Isn't it too bad that it sometimes takes adversity to force us to trust God?"[38]

Jim managed a nervous laugh as he muttered, "It sounds like problems have actually brought you closer to God and deepened your spiritual life. Well, frankly, my faith isn't that strong. I'm not holding up very well under the sledge hammer of adversity.[39]

"I'm trying to keep my eyes focused on the Lord.[40] But, boy, that's tough to do. Worry[41] and apprehension[42] seem to follow me wherever I go. And, I'm finding it extremely difficult to be the pa-tient,[43] joyful,[44] courageous[45] and persistent[46] kind of person that the Bible urges me to be.

"Because I believe in prayer, I've spent long periods of time talk-ing to the Lord.[47] I've pleaded with Him to heal Brenda and demol-ish my other problems. In desperation, I've even bargained with God and promised Him that I would be more faithful, if He would just help me negotiate my way through some of the mine fields that I'm facing.[48]

"But my prayers seem to go unanswered.[49] So, lately, my pleas have become laments. In fact, sometimes I find myself complaining to God so frequently and so bitterly that I scare myself."[50]

TRUSTING GOD

By the time Jim had finished voicing his anguish, he was sobbing uncontrollably.

Bob hugged the shoulder of his friend and tried to reassure him. "I know, Jim. I know. Sometimes it's hard to maintain our faith in God—especially when it seems like He's not listening,[51] He's moving very slowly,[52] or He's miles away.

"It's much easier to trust in things that we can hear, see, touch, and control. That's why so many people put their faith in tangible things like material resources,[53] money,[54] and power.[55]

"However, these things aren't as reliable as some may think. Power can vanish overnight. Money can be lost in bad investments. Facilities, equipment, and supplies can break down, rust out, or burn up."

Jim could identify with that. "Yeah, I know. I've work with enough computers and slide projectors to realize how finicky they can be."

"If you trust in people," Bob continued, "they can let you down too.[56] Their minds and moods change. They sometimes lie, cheat, and steal. Even if normally reliable people offer to help us, they may default on their promises because they become sick or they have an accident."

Again, Jim nodded his head in agreement. "Tell me about it. Ninety percent of my problems are people-problems."

Bob continued. "Despite all of our skills, background, and training, we can't even fully depend on ourselves. We're not always as wise as we think.[57] And, we're subject to all of the same frailties as other people are.

"That's why it's so important to trust God. He specializes in using impossible situations and improbable people to reveal His power.[58] This way, He receives the glory and honor that is due Him for the success of a task.

"Jim, I've learned to rely on God because He knows me and my future intimately; He's powerful; He's consistent; and He's faithful. Those are sterling qualifications . . ."

Jim interrupted Bob long enough to ask: "So what am I supposed to do when people like Helen and Holly let me down? Just sit back and ask God to take care of things?"

"Sometimes, if that's what God requires,"[59] said Bob. "However, most of the time, He wants to work with people in a collaborative effort.[60]

"For example, when God leveled the walls of Jericho, the Israelites still had to march around the city, shout, blow their trumpets, and take possession of what God had given them.[61]

"The same principle is illustrated in the story of Naaman's miraculous healing.[62] Even though God took away his leprosy, this mighty warrior had to first humble himself, listen to Elisha, and dip himself into the Jordan River seven times before he was cured.

"Notice two important principles can be seen in both of those cases.

"First, when I talk about a cooperative venture, I don't mean that God and man are on an equal footing. Only God could have brought down the walls of Jericho or cured Naaman of his dreaded disease. Still, God required people to do their part.

"Secondly, God has no intention of merely rubber-stamping the plans that we develop and then bring to Him for His approval. He is in charge and gives the orders. We need to discern His will correctly and obey it faithfully. Then, God will give us the wisdom, the resources, the power, and the courage to successfully accomplish the task that He has given us.

"You know, Jim, as you continue to face problems at home and at church, you might want to memorize some poignant promises that the Bible gives us.

Nothing is impossible with God.[63]

Jesus said, "I am the vine; you are the branches. If a man remains in me and I in him, he will bear much fruit; apart from me you can do nothing."[64]

If God is for us, who can be against us?[65]

I can do all things through Christ which strengtheneth me.[66]

Jim felt a little guilty to be reminded, by his friend, of the need to trust in God. He said: "Believe it or not, Bob, Jill and I adopted Proverbs 3:5-6 as our life verses when we were married. As you know, this passage says: 'Trust in the Lord with all thine heart; and lean not unto thine own understanding. In all thy ways acknowledge him, and he shall direct thy paths.'[67] But, as is true of so many Bible passages, these verses are easier to preach than to practice."

POINTS TO PONDER

1. How do you know when to handle a problem yourself or to let God or other people handle it?

2. How long should new leaders wait before they make major changes in their organization?

3. Why is it so hard to trust God?

4. If a pastor or church staff member is thinking about leaving a church because he's encountering difficulties in his ministry, what kind of factors should he consider making that decision?

PRACTICAL PROJECTS

1. Write down, in a short term-paper, what you would say to and do for the people involved in the following situation.

   Imagine that you are a leader who takes your twenty-member youth group to a skiing activity on your church's bus. On your trip, the bus driver hits a patch of ice. After hitting an oncoming van with five people in it, the bus leaves the road, overturns, and slides down a steep embankment.

   The accident kills one person and injures two people in the oncoming vehicle. It also kills five people (four teenagers, one sponsor) and injures seven people in your group. Both the bus driver and you survive the crash but are injured.

2. Interview two leaders who have faced a crisis situation in their ministry. As you talk with them, ask: "What helped or hindered you in the resolution of your problem? In retrospect, what would you have done differently if you could work through the problem again?"

14

Loners Lose

(DELEGATION)

"**W**hat do you mean you're not going to be home tomorrow evening?" exploded Jill. "That's the fourth night this week that you've been out doing your 'precious' church work.

"I never see you anymore. Neither do the girls. I feel like I have to make an appointment to talk to you."

"Listen. I never complain when you're gone because you have to work a graveyard shift at the hospital," Jim countered. "And, this is the Lord's work!"[1] he shouted with a self-righteous tone in his voice.

This wasn't the first time that Jim and Jill had had this "discussion." Every since Brenda's accident, their arguments over his schedule had grown louder, longer, more frequent, and more vehement.

As they ate the rest of their meal in stony silence, Jim finally came to a long-overdue realization. *You know, Jill's right,* he thought. *I have been spending too much time on church activities and too little time with the family. Ever since I've immersed myself in God's work, I seem to be drowning in conflict, unfulfilled goals, anxiety, and adversity.[2] That simply doesn't seem to square with the abundant living[3] and the gentle, supportive leadership[4] that Jesus had promised to provide.*

In the deep crevices of his soul, Jim knew that he was being pulled into a whirlpool. He recognized that he would have to change his lifestyle and learn to manage his time better if he was going to escape its tug. However, he hated to admit that he had a serious problem. So he voiced his conclusion to no one but himself.

THE NEED FOR DELEGATION

Although Jim was reluctant to confess his need, most of those around him could see that he was suffering from a "Messiah complex." He sincerely felt that the Lord's work couldn't move forward without his intimate and frequent intervention.[5] His symptoms were classic.

- He frequently complained, "There just aren't enough hours in the day to get everything done."

- He didn't have enough time for his family, for relaxation, or for exercise.

- He spent many of his evenings and weekends doing church work. He was afraid to take any kind of trip because something might go wrong while he was away from his post. If he did take a little time off, he felt guilty.

- He continually fell behind in his work.

- Unexpected interruptions or crises disrupted his schedule so much that he never seemed to get caught up again.

- He was interested in the most minute details of any project.

- He was reluctant to ask others for help (even when people offered their assistance).

- His projects would suddenly come to a standstill if he was gone or became sick.

- Some aspects of his job were being done poorly because he just didn't have enough time to spend on them.

THE IMPORTANCE OF DELEGATION

The loud knock on his office door startled Jim. He had come into the church early Saturday morning to finish preparing a training lesson. And, he was so engrossed in his work that he hadn't realized that someone else was in the building.

He sat up straight in his chair, turned to the left, and saw Pastor Grant's large frame filling the doorway.

"Hi Jim," said Pastor Grant. "My, you're here kind of early, aren't you? And, on a Saturday?"

"I suppose so. I have a lot of work to do. Things have really been piling up lately."

"I know. That's one of the reasons why I wanted to talk to you. Do you have a minute?" asked Pastor Grant.

"Sure. What's on your mind?" answered Jim somewhat grudgingly. Jim could tell from the tone of his voice and the expression on his face that Pastor Grant wasn't there just to squander his time in idle conversation. Besides, a chat with Pastor Grant *never* lasted just "a minute."

"Jim, I've noticed that you've been working pretty hard lately. Setting up our new computer system has especially taken a lot of your time. I want to commend you for your commitment to your job. However, at the same time, I'm a little worried about you."

"Has Jill been talking to you?" asked Jim defensively.

"No. Have Jill and you been discussing your workload recently?"

"A little bit," replied Jim nonchalantly, trying to hide how serious this problem had become. He also tried to conceal his annoyance at Pastor Grant's interruption. His seminar preparation would never get done this way. But, Jim figured that he would only make matters worse if he disclosed his displeasure.

"Jim, you've really been driving yourself hard. And, I don't think that it's healthy or necessary. If you keep this pace up much longer, you're going to be totally exhausted, your family is going to resent your work, and your attitude toward the ministry is going to sour.

"You have to learn to delegate more. That is, you need to share your workload with others so that your team can accomplish more than you can do by yourself.

"Let me share with you a few of the reasons why I believe so strongly in delegation.

- Biblical leaders such as Moses,[6] Nehemiah,[7] Jesus,[8] the apostles, and Paul[9] frequently used delegation in their ministries.

- Sheer necessity demands it. There's a limit to the amount of work that you or any other leader can do.

- Delegation makes people feel needed and gives them a strong sense of belonging—something all of us crave. When church members know they're part of the team, they're also less likely to leave the church.

- Delegation shows that you trust other people. That display of confidence makes people feel important and motivates them to live up to your expectations.

- Delegation capitalizes on people's special skills. We may not be able to play musical instruments, paint pictures, fix machines, build storage cabinets, drive a bus, sew a costume, or balance a group's financial books. But others can.

- Delegation will free you from minor details so that you can keep your eye on the big picture and your overall strategies.

- Delegation develops future leaders who will be equipped for more and bigger jobs.

- Delegation reduces the stress and pressure that you, as a leader, feel.

- Delegation allows the scope of your ministry to grow."

FAILURE TO DELEGATE

"Okay, okay, I get the idea," responded Jim with one hand raised. "Delegation can help me. So I need to do more of it."

Jim was impressed with Pastor Grant's long list of benefits. He also appreciated his supervisor's concern for his health and welfare. However, he wasn't fully convinced that delegation was the answer to his problems.

"What you've said sounds good, in theory," Jim continued. "But let's face it. There simply aren't enough people who want to participate in our educational ministry. It's incredibly painful to call people, ask them to help out, and then face their rejection. I'm sick and tired of that."

"You're right, Jim. Recruiting is a difficult task. Maybe we need to consider some other alternatives. We could streamline or drop some of our programs. We could limit our outreach efforts and church growth so that you wouldn't have to find so many new workers. We could remove some of our classroom walls so that our teachers can use methods which are designed for larger groups. Or, maybe we should pay some people to help you out; for example, I think that we should hire a summer youth worker next year.

"Those ideas are pretty drastic," objected Jim. "I don't think our church members would accept them."

"Perhaps," continued Pastor Grant, "but the congregation needs to face the fact that their lack of participation may force us to take unpleasant but necessary steps.

"By the way, have you ever talked to Rich Cooper about taking your place on the computer committee or Rose Adams about leading a teacher training workshop? Both are well qualified and would do a superb job."

"Well . . . no," answered Jim sheepishly. Pastor Grant's question had cut to the core of the problem.

"I know I'm busy," conceded Jim. "But I really enjoy leading training seminars and working with the church's computer system."

"You've just cited a second major reason why some people don't like to delegate," explained Pastor Grant. "They enjoy doing a specific job so much that they won't let others help.

"But, Jim, delegation separates a 'leader' from a 'doer.' Just think of all the time that you could save if you would enlist the assistance of other people."

"That's true," said Jim. "However, lay people don't have the education or the experience that I do."

"In other words, Jim, you subscribe to the adage, 'If you want something done well, then you have to do it yourself.'"

Pastor Grant paused for a moment as he remembered some of his past struggles with this issue. "That's what I used to think—until my heart attack. "Then I was forced to lean on others. I created a worship team to help me out in the Sunday services. My deacons stepped in and started to assist me with my counseling responsibilities. The church decided to hire you so that I wouldn't have to spend so much time in Christian education work.

"And just look at the marvelous visitation team that we've formed. Kathy lost her husband recently to cancer. Tom is a counselor at Washington High School. Ted is a great listener. Vicki has a marvelous gift for evangelism.

"I hate to admit it, but they're doing a better job reaching out to others than I was doing before I became sick. In addition, they've multiplied my ministry.

"It's amazing what people can do if they're properly trained and motivated. Read Acts 4:13 and you'll see what I mean.

"When most teenagers start to look for their first job, they're often rejected because they don't have any prior work experience. They're bewildered by their rejection and ask, 'How can I gain the experience if nobody will give me a chance to perform?'

"The same question is being asked in church circles as well. People have to begin somewhere to gain the knowledge and experience that they need to undertake new and more demanding jobs.

"Of course, some people already have the experience, training, and knowledge to tackle difficult tasks. Katie Miller, our treasurer, is a professional accountant. Mary Black, our Sunday School director, is a school teacher. And, Fran Cooper, our church librarian, is a retired bookstore manager. All of them are very qualified.

"Jim, another thing that I had to learn was: getting others to do ten jobs that are slightly flawed is much better than doing one job myself—even though it's done absolutely perfectly.

"The first time someone attempts to do something new, he probably won't be fast or as competent as you would like. The next time he does the same job, however, he's going to be much more proficient.

"When leaders lighten their loads, the jobs that they delegate might not always be done as well as they would like. However, more work certainly is accomplished than if they tried to do everything by themselves.

"If you're worried about other people's performance, you can reduce the risk of failure by taking a few simple precautions. Give clear and detailed instructions. Provide adequate training. Supply your workers with the necessary resources that they need to carry out the task. Start them out on an easy job before giving them a more difficult one. And closely supervise them until they feel comfortable with their new responsibilities and you feel comfortable with them."

"But all of that takes time, and I don't have any time to spare," argued Jim. "Frankly, it's much easier and quicker if I just do the job myself."

"Sometimes that's true if the job is a one-time task," agreed Pastor Grant. "However, if the task is repetitive, you'll save time in the long run."

SELECTING ACTIVITIES TO BE DELEGATED

During the next couple of days, Jim spent a lot of time reflecting on what Pastor Grant had said. Finally, he realized that his boss was right. Delegation is a crucial ingredient in a productive ministry, a happy home, and a healthy outlook.

Once Jim had reached this conclusion, he began to write down everything that he did on a regular basis. His job description, calendar, and goals were helpful in constructing this mammoth list.

Next, Jim examined each activity and asked himself if it was one that he could delegate. As he looked at his workload, he discovered that his tasks could be grouped into three basic categories: (1) jobs that only he could do, (2) jobs that someone else could do immediately, or (3) jobs that other people could do if they were properly trained.

He determined which tasks fell into the last two categories by asking some of the following questions.

- Is the job routine and repetitive?

- Does the task deal with minor matters that are not central to my ministry?

- Can someone else do this job as well or better than I can because of their relationships, skills, available time, or access to resources?

- If delegated, will this job contribute to another person's training and prepare him for greater service?

- If delegated, will it allow me to get more work done?

- Can someone do this more efficiently or less expensively than I can?

- Does this job take a large portion of my time or demand frequent attention?

By the time Jim had finished evaluating his workload, he was amazed at the number of jobs that he felt he could transfer to other people. Jim was simultaneously shocked and relieved by the realization that he didn't have to teach every lesson, write every training manual, select every piece of equipment, and plan every youth activity.

That evening, Jim surprised his wife by coming home early. Immediately, Jill jumped to the conclusion that something was wrong. However, Jim quickly quieted her fears.

"Jill, why don't we take a couple of days off next week and go up to the mountains—just the two of us," offered Jim.

Jill was astonished, especially after their recent argument. "Really? Do you have the time? I mean you were going to make a big presentation to the church council on Tuesday about painting the educational wing."

A broad, relaxed smile widened across Jim's face. "Well, I decided that Fred Thomas could make that presentation just as well as I could. Did you know that he repainted his whole house by himself a number of years ago? Besides, this will give him a chance to find out what happens at a council meeting."

"Is that good or bad?" laughed Jill. "You know, those meetings can be pretty discouraging."

"Well, I hope it will be a good experience for him," Jim said as he tried to maintain a serious tone. "Who knows, maybe he'll start getting more involved in the church's ministry."

GUIDELINES FOR EFFECTIVE DELEGATION

When Jim returned from his mini-vacation, he was refreshed and ready to tackle his job with renewed vigor. His enthusiasm dissipated rapidly, however, when he saw the stack of telephone messages that Shirley had left for him and when he realized how many tasks he had left undone.

Jim decided that the only way to shrink his oppressive pile of responsibilities was to continue the delegation process which he had started before his trip.

It seemed like a terribly formidable job for an activity-junkie like himself. However, it had to be done.

One of the first jobs that Jim wanted to assign to someone else was his role as children's choir director. Although he derived a lot of satisfaction from this ministry, it took a great deal of his time and there were other people who could do the job almost as well as he could.

The first question that Jim faced in turning over his responsibilities to someone else was: "Who's going to replace me as director?" After mulling over the situation for a while, he decided that Clint Wagner would be the best person for the job. Even though Clint was new to the church, he had already built an impressive track record in the six months that he had served as the choir's assistant director.[10] Although he was a very capable musician,[11] he was still eager to learn and to grow.[12] He loved working with both children and adults. His faithfulness was exemplary.[13] Furthermore, Jim and Clint got along very well together.

So Jim called Clint and made an appointment to see him at the end of the week. Although the call was short, Clint sounded interested in the job.

The first thing that Jim emphasized when Clint and he met together was the importance of the children's choir ministry. Jim stressed the tremendous impact that the choir was having on the church's outreach, the families involved, the children themselves, and their audiences.

After making this point, he challenged Clint to become the new choir director. Clint hesitated for a moment and then told Jim that he would like more information before making a decision.

Jim, ready to respond, started to explain the job in great detail. In addition to giving Clint a comprehensive job description, he also shared his personal hopes and expectations for the coming year. To these goals, Jim added some information about the program's history, the time commitment that was involved, and some of the challenges that Clint might face.

"Sounds like a pretty demanding task," said Clint. Although Jim didn't want to overwhelm his recruit, he was not about to back down and assure Clint that the job was easy and took no time at all. Jim wanted a quality program and that would demand a high level of commitment and sacrifice.[14]

Instead of retreating from his standards, Jim expressed his belief in Clint's ability to get the job done and delineated the specific reasons why he had chosen Clint for the position.

To further bolster Clint's self-confidence, Jim pointed out some of the resources that were available to Clint. This included the music and tapes that the choir had used in the past, the choir's budget, and the people in church who might be willing to help.

Jim also promised to provide Clint with a three-pronged training program.[15] First, Jim volunteered to spend some time showing Clint how to select songs, rehearse the choir, manage discipline, and direct music patterns. Second, he pledged to let Clint know when church music seminars were being held in the community. Third, he offered to give Clint a year's subscription to an excellent monthly magazine for church choir directors.

Ordinarily, Jim would have given Clint some time to think about the job. Apparently, however, Clint had already given the offer a great deal of thought. When he realized what the job would entail and the amount of support that he would receive,[16] he paused only a brief moment before accepting the position.

Jim smiled, thanked Clint, and again voiced his confidence in Clint's skills. He wished that all recruitment interviews would go as smoothly as this one had.

Before Jim left, he wanted to cover one more item on his agenda. Jim knew that delegation didn't mean abdication.[17] Inattentive leaders who abandon their responsibilities can encounter some pretty unpleasant and unwanted surprises.

Assigning others a part of your workload requires vigilance.[18] Therefore, Jim told Clint that he wanted to get together with him at the beginning of each month to discuss the choir's progress.

"Of course, I'd be glad to meet with you at other times as well," Jim added. "If you have some questions that I can answer or if you encounter a problem which needs my attention,[19] just give me a call."

Jim liked the idea of meeting with his team members on a regular basis. These rendezvous gave him a chance to accomplish several things. First, since his workers weren't likely to come to him with their troubles and mistakes, Jim's appointments with them acted as an early warning system to detect any problems. If necessary, Jim could step in and suggest remedial action before major calamities occurred.

These meetings also kept Jim informed. If the church council, parents, or other interested individuals asked about the choir's activities, he'd be able to give them a knowledgeable reply.

Jim's attention also said to his workers: "Your job is important. I care about you and your group."

Jim's get-togethers also let his workers know that they were accountable to him and to the church. Since the educational staff knew that they had to periodically report back to Jim, they were motivated to stay on track and do a better job than if they were simply left alone.

Jim had a natural opportunity through such meetings to encourage and motivate his workers. He wanted to remind them periodically of the importance of their jobs, applaud them for their efforts, and urge them to keep up the good work.

Of course, Jim didn't want to make it look like he was a "back seat driver." As Bob Sparkman had pointed out to him, that kind of close supervision negates the benefits of delegation, stifles creativity, and demotivates people. So his goal with Clint was to achieve a healthy balance between deserting his new director and staying involved in every aspect of the choir's program.

Although Jim suggested some goals for Clint to consider, he also told his young protégé that he should use his own style and methods to reach the choir's objectives. "After all," said Jim, "you're a unique individual with your own way of doing things. So don't try to copy me."

Since Jim had led the choir for most of the year, he knew that people would be tempted to come to him for answers and ideas. They might also make comparisons between his leadership style and

Clint's. To avoid those problems, Jim promised Clint that he would call a meeting in the near future to let the choir team know that Clint was now in charge and that they should give him their full support.[20]

In the weeks that followed, things went rather well. Clint dove into his job like a child enjoying a delicious bowl of ice cream. The children, parents, and members of the choir team liked Clint's warm and friendly style. In fact, things were going so smoothly that Jim felt a little jealous. It was hard to admit that the choir could function without him.

After a while, however, Jim realized that a slight problem was developing. Clint was constantly coming to him for advice and instructions. He wanted Jim to make most of the major decisions or, at least, approve decisions before they were announced. It was as if Clint was trying to reverse the delegation process.

Initially, Jim wasn't too concerned. It's natural for a rookie to seek out information and advice. Clint also harbored a blemished self-image and, therefore, was slightly insecure about tackling new responsibilities.

However, Jim didn't want to become Clint's permanent answer-man or problem-solver. That would have defeated the purpose behind Jim's delegation.

So Jim took several steps to encourage Clint to become more self-reliant. He provided more training, pointed out Clint's strengths and abilities, and applauded his accomplishments. Jim also outlined Clint's authority, responsibility, and accountability more clearly. Sometimes, Jim even became quite blunt and told him, "Clint, you need to make that decision; not me."

Most of the time, however, Jim guided their discussions with questions that encouraged Clint to discover his own answers. When, for example, Clint consulted Jim about choir uniforms, Jim asked Clint questions like: "Who are some good seamstresses in the church that can give you some help in this area?" "What colors do you think would be appropriate?" "Why?" "What kind of outfits do other churches use?" "How are you going to pay for the outfits?"

After Clint had become accustomed to his new role and had set his goals for the school year, Jim furnished him with the following form and asked him to fill it out before each of their monthly meetings.

Goal #1

Goal Statement:
Current Status:
Plan of Action:

Goal #2

Goal Statement:
Current Status:
Plan of Action:

Goal #3

Goal Statement:
Current Status:
Plan of Action:

Since Jim expected Clint to map out the progress that he had made toward each of his goals before they met together, Clint was forced to take the initiative and become more independent.

Thankfully, most people on Jim's team were more self-sufficient than Clint. Therefore, as Jim delegated an increasing amount of work, he was able to accomplish more, he had more time for Jill and his two girls, and he functioned more as a leader than a technician.

When Jim looked back at his life B.D. (before delegation), he only had one regret. He wished that he had recognized the importance of delegation before he became so snowed under. If he had delegated more things earlier in his ministry, he could have saved himself a lot of time and stress.

POINTS TO PONDER

1. Why do people engage in reverse delegation?

2. What is the difference between authority, responsibility, and accountability?

3. Why is the seemingly simple task of delegating so difficult?

4. Do pastors have an easier job delegating tasks than their staff members? Why or why not?

5. Are there some jobs that a pastor or church staff member shouldn't delegate? If so, which ones?

PRACTICAL PROJECTS

1. Have a pastor whom you know list all of the things that he does in a typical month. Examine this list for three responsibilities that he could delegate. Then ask him why he doesn't assign these jobs to other people.

2. Interview three pastors and ask them about their experiences in delegating tasks. Find out what principles they've learned in the process.

15

All in Good Time

(TIME MANAGEMENT)

"**W**ouldn't it be great if we could live as long as Methuselah[1] or if God would suspend time for us like He did for Joshua?"[2] speculated Jim, as he talked with Doug Saxby after a church council meeting.

"Yes, that would be great!" affirmed Doug. "However, barring the miraculous, we need to make good use of the time that God *has* given us.[3] As the philosopher Seneca once said, 'We're always complaining that our days are few, and acting as though they would never end.'"

"Well, that's not going to happen to me," asserted Jim. "Brenda's accident has reminded me how short,[4] precious, and uncertain[5] life is. That's why I've vowed to make every moment of my life count. I don't want to echo the words of one of Shakespeare's characters who said: 'I wasted time and now doth time waste me.'"[6]

"Well, it sounds to me as though you've discovered two of the primary principles of time management," said Doug. "You've learned how valuable your time is, and you've committed yourself to using it wisely."

"Since I've started working here, I've also learned to use some valuable time-management tools," said Jim. "Setting goals and establishing priorities have helped me to concentrate on the important things in my ministry. Planning has allowed me to accomplish my tasks efficiently. Delegating has helped me to multiply my time. And, most importantly, relying on God has allowed me to achieve more than I ever would have done if I had relied on my own strength.

"Still, I wish I could do an even better job of governing my time. Sometimes my schedule looks like an over-packed suitcase. I keep trying to squeeze too many activities into too little space."

TIME ANALYSIS

"If you're really serious about refining your time management skills even further," said Doug, "I have two suggestions for you.

"First, keep a time log for two weeks. Most of us think we know how we spend our time. However, that's not always true. When I've used this technique in the past, I've been astounded to learn where my time goes. And unless I know that, I really can't control it properly."

"Back up for just a minute," Jim urged his friend. "What's a time log?"

"A time log is a record of how you spend your time," explained Doug. "I think I have a sample sheet with me." After Doug went on a short scavenger hunt through his briefcase, he handed Jim the following document.

TIME LOG		
Date: Day:		
6:00	12:00	6:00
6:15	12:15	6:15
6:30	12:30	6:30
6:45	12:45	6:45
7:00	1:00	7:00
7:15	1:15	7:15
7:30	1:30	7:30
7:45	1:45	7:45
8:00	2:00	8:00
8:15	2:15	8:15

8:30	2:30	8:30
8:45	2:45	8:45
9:00	3:00	9:00
9:15	3:15	9:15
9:30	3:30	9:30
9:45	3:45	9:45
10:00	4:00	10:00
10:15	4:15	10:15
10:30	4:30	10:30
10:45	4:45	10:45
11:00	5:00	11:00
11:15	5:15	11:15
11:30	5:30	11:30
11:45	5:45	11:45

After scanning the sheet, Jim thanked Doug and then asked his friend another question. "Okay, what's your second suggestion?"

"Come with me to a workshop on time management at the end of this month," invited Doug. "You'll have a great time, meet some interesting people, and learn some important principles."

"It's a deal," said Jim. He looked forward not only to the information that he would gain but also to the opportunity of getting to know Doug better.

After Doug left for home, Jim headed back to the church office. He wanted to make several copies of Doug's time-inventory sheet so that he could begin his time-analysis project the first thing in the morning. Since an upcoming missionary conference would make unusual demands on his time, Jim worried that, if he delayed too long, this exercise wouldn't really reflect his normal schedule.

For the next two weeks, Jim faithfully recorded everything that he did: his trips, correspondence, planning, teaching, reading, sleeping, and eating.

At first, Jim found it difficult to record what he was doing every fifteen minutes. However, he realized that if he didn't write down each activity as it occurred, he either forgot what he had done or he incorrectly estimated the time that he had spent on the task.

In the beginning, Jim was also reluctant to keep track of what he thought were minor events. Things like casual chats, coffee breaks, and interruptions seemed insignificant. However, by the end of the week, Jim noticed that these activities, when they were all grouped together, took a large chunk of his time.

Doug was right, Jim thought. *A time log can be both revealing and surprising.*

As Jim kept track of his activities, he was often tempted to alter his record to make his schedule look good. However, he was also wise enough to resist that urge. It would have foolishly defeated the purpose of his exercise.

In fact, after a couple of days, Jim made an interesting discovery. He found out that, because he didn't alter his records, his records began to alter him. The more he became aware of time, the more carefully he used it.

TIME WASTERS

At the end of two weeks, Jim sat down and examined his time log. As he did, he wanted to find out the answers to three important questions: "How did I waste time?" "How did others waste my time?" and "How did I waste other people's time?"

As Jim looked at individual activities, he also asked himself: "Can this task be eliminated, delegated to someone else, or be done more efficiently?" and "What did this activity contribute to the attainment of my yearly goals?"

To see the big picture, Jim also looked at the total amount of time that he spent during the week in each of the following areas.

Sleeping	Yard Work
Eating	Shopping
Grooming	Visits
Committee Meetings	Cooking
Correspondence	Housecleaning
Leisure Reading	Church Services
Work-Related Reading	Lesson/Workshop/Sermon Preparation

Driving	Radio/Music Listening
Telephone Calls	Participant Sports
Planning	Hobbies
Watching Television	Parties
Concerts/Plays	Family Outings/Trips
Prayer	Miscellaneous

Jim was stunned by the results of his time inventory. According to it, there was more room for improvement than he had first thought. To rectify the deficiencies that he had spotted in his schedule, Jim pulled out his leadership diary and jotted down the following observations and instructions to himself.

Time Bandit	Recommended Security Measures
Television	Reduce the time that you spend watching sports. Having fun with your family can be just as relaxing and entertaining.
	Record interesting programs on your VCR for later viewing. You probably won't replay most of them. Those that you do watch will be less time-consuming because you can skip over the commercials or other unwanted portions of the program.
	Try to do without television—except for the news—for two weeks. The experience will probably be painful for you but wonderful for Jill.
	Turn off the television during mealtime.
	Take the amount of time that you spend watching television, and double it, spend it with your family.
Clutter	Since Shirley is already quite busy, ask someone in the congregation to help you set up an efficient filing system.
	Answer your letters immediately.
	Never handle a piece of paper more than once. Act on it, file it away properly, or throw it in the wastepaper basket.
	Leave each day with a clean desk.
	Ask for written reports only when you really need them.

Writing	Use the telephone instead of writing a letter.
	Avoid flowery prose. Make your points in outline form.
	Write an outline before you begin to compose your letter.
	Don't waste time revising a document for a third and fourth time.
	Limit reports to one page.
	Dictate letters and training manuals.
	Communicate clearly to avoid future questions or mistakes.
	Write your replies directly on the original letter itself. This is tacky but efficient.
	Write an outline or rough draft of your letters. Then, let Shirley smooth out the wording and check for spelling errors.
Interruptions	Discourage impromptu visitors by making your office less "homey" (in other words, remove extra chairs, personal knickknacks and other items which encourage people to stop by and chat).
	Rearrange your office so that your desk faces away from the door.
	Ask Shirley to hold your calls when you're involved in an important project which needs your undivided attention.
	Close your door when you're busy with important matters.
	Be candid with your visitors. If someone asks you if you have a minute to spare, politely tell them: "I'm right in the middle of an important project. Can I talk to you later?"
	Go to the public library or a park when you need a string of uninterrupted hours.
	Encourage people to make appointments rather than dropping in unexpectedly.
	If a long-winded visitor stops by the office to talk about trivial matters, gently encourage him or her to make the stay brief. Don't offer a seat, talk standing up, and contribute little to the conversation. If all else fails, remind the person of your busy schedule and excuse yourself.
	Tackle your important or complex projects when you are least likely to be interrupted.
	Have Shirley or your telephone answering machine at home screen your calls.
	Let others know that you need an uninterrupted block of time in the morning for studying and planning.
	Don't interrupt yourself. Once involved in a project, don't stop until you've finished it.

Mail/Reading	Take a speed reading course.
	Put your magazine subscription list on a diet and give up the paper totally—in favor of taped television broadcasts.
	Scan letters for major ideas (look at the introduction, conclusion, headings and bulleted or numbered points).
	Read letters during your spare moments rather than in your most productive hours.
	During extremely busy periods, skip reading totally.
	Read condensed versions of books or children's books when exploring historical events or interesting biographies.
Perfectionism	Don't use large amounts of time trying to turn an excellent job into a perfect job. The laws of diminishing returns and limited resources urge you to get the most done with the least amount of effort.
Meetings	Don't call unnecessary meetings if you can achieve the same results with less effort.
	Start and stop meetings on time.
	Prepare an agenda which specifies how much time will be spent on each item and then stick to it.
	If possible, send someone else in your place.
	If you are in charge, encourage people to stick to the subject.
	Make sure that people have the information that they need to make a decision.
	Avoid establishing regular meetings when there usually isn't enough business to warrant doing so.
	Limit the number of committees to which you belong.
	Be prepared.
	If you've been invited to a meeting but you can't contribute anything, don't attend. Likewise, ask other people to attend a meeting only when they are needed.
	Put slightly uncomfortable chairs in the meeting room.
	Consider holding a meeting while everyone stands. This will encourage people to keep it short.
	During long meetings, take a ten-minute break every hour-and-a-half.

Worry, Regret, and Daydreaming		Work to correct the situation, ask God for help, ask for forgiveness, concentrate on the future or accept what you can't change.[7]
Sluggish Performance		Avoid heavy lunches. Eat salads instead.
		Get enough sleep.
		Exercise regularly.
		Take a brief break every hour or so to refresh your mental machinery.
		Don't waste the first hour of your workday. Use this time to launch into important tasks rather than drinking coffee, reading a newspaper, or chatting with Shirley.
Travel time		Consider moving closer to work.
		Telephone or write rather than visiting someone in person.
		When traveling long distances, use the quickest mode of transportation and the most direct route.
		Make better use of your travel time by listening to training or foreign language tapes.
		Group your tasks so that you can make all of your trips at once.
Mistakes		Concentrate on doing something right the first time.

CRITICAL ACTIVITIES

As Jim reviewed his time log, he was shocked not only by how he spent his time but also by what he left out of his schedule. He could see clearly that some areas of his life deserved more attention.

For example, Jim realized that his prayer life and personal Bible study lagged far behind the time that he spent watching television and eating. Before the survey, he thought he was putting Christ first in all that he did.[8] Now he wasn't so sure.

If I don't spend enough time with the Lord, thought Jim, *how can I expect others to do so?* Realizing that he needed to carve out more time for his personal devotional life, he promised God that he would use the first hour of every day to study the Scriptures and pray.

Jim also discovered that Jill's complaints were absolutely correct. He wasn't spending enough time with the family. Therefore, he vowed to stop working on Saturdays, spend at least one full day every month alone with Jill, and take Brenda and Barb (individually) out for lunch each month.

At the beginning of the year, Jim had set three physical fitness goals for himself. However, as the pressure of his job had increased, his exercise regimen had decreased, and his goals had been forgotten.

Jim recognized that a healthy body would allow him to live longer and tackle his jobs with more vigor. Therefore, he renewed his commitment to a walking and swimming program that was designed to keep him in shape.

From his study of the Bible, Jim knew that God detests both the idleness of the sluggard[9] and the unrelenting pace of the workaholic.[10] However, his stressful schedule revealed that he was no longer steering a course between those two extremes.

To remedy the situation, Jim recognized that he had to change not only his schedule but also his attitude. Before keeping his time log, he used to feel guilty whenever he stopped to relax. He viewed rest time as waste time.

Now, however, Jim realized that he needed to reap the benefits of relaxation. Rest would rejuvenate his body and renew his mind. It would also force him to set his priorities more carefully, since more rest would mean less time for work.

Furthermore, Jim decided to reserve more time for thinking and long-range planning. His time log had revealed that he was so involved in the day-to-day details of his job that he was beginning to lose some of his perspective. He no longer saw the big picture, developed innovative programs, nor planned far enough in advance to bring about meaningful change.

To pull himself out of the quagmire of daily trifles, Jim decided to set aside the first Tuesday of every month as "Think Tank Time." He vowed to devote this day exclusively to attacking the long-term needs and the recurrent problems of the church's educational program.

THREE MISCONCEPTIONS

As Doug Saxby and Jim examined the materials that they had been given for their time management workshop, Doug poked his companion in the ribs and asked: "Well, what do you think?"

"From what I've seen so far," said Jim, "I'm impressed. The workshop manuals look very professional. The staff is friendly, helpful, and well-organized. And . . ."

While Jim was sharing his evaluation with Doug, the room's lights began to dim and the screen in front of them started to display the life of a beleaguered executive trying to negotiate his way around several document skyscrapers on his desk. "The workshop is starting right on time!" exclaimed Doug in a hushed tone.

"Now, I'm really impressed," said Jim with admiration.

After the opening video tape, Vance Crawford (the workshop's leader) launched into his presentation by debunking several misconceptions about good time management. "From the outset," he said, "I want you to know that you don't have to become a nervous, compulsive clock watcher to manage your time well. That's a myth.

"Neither do you have to organize your day so completely that you end up with a schedule like the following one.

6:00   Wake up

6:01   Turn off alarm

6:02   Open right eye

6:03   Open left eye

6:04   Yawn

6:05   Rub eyes

After the crowd's laughter had died down, Vance explained, "I want you to learn how to control, not straightjacket, your time. That means that your schedule should be neither so tight that you can't enjoy life nor so loose that you can't accomplish anything.

"I want to demolish the notion that 'activity equals accomplishment.' Leaders who accept that myth are just like caged animals on a treadmill. They're always running but they're never getting anywhere.[11]

"They think they can achieve more by doing more, and more, and more. However, that approach leads to exhaustion, heart attacks, ulcers, and strained relationships.

"That's why, during this workshop, I'm going to show you how to work 'smarter not harder.' I want to help you to do right things rather than more things.

"I want you to dismiss the idea that 'urgent activities are always important activities.' As one philosopher has said: Important things are seldom urgent. And, urgent things are seldom important.

"The ability, therefore, to deal with minor problems quickly is an asset and devoting large blocks of your time to important, long-range projects is essential. In fact, the more time that you spend developing long-term solutions, the less time that you'll have to spend dealing with short-term crises. In other words, being proactive instead of reactive pays off handsomely."

As Vance continued to dispense ideas, principles and suggestions, Jim turned to Doug and flashed a 'thumbs-up' signal. He wanted Doug to know how much he appreciated the opportunity to come to the workshop. It was turning out to be an excellent use of Jim's time.

TIME SAVERS

After lunch, Vance divided the workshop participants into ten discussion groups. Gathered around Jim's table were six people from very diverse walks of life. Sharon Kruger was a high school principal. Sam Cummings owned a print shop. Boyd Winston was a financial analyst who had written several books. And Marcia Timmons was a surgeon.

Wayne Freelander, a real estate broker who had been appointed the group's facilitator, started the discussion with a simple but effective question: "How can we save time in our lives?"

"We can save time by establishing good habits," said Sharon. "For example, I have a definite routine that I go through every morning. That way, I don't have to waste time deciding when and where I should jog, what I should eat, or what I should do when I first arrive at the office. Once at work, I spend 60 percent of my time using well-established procedures that I've developed to handle routine matters."

"Setting deadlines has enabled me to pack more things into my schedule," said Sam. "If I tell my wife that I'll build a new bookcase 'sometime' during the next month, I'll eventually get the job done. However, I'll do it more quickly and efficiently if I commit myself to a specific completion date."

"I've found that doing two things at once can save a lot of time," said Jim. "For example, I take a small book with me wherever I go. Then, if I have to 'cool my heels' in a waiting room or in a long line, I use that time to catch up on some of my reading."

Sensing a good discussion topic, Wayne asked a follow-up question: "How else can we 'double-up' our activities?"

The group's response was fluent and lively.

"I handle my correspondence while I watch television."

"I listen to tapes or practice my speeches while I drive. However, sometimes that can be dangerous. I've almost been in a couple of accidents because my mind was preoccupied with things other than driving."

"I take long strolls with my husband. Those walks improve not only my physical fitness but also my relationship with my sweetheart of twenty years."

"I knit when I attend meetings. At first, my fellow board members didn't like that. However, now, I think they secretly admire my ability to redeem some of the time that they think they're wasting."

"I watch television and iron at the same time."

"I use my rides on the bus each morning to learn German and do some planning."

"Last night, I did six things at once," bragged Boyd. "I typed on my computer, printed my manuscript, listened to a television program, talked with my wife, washed the dishes (with the help of the dishwasher), and washed my clothes (with the help of the washer and dryer)."

"Maybe that's taking things a little too far," cautioned Sharon. "Remember, Vance said that both quality as well as quantity matter in the management of our time."

"Sometimes, when people try to waste my time by making me wait," said Marcia, "I just sit back, relax, and meditate."

"What a novel idea," said Sharon, with an impish laugh.

To keep things moving, Wayne broke into their discussion and brought them back to his original question. "How else can we save time?" he inquired.

"I've learned to say no to people," said Boyd. "That saves me an immense amount of time."

"That may be easy for you," said Sharon. "But if I say no too often, I'm going to have some angry teachers, parents, or influential supporters on my hands. You see, it's my job to say yes and to help other people. If I don't, I'll end up standing in the unemployment line."

To explore this subject further, Wayne asked: "What are some other reasons why we're so afraid to say no?"

The group was eager to respond.

"We don't like saying no because people might not ask us again."

"We don't want to admit to others that we can't cope with our schedule. Saying no tarnishes our image as hard-working, well-organized workers."

"We hesitate to say no because we want to say yes. It's wonderful to be needed."

"What are some ways that we can say no gracefully?" asked Wayne.

"To discourage last-minute requests by procrastinators, you can say: 'I'm sorry. If you had asked me sooner, I might have been able to do it.'"

"To encourage people to ask again (when you have more time), you could say: 'Thank you for asking. My schedule is pretty packed right now but maybe we could arrange something in the future.'"

"Maybe you could propose an exchange. You could say something like, 'I'd be glad to help you out with the bake sale if you'll mow my lawn. Otherwise, I just won't have enough time to make the cookies.'"

"I have a surefire way," said Marcia, "but it probably won't win you too many friends. Volunteer others. Say something like: 'Unfortunately, I can't do that right now. However, Rick might be able to help you.'"

To keep the group focused on the main question, Wayne once again asked: "Okay. What are some other ways of saving time?"

Boyd recommended that the group should continually *ask the question, "What is the best use of my time right now?"*

Sharon suggested, *"Learn to use other people's ideas instead of continually reinventing the wheel.* Why should you start from scratch, when somebody has already developed materials or a program that suits your needs?"

"In our modern, technologically oriented world, *there's a host of labor-saving devices that we can employ*—devices like VCRs, fax machines, computers, and photocopy machines."

"One great labor-saving device is the telephone. Now, I know that a lot of time management people call it a 'time-waster,' and, it can be, if it's always interrupting your train of thought. However, I've found that the telephone is much cheaper and faster than writing or traveling."

"I save a lot of time by starting a project early and then letting my subconscious develop ideas while I'm doing other things."

"I try to do similar tasks at the same time," said Sam. "For example, instead of writing a letter here and writing a letter there, I take care of all of my correspondence at the end of the day. That way I don't waste time and mental energy shifting gears from one thing to another."

"That can also apply to things like making telephone calls, visiting people and going on buying trips," said Jim.

"Of course, there are times during the day when it's important to shift gears," said Marcia. "Taking strategic pauses during the day, for example, serves to renew my energy."

"Just don't forget to keep your breaks short!" cautioned Sam. "Otherwise, they will become well-defended but poorly advised excuses for procrastination.

SCHEDULING

After the workshop was over, Jim was eager to apply the principles that he had learned. So, immediately after he arrived at home, he pulled out his pocket calendar and started planning his next month's activities. As he mapped out his agenda, he frequently referred to the following handout that he had received at the time-management seminar.

1. Select one good calendar and keep your entire schedule in it. Because it's so valuable, don't misplace it. In fact, just to be safe, you might even want to make copies of it every once in a while.

2. Use your prime time effectively. Some people are "night people;" others are "morning people." Decide when you function best and use that time of day to handle your most difficult assignments.[12] Easy, routine tasks should be reserved for your most unproductive hours.

3. Allow for the unexpected. Because your schedule may be subject to emergencies over which you have no control, leave some slots in your calendar open. Then, if a crisis develops, you can deal with it during these 'free' periods. If no emergency comes up, use that block of time to work on optional items.

4. Be realistic. When developing your schedule, you may attempt to do too much in a day or underestimate the time that an activity will demand. If you find that this is happening to you, start allowing twenty percent more time than you think it will take to complete a task. With experience, your time estimates will improve.

5. Follow your schedule. During the day, many temptations will try to sidetrack you by offering pleasant diversions. Resist their allure.

POINTS TO PONDER

1. When does being friendly and meeting people's needs degenerate into wasting time? Did Jim go too far in attempting to discourage interruptions?

2. Why do some people spend more time watching television than reading the Bible and praying?

3. Why do people procrastinate?

4. Why do some people find it hard to relax?

5. How would you deal with a person who wastes your time by habitually arriving late?

6. What are the benefits of being lazy?

PRACTICAL PROJECTS

1. Keep a time log of your activities for two weeks and then write an analysis of how you spend your time.

2. Ask two pastors to keep a personal time log and then share the results with you.

3. Write a short paper describing how to deal with procrastination.

16

Reach Out
and Touch Someone

(OUTREACH)

As Bill Chamberlin walked through the door of Manfred's German Restaurant, Jim stood up to greet him. "Thanks for taking time out of your busy schedule to meet me here."

Bill, who was used to business luncheons, didn't mind at all. He said, "Oh, I'm always happy to get together with you—especially when you're paying the bill."

Jim chuckled. He had discovered that getting together with businessmen during the lunch hour was a natural way to get acquainted with them. He wasn't always sure, however, that his budget could take the strain.

After Bill and Jim were ushered to their table and had looked over their menus, a friendly waitress greeted them. "Welcome to Manfred's. How may I help you?"

After Jim and Bill placed their order, they were treated like royalty. The restaurant's service was speedy, pleasant, and attentive. Their surroundings were stylish, clean, and attractive. Their food was delicious, inexpensive, and served with flair.

From experience, Jim and Bill knew that once they had finished their meal, they would be sent on their way with a few after-dinner mints and the words: "Thanks for coming. Have a nice day and come back soon."

With this kind of pampering, Bill couldn't help observing: "Boy, I wish our church would treat its visitors like this."

"Well, now that you've agreed to coordinate our church's outreach activities," said Jim, "you'll be in a position to influence how we take care of both our guests and our members."

AN EVANGELISTIC ATMOSPHERE

"I know," said Bill. "And, I'm really looking forward to serving God in this way. Ever since my brother died, I've had a renewed interest in reaching out to those who don't know Christ.

"I'm also excited about the job because I know that you and Pastor Grant are deeply interested in outreach. Both of you have stressed the importance of evangelism in your teaching and preaching.[1] You've set growth goals and made plans that encourage and anticipate expansion. Best of all, you've shown us by your example that we should be talking to others about Christ wherever we are.

"With that kind of support, it'll be easier to get members involved in the church's outreach program."

"I hope so," said Jim. "Despite our best efforts, however, most of our members aren't very excited about evangelism. Some are content to let Pastor Grant and me do most of the witnessing ourselves; after all, they say, that's our job. Some believe that reaching out to nonbelievers takes too much time, costs too much money, and invites too many problems; these members are perfectly comfortable with the status quo. Still others are so preoccupied with their own selfish pursuits that they don't seem to care that people around them are going to hell."[2]

"Isn't it a shame that we don't share the gospel with the same kind of gusto and ease that we do when we talk about politics, sports, or our children?"[3] asked Bill.

"It sure is," agreed Jim. "You know, sometimes I get pretty discouraged. I don't think that we've done nearly enough in this area yet."

"Oh, I don't know," said Bill. "I think you and Pastor Grant have done a great job so far. In order to reach our community for Christ, Pastor Grant has used evangelistic preaching, supported city-wide revivals, organized a bus ministry, conducted door-to-door evangelistic surveys, and established a day-care center.

"I think that his creation of two different worship services—one designed for traditional-minded Christians and the other designed for nonbelievers—was a great idea. A couple of weeks ago, I brought my nephew, Collin, to our Saturday-night seeker service and he hasn't missed one since. He likes the fast-paced, informal worship atmosphere that we've created. He also enjoys our thought-provoking skits, contemporary music, and practical emphasis on relationships."

"I'll bet the fact that Pastor Grant's talks are short and that his emphasis on offerings is nil doesn't hurt," joshed Jim.

"Not at all," laughed Bill.

"Of course, Pastor Grant isn't the only one who's been helping our church grow. Since you've started working at Bethel, we've really expanded our outreach efforts. You've started new groups. You've introduced us to friendship evangelism. You've increased our advertising. And, you've used a divide-and-multiply strategy in the reorganization of our Sunday School's structure.

"As if that weren't enough, now you're helping us experiment with special-event evangelism.

"By the way, my son Stan loved the sports workshop that you conducted for the youth group. He didn't even mind the fact that he had to bring two nonChristian friends in order to attend.

"In fact, as I think about all that's been accomplished so far, I'm not sure that I can make much of a contribution."

"Oh, there's still plenty of work to do," laughed Jim. "We need to enlarge our visitation program, organize outreach teams in our Sunday School classes, and train people to witness to their friends, coworkers, and neighbors.

"But we can talk about that later. Right now I want to share with you what we have planned for our upcoming children's crusade. It's the biggest outreach event that we have scheduled for this year."

PUBLICITY

Jim was excited about what the church was calling "Adventure Week." For this special occasion, he had been fortunate enough to enlist the services of "Uncle Andy" Nelson. This enthusiastic evangelist possessed a tremendous passion for the lost and a remarkable ability to share biblical truths with children. His programs were fast-paced, Christ-centered, biblically-based, and evangelistically-oriented.

Of course, if people didn't come to the crusade, they wouldn't have a chance to see Uncle Andy's spell-binding presentations. That's why Jim was so happy that Ed Sanders had agreed to become the publicity coordinator for the crusade.[4]

As Jim talked about Ed Sander's role, he handed Bill a thin booklet and said, "When I recruited Ed, I gave him this manual. I thought you might be interested in it."

Bill was interested. He could see that its contents could help him in his new job. One of the first things that caught his eye was Ed's job description as outlined below.

PUBLICITY CHAIRMAN

Basic Responsibility: To create an interest and involvement in our upcoming children's crusade (otherwise known as "Adventure Week").

Specific Responsibilities:

1. Pray weekly for the children's crusade.
2. Plan a comprehensive publicity campaign for the crusade.
3. Participate in all planning meetings for the crusade.
4. Attend the crusade's evaluation session.

Procedure:

1. Acquaint yourself with the following information about the
children's crusade.

    a. What? "Adventure Week"

    b. When? November 19-22, 7:00 P.M. to 8:15 P.M.

    c. Where?
    Bethel Church (in the sanctuary),
    3512 Blossom Way,
    Cody,
    284-4661

    d. For whom? Grade school children and their parents No care for preschoolers will be provided.

    e. Theme? Heroes of the Bible

    f. Attractions?

    | Puppets | Bible Stories | Prizes |
    | Skits | Refreshments | Magic |
    | Singing | Quizzes | Crafts |
    | Games | Contests | |

    g. Contact Person? For further information, call me at 284-4452 or talk with Shirley.

2. Set your goals after asking: "Whom and how many do I want to come?"

3. Analyze your audience (whom are you trying to reach and what will motivate them to attend).

4. Determine your message (what do potential participants need to know and which parts of the Adventure Week program do you want to emphasize). To be effective, you may have to design different approaches for different audiences. For example, if you're trying to reach children who attend our church, then you'll need to gear your message and methods toward them. If, however, you're trying to appeal to parents who are nonbelievers, your style and strategies must suit their needs and interests.

5. Determine your media.

   a. List all of the ways that you can promote our children's crusade.

   b. Estimate the resources that you'll need to carry out each idea (time, people, artwork, and money).

   c. From your list of potential publicity methods, select and schedule the ideas that will best bring children and their parents out to the program. In scheduling your plans, remember to start early, keep the program in front of the people and plan the campaign so that the publicity builds in excitement and intensity as the time for the program gets closer.

6. Obtain my approval for your budget and publicity plan before you begin.

7. Execute your plan.

   a. Recruit your team.

   b. Plan the design and wording of your announcements.

   c. Print and distribute your advertisements.

8. Keep me informed of your activities.

9. Evaluate the results of your publicity efforts after the crusade is over. Ask yourself:

   a. How effective was the publicity campaign?

   b. What would you do differently the next time (what would you add, eliminate, expand, or reduce)?

10. Save examples of your publicity efforts and a record of your publicity schedule so that other publicity chairmen can learn from your efforts.

Resources:

1. The Resource Center contains many of the materials that you'll need to make your posters and brochures: posterboard, paper, paints, or markers.

2. Our church secretary will be glad to help you out with clip art and any office supplies that you need (the church's computer and photocopy machine can help you reduce and enlarge your artwork). She is also willing to print any flyers that you may need.

3. I've included in this manual some ideas and samples that previous publicity chairmen have used to promote a variety of church events.

4. If I can be of any help, please give me a call.

5. Artistic people in our congregation include Dan Rivers, Rita Nelson, and Harvey King.

The Importance of Your Job

Your job is vital to the success of our crusade. Unless children are invited, they won't come. And, if they don't come, they may not get another chance to hear the gospel so vividly and clearly portrayed.

Also, your publicity may be the first contact that some people will have with our church. Those first impressions are extremely important because they'll linger so long.

After Bill had studied Ed's responsibilities for several minutes, Jim turned his colleague's attention toward another section of the manual. "As you can see, I've also included a list of publicity methods. As our new outreach director, you might want to use some of the following ideas yourself."

Suggested Means of Promotion

1. Announcements
   a. Place
      (1) Worship Services
      (2) Midweek Clubs
      (3) Children's Church

  (4) Women's and Men's Groups

  (5) Sunday School (general assemblies, department openings or individual classrooms)

  (6) Bible Study Groups

 b. Type

  (1) Use pulpit announcements.

  (2) Plan a dedication service for the workers.

  (3) Flash announcements on an overhead projector before the worship service.

  (4) Use a play or skit to highlight the crusade.

  (5) Show slides or filmstrips from Uncle Andy's previous crusades.

  (6) Ask children or parents who have attended Uncle Andy's crusades in the past to share what his programs have meant to them (some people may prefer giving a testimony while others may prefer being interviewed).

  (7) Ask Uncle Andy to come and make a presentation the Sunday before his crusade begins.

  (8) Pray for the crusade and encourage others to do the same. Organize special prayer chains and prayer meetings or use the ones that are already in place.

  (9) Leave brochures on the table in the church's foyer.

  (10) Ask Pastor Grant to refer to the crusade in his sermon (use Uncle Andy as an illustration or mention the need to expose children to good to Christian entertainment).

  (11) Present a slide show in the church's foyer.

  (12) Put inserts or notices in the church's bulletin or order the bulletin covers that Uncle Andy sells.

  (13) Show the promotional video that Uncle Andy sells.

  (14) Conduct a "Make a Poster" contest and display the posters around the church and the community.

2. Posters, Flyers, Displays and Banners

 a. Outside the church

- Christian bookstores
- Grocery stores
- Department stores
- Dentist's and doctor's offices
- Telephone poles (with the city's permission)
- Laundry-mats
- Beauty parlors and barber shops
- Libraries
- Schools
- Other churches
- Doors or windows of church members' homes
- Information booths and bulletin boards at shopping malls
- Windshield wipers or cars parked at stores or malls (with the mall's permission)
- Church buses, city buses, or other transit cars
- Local schools
- Community or recreational centers

b. Inside the church
- Bulletin boards
- Church foyer
- Sunday School classrooms

c. On the church's property (use the church's outdoor sign or string a banner across the front of the church)

3. Flyer Distribution

a. On the street corners near our elementary schools (check with the city police first) and in shopping malls (with their permission)

b. From house-to-house

4. Personal Invitation. We should encourage our church members to invite their friends, family members and neighbors.[5] One way to do this is to run a contest and give out prizes to those who bring the most people.

   We could also help our church members by giving them flyers and posters to hand out.

5. Direct Mail and Telephone Calls. Mail invitations to people who have attended our children's programs in the

past. You can get a list of students who have previously attended our VBS program by talking to Shirley.

6. Mass Media

   a. Types

      - Advertisements

      - Special interest or news articles (I've included Uncle Andy's picture and some biographical material at the back of this manual).

      - Interviews with Uncle Andy

      - Program previews

      - Public service announcements or coming-events calendar

      - Religious columns

   b. Methods (Christian or secular)

      - Newspapers (city, community and school)

      - Radio

      - Television (regular or cable)

7. Other Means:

   a. Buttons (inside and outside of church)

   b. T-shirts

   c. Bumper stickers

   d. Give aways (buttons, pens, cards)

   e. Balloons

Bill looked at the publicity methods with interest and then turned to Jim and asked, "Out of all these options, which ones do you think will produce the best results?"

"Frankly, I don't know," said Jim.

Bill responded to Jim's uncertainty by scribbling something on a sheet of paper which he had pulled from his briefcase. Then he said, "I have an idea. Why don't we include a little addendum like this on the back of our registration cards.

What brought you to our Adventure Week program?

[ ]   a poster   [ ]   a flyer   [ ]   a bulletin announce-ment

[ ]   a friend   [ ]   a newspaper advertisement

[ ]   Other:

"That's an excellent idea," said Jim. "We can use the information garnered from this survey to help us decide where we're going to spend our time and our money in the future.

"We can also capitalize on our crusade in several other ways. We can take slides of Uncle Andy's presentations and show them later when we want to generate interest in our next crusade. We can ask those who attend if they'd like to receive more information about our children's program. In addition, we can give our Sunday School and midweek club coordinators a list of those who came; then our leaders can invite these children to attend their programs.

PROSPECTS

"By the way, do we have a mailing list or a prospect list which we can use to invite children to the crusade," asked Bill.

"Unfortunately, we don't," said Jim. "However, that sounds like a good project for our new outreach director. We could compile a list from our Sunday School, VBS, midweek club, choir, and day-care and camping records."

"Don't forget. Our prospect list should also include adults," suggested Bill.

"Right," concurred Jim. "And we could collect their names in a number of different ways. We can use our church directory. And we can ask people who come to musical concerts to sign a visitor's card. We can add the names that we've gathered from our house-to-house surveys."

"We can even conduct an in-house survey," said Bill. "That is, we can ask our members to suggest the names of people who might be interested in attending some of our church activities."

"We could also try to obtain the names of people who are new to the community," remarked Jim.

"How can we do that?" asked Bill.

"Well, we can call Welcome Wagon or we can obtain the lists of new water and electrical connections from the city."

"You're right," said Bill. "There's still plenty of work to do."

VISITORS

Two weeks after Bill Chamberlin assumed his new job as outreach director, Jim decided to give him a call and find out how he was doing. When Jim asked his friend if he was having any difficulties, Bill was surprised. "Not in the least," he said. "I'm thoroughly enjoying my new responsibilities.

"Last night, for example, I was thinking about how crucial it is for me (as a salesman) to make a favorable first impression. Then I began to ask myself: 'How can our church make newcomers feel welcome from their very first contact with us?'

"Well, after twenty minutes of brainstorming, I was able to compile a long list of ideas. Would you like to hear some of them?"

"Sure," said Jim. "I'm always interested in finding out how we can improve our programs."

"Good!" responded Bill, sensing that he had a supportive ally in Jim. "If we're going to make favorable first impressions, we need to:

1. Beautify the exterior of our church, including the improvement of the landscaping.

2. Construct a bigger and more attractive church sign that will capture people's attention, boldly identify our church, and advertise our Sunday services.

3. Provide special parking spaces near the front door for 'visitors only.'

4. Place a welcome booth near the church's main doors.

5. Post conspicuous signs to guide people to our sanctuary or welcome booth.

6. Recruit members to greet people as they come into the church and answer any questions that newcomers might have.

7. Provide these greeters with information packets which describe our church's activities and provide a map of our

facilities. Of course, these materials would include a brochure listing the topics, ages, and locations of our Sunday School classes."

"That's a good idea," interjected Jim. "However, wouldn't it be better if the greeters would personally escort visitors to their classrooms?

"Maybe we could even station greeters at the entrance of our Sunday School classes or departments. They could introduce newcomers to other class members and make them feel at home.

"That sounds good, in theory," said Bill. "However, I'm not sure whether we can recruit enough people to do that right now. Maybe I can include those ideas in my long-term goals."

"I have another idea," said Jim. "Maybe we could identify our visitors with special name tags or introduce them in Sunday School or in our morning worship services."

"Wait a minute!" said Bill. "I know from personal experience that most visitors don't like to be put on the spot. More than likely, they're already uneasy about coming to Sunday School. And, if we make them feel more uncomfortable, they won't come back."

"You're absolutely right," conceded Jim, realizing that he needed to listen more and speak less. "What are some other ways that we can 'roll out the red carpet' for our guests?"

"Well, after the class is over," continued Bill, "we need to befriend newcomers and let them know how much we've appreciated their visit.

"We could do this in a number of ways. We could simply say 'thanks for coming.' We could engage them in a casual conversation and find out more about them. We could escort them down to the sanctuary or over to their children's classes. Or we could invite them out for lunch after church.

"Of course, to make this work, we have to encourage our regular class members to move beyond their comfortable cliques and demonstrate their interest in newcomers."

"How do we do that?" asked Jim.

"I'm not quite sure," admitted Bill. "But I'll work on the problem.

"We also have to persuade our teachers to treat visitors with care. Asking them to find Bible passages, read a paragraph in a curriculum book, or answer a question that requires Bible knowledge is asking for trouble."

There was a small lapse in the conversation while Bill tried to remember if he had forgotten anything. Then he made one more suggestion. "If we want to be really formal, we could send our visitors a note or a card in which we thanked them for coming and expressed our hope that they would return. Or, we could even set up an appointment and visit them in their homes."

"Bill, you have some good ideas," said Jim. "Now, we need to translate them into action. Why don't you drop by my office next week and we'll discuss your plans in a little bit more detail.

"Some of them, like the welcome booth and the landscaping project, will require committee approval. However, if we work together, I'm sure we'll be able to convince the appropriate people of their importance."

ABSENTEES

A couple of days later, Bill came by the church office to discuss his outreach proposals with Jim. In the middle of their discussions, however, Bill started to pursue another avenue of thought.

"Since we talked Jim, I've been thinking about our absentee problem. We lost a lot of good families last year. And, frankly, our efforts to attract new people will be meaningless if people leave through our back doors faster than we can bring them in our front doors."

Jim didn't accept Bill's assertion that their efforts would be 'meaningless.' However, he did agree with his friend's concern. So he asked Bill: "What would you recommend?"

Bill had given this a lot thought, and he said, "As I see it, we need to do five things.

"First, We need to establish an AWOL warning system so that we know when class members are missing. That requires good records and watchful teachers.

"Second, We need to contact absentees and let them know that we've missed them. The first time that they're gone, we should send them a card. The second time that they're absent, we should call them and see how they're doing. Then, if they miss a third time in a row, someone in their class should visit them in their homes.

"Some may think that's overkill. However, by the time most of our members think to ask: 'Whatever happened to Jack and Jill?' it's probably too late to win these absentees back. More than likely, they've already decided that they're not going to come back to our church."

"Of course, when we contact people, we have to be careful about how we approach them," cautioned Jim. "A casual, friendly 'we missed you' is preferable to a grilling from a nosy or critical class member."

"Absolutely," said Bill.

A slight pause ensued. Sensing that he might have disrupted Bill's train-of-thought, Jim quickly added, "You said that we need to do five things to reclaim our absentees. What are the other three?"

"Thirdly, We need to find out why people aren't coming as regularly as they should," Bill continued. Maybe they're sick or having problems at home; if so, we need to minister to them. Maybe they've been on a trip; then, we should show interest in their travels. Maybe they're working in another classroom; if so, we need to let them know what we're doing and remember to invite them to our socials. Maybe they're serving in the military or attending a university outside of Cody. If that's true, we should pray for them, stay in touch with them, and periodically do something that shows that we're still interested in them.

"Perhaps they simply don't like our church or its programs. If that's the case, then we need to take another step—we need to identify and correct our weaknesses.

"Fourthly, Pastor Grant has really worked hard to improve the quality of his speaking and the competence of our choir. Now we need to do the same kind of thing for our educational program.

"Poorly-trained workers, ill-prepared teachers, inadequate facilities, and irrelevant materials don't attract or keep newcomers. We need to strive for excellence in everything that we do."

"We also have to provide programs that meet needs," added Jim. "That's why I'm really enthused about the new groups that we've started this year—groups for the hearing impaired, for the athletically inclined, and for single adults who attend Christopher College.

"Of course, next year, I think we can do even more. I'd like to start some groups that would be designed to meet the needs of widows, divorcees, parents of blended families, and substance abusers. Maybe we could even begin a program for freshman at Christopher College with a title something like: 'How to Survive Your First Year at College and Love It.'"

Bill liked Jim's ideas and told him so. Then he directed their discussion back to its original train of thought. "Another reason why some people stop coming is that they don't feel wanted. People may put up with a few deficiencies in a church's program, but they will not tolerate an unfriendly church.

"So lastly, We need to improve the way that we assimilate people. Unless we can transform an outsider into an insider, we're going to lose a lot of people.

"Right now, I'm not sure how we're going do that but, as with the other gaps in our outreach program, I'm working on it."

"Sounds like a big challenge," said Jim. "However, I'm confident that you can do the job."

GOSPEL MESSAGE

Initially, Jim was disappointed when only four of his church members agreed to counsel at the children's crusade. However, he was determined not to let his disappointment get in the way of providing these volunteers with a top-notch training experience. So, when he brought them together for a workshop on "How to Lead a Child to Christ," he began on a positive note.

"During our children's crusade or what we're calling 'Adventure Week,'" said Jim, "you're going to have one of the most thrilling experiences of your life. You're going to get an opportunity to lead a child to Christ. What you say and what you do will determine their eternal destiny.

"That sound's like a big responsibility," said Sandra Sutherland apprehensively.

"It is," replied Jim, "but it's also a rewarding one because children are so open to the gospel and because they have so much time left with which to serve Christ."

After Jim finished explaining the importance of evangelizing children, he went on to share with his workers the procedures they would be using during Adventure Week.

"At the end of each program during our crusade," Jim said, "we're going to invite children and their parents to make Christ the Lord of their lives. However, we're going to do this in a way that is probably unique for our church.

"Some adults try to manipulate children into God's kingdom. They twist arms, so to speak, by making emotional appeals and offering seductive gifts that youngsters find hard to resist.

"And, if those things don't work, these manipulative adults enlist peer pressure to achieve their goals. That is, they urge children to 'join the bandwagon' and come forward to accept Christ with the rest of their friends. In fact, I've even seen some evangelists seed the audience with a few confederates who prime the pump by 'coming down to the front and accepting Christ' (even though they're already Christians).

"During our crusade, however, we're not going to usurp the Holy Spirit's role by using these tactics.[6] In my opinion, they'll never produce the kind of solid, life-changing commitment that we want.

"This year, we're actually going to make it a little difficult for children to become Christians. We're going to ask those who are interested in accepting Christ as their Savior to go directly to our library after our program is finished. That means that they'll probably miss the refreshment time. It also means that eager parents who want to go straight home will try to dissuade them from going to the library.

"However, I'm convinced that, if their desire is genuine and the Holy Spirit is really prompting them to make a life-changing decision, they'll make the effort to come.

"Once a child enters the library, your job begins. The first thing I want you to do is greet that child with a smile and a short welcoming phrase. I also want you to find out his or her name so that you can use it throughout the rest of the conversation.

"Then, I want you to ask the child why he came. That's important because children will come for a variety of reasons. Maybe they'll want to see what the room looks like or ask a question about something that was said or done in the program.

"If a child comes for one of these reasons, answer his question or show him the room. Then, explain to the child: 'This week we're using the library to show people how they can become Christians. Would you like to know how to do that?'

"If he says no, don't pressure him. Just thank him for coming and invite him to return if he has any questions.

"If he says yes, then explain to him the following plan of salvation.

1. God loves you and wants the very best for you (John 3:16; 10:10).

2. But you've sinned and your sin has separated you from God (Rom. 3:23; 3:10; 6:23).

3. Jesus died on the cross to take the punishment for your sins (Rom. 5:8-9; 1 Tim. 2:5; 2 Cor. 5:21).

4. Jesus' death on the cross is God's only provision for your sin (John 14:6; Eph. 2:8-9; Titus 3:5; Acts 4:12).

5. Now God wants you to accept what Jesus has done for you and to become His follower (Acts 16:31; John 1:12; Rev. 3:20; Rom. 6:23).

"In the counseling packets that I've given you, you'll notice that I've provided you with several gospel tracts and flash cards to help you remember these steps. In addition, we've printed up some Bible bookmarks with the gospel outline printed on them. Look over these tools and select the one with which you feel most comfortable.

"You might also want to write some notes in the margins of your Bible. For example, next to John 10:10, you could jot down Romans 3:23 which is the next verse that you'd probably use in your gospel presentation."

Jim paused momentarily to see if he still had his team members' attention. Then he continued.

"Okay, the big moment has arrived. You've shared the gospel with your child and then you ask him, 'Do you want to accept what Jesus Christ has done for you on the cross and let Him control your life from now on?'

"The child pauses for a second to consider the matter. Then he looks up at you, smiles, and says: "Yes."

"Your heart skips a beat, you feel like shouting 'that's terrific,' and then you panic because you're not sure what to do next.

"Well, when you come to this joyous point in your presentation—and you will, I'd like you to follow a nine-point procedure.

1. Affirm his decision. Let him know that he's taken a wonderful and an important step in his life.

2. Pray with him. Thank God for his decision and then allow the child to pray a prayer of commitment.

3. Have him write the date and sign his name underneath the phrase 'today I decided to let Jesus be the Lord of my life' in the New Testament that you'll be giving him.

4. Assure him of his salvation by quoting Hebrews 13:5, John 10:28, or 1 John 5:11-13. Better yet, have him read one of these verses from his New Testament.

5. Record his decision. In your counseling packets, you should have a number of decision cards. Please fill out the information on this card completely and clearly. We'll need it for our follow-up program.

6. Prepare him for a follow-up visit. Explain to your child that the church would like to help him as he grows in his Christian life. Let him know that you or someone else from the church will be stopping by to see him and that this person will be giving him a little booklet which talks about his new life in Christ.

7. Write down, on the decision card, any information that might be helpful in following up the child—facts about his family, his interests, his church background, or his questions.

8. Urge him to tell somebody else what he has done after he leaves the library.

9. Tell his Sunday School teachers, if the child has some, so that they can encourage him in his new faith.

Seeing that his first session was almost half over, Jim said, "Okay, I've talked long enough. Now I want you to practice the principles that I've taught you.

"Sandra and Rita, I want you to go into the classroom next door and share the gospel with each other. As you do, pretend that your partner is a child who has come to you for counseling. Bev and Diane, I want you to do the same thing in this room. Then, we'll get together again and learn some more about counseling children."

After twenty minutes, Jim reconvened his group and continued his lecture. "In a moment," he said, "I want you to change partners and share the plan of salvation again. However, this time, I'd like you to keep in mind the following principles.

- Keep your presentation short and simple. Don't confuse or complicate the gospel by endless verses or illustrations.

- Avoid religious jargon. Children have difficulty understanding big words like *redemption, salvation,* and *justification.* So, instead of using long explanations to define these terms, use simple words in the first place.

- Avoid metaphors and abstract concepts like 'let Jesus come into your heart' or 'sin is like an ink stain.' Since children are literal-minded, these expressions tend to confuse them.

- Use Scripture verses, visuals, and illustrations to convey the gospel story.

- Periodically, during your presentation, ask questions to test your listener's understanding. You might ask: "Do you believe that all of us including yourself have done things that are wrong?" "Are you sorry for your sins?" "Do you believe Jesus died to take the punishment for your sins?"

- Don't force children to accept the gospel.

- Don't manipulate children by asking them leading questions, such as: "You want to become a Christian, don't you?"

- Be sensitive to your child's needs and remain flexible in your presentation. Children will probably have questions which they want to ask or problems about which they want to talk. So don't be afraid to deviate from your outline to clarify a point or to help your child with something that is troubling him or her.

- Throughout the counseling session, rely on the Holy Spirit to empower you and to give you the right answers. John 16:8 tells us that it's the Holy Spirit's job to convict people of their sins. Therefore, we need to rely on His strength and not ours.

FOLLOW-UP

After ten more minutes of lecture and fifteen more minutes of practice, Jim and his trainees broke for lunch. Surprisingly, Jim's workers asked more questions during the break than they did during their actual training session.

Jim thought to himself, *Evidently, in my next workshop, I'll need to leave more time for discussion.*

As he tried to answer the practical questions that his workers fired at him, he realized that they weren't there just to learn how to lead a child to Christ during the crusade. They also wanted practical suggestions on how to lead their family members and their neighbors to Christ.

This prompted Jim to make another mental note: *I'll need to widen my focus the next time I talk about this topic.*

Because of his worker's concerns, Jim began the second part of his workshop with a lengthy period of prayer. What a wonderful time they had. It was exciting to hear people pray so fervently for witnessing opportunities, for people's salvation, and for the wisdom to know what to say.[7]

Invigorated by this time of intercession, Jim launched into his training with renewed energy. "Once children have made a decision to accept Christ," he said, "your job isn't over. In fact, it's just beginning.

"When Brenda was born, Jill and I didn't just bring her home, set her on the kitchen table, and say, 'There's the refrigerator. Help yourself.'

"Just the opposite happened. We spent long hours looking after Brenda's most basic needs and protecting her from harmful situations.

"We need to treat young Christians with that same kind of care. We need to help them, support them, protect them, teach them, and guide them in the formative stages of their Christian life.

"That's why, immediately after Adventure Week is over, I want you to follow up those who have become Christians during the crusade.

"You can prepare yourself for this task in several ways. Pray that your visit will be fruitful. Contact your families and arrange a mutually acceptable time to visit. And familiarize yourself with our church's programs so that you can invite people to get involved in these activities.

"I'm rather shy about talking to strangers," said Rita Brown. "What am I supposed to say after a family invites me into their home?"

"You need to get acquainted with the family that you're visiting," explained Jim. "After you've introduced yourself, spend some time talking about such general topics as the weather, the house, work, hobbies, and school. Once you've established a rapport with the family, then you can go on to discuss other matters like the Adventure Week program and our church.

"Next, you need to focus on the child whom you came to visit. If you're visiting a child whom you didn't counsel personally, say something like: 'Bobby, I understand that you made a very important decision during Adventure Week. Can you tell me about it?'

"His reply will help you discover how much he remembers and understands. However, don't expect profound answers. The child may not be accustomed to talking about spiritual matters.

"To help cement the child's decision, applaud the child for taking such an important step, review the plan of salvation, and share with him some of the assurances verses that we mentioned earlier.

"Then, explain to the child how important it is to grow in his Christian faith. Urge him to read his Bible, pray, and get involved in our church's educational activities. To remind him of the necessity of spiritual growth, you might even want to write Colossians 2:6-7 in the flyleaf of his Bible. That passage says:

> So then, just as you received Christ Jesus as Lord, continue to live in him, rooted and built up in him, strengthened in the faith as you were taught, and overflowing with thankfulness.

"If the child comes from a Christian home, emphasize the parent's responsibility in the child's upbringing.[8] Encourage them to attend church regularly, have family devotions, and be a good example. Tell them about our church's collection of books and videos.

Talk about the importance of establishing good friendships and ways our church programs can help the child in that area.

"To help you in your discussion of Christian growth, I've provided you with several copies of a booklet called: 'New Life in Christ.' It's a terrific pamphlet designed for children and covers the essentials of the Christian life.

- It reviews the plan of salvation.

- It talks about the person's relationship with Christ.

- It covers the five basics of the Christian walk: prayer, Bible study, fellowship, witnessing, and obedience.

- It outlines, in exquisite simplicity, the basic doctrines of the Christian faith.

- It also prepares children for the temptations that will come their way and how to ask God for forgiveness.

"We'll be going over that booklet in a few minutes. However, before we do that, let me share with you some more tips about visiting in the home. As you talk with the child's family, make sure to:

- Wear a friendly and sincere smile.

- Stand and sit tall.

- Speak clearly and pleasantly.

- Avoid religious jargon.

- Be positive. Don't argue with the family and don't criticize people or churches.

- Use a "soft-sell" approach. Don't carry a large Bible or "hit people over the head" with religion.

- Show a personal interest in the child's family and make them feel worthwhile.

- Use the names of the family members in your conversation.

- Get the family members to talk and then be a good listener.

- Take along a good friend. Two can keep the conversation going much better than one can.

- Keep the visit short. It's better to leave while they still want you to stay than to stay and have them wish that you would leave.

- Make a graceful exit. Watch for a natural break point, thank the family for their time, and leave on a positive note.

"Before you leave, answer any questions that the child has and assure both him and his family that the church stands ready to assist them in any way possible.]

"Immediately, after your visit, fill out the follow-up cards enclosed in your counseling packets. On them, write down as much information as you can remember about the family: names, approximate ages, church affiliation, hobbies, interests, and their response to your time with them.

"During the ensuing weeks, follow up as the situation allows. When you see the family at church, make a special point of talking with them. If you've promised to send them some information or provide them with a ride, make sure you do so.

"Now, let's get back to the booklet that I mentioned earlier, 'New Life in Christ.'"

As Jim discussed the pamphlet's features and allowed his trainees to role play their follow-up visits, he became increasingly excited about the grounding that each new Christian would receive. He could tell that the workshop's participants were eager to put their new knowledge and skills to work.

POINTS TO PONDER

1. Imagine that you're a nonChristian who is visiting a home Bible study or a Sunday School class for the first time. How do you feel? What questions do you have? What would make you feel at home? What would make you feel uncomfortable?

2. Why do people refuse to become Christians? How can you overcome these barriers?

3. How can you follow-up a new Christian who comes from a home that is hostile toward Christianity?

4. Do you think it was right for Jim to make it difficult for children to accept Christ during his church's crusade?

PRACTICAL PROJECTS

1. Make a gospel tract of your own. Be creative.

2. Visit three different churches. Then write a paper which describes your experiences and your evaluation of how you were treated as a visitor.

3. Share the gospel with someone you know. Then write an account of your experience. Tell your reader how you felt and what you would do differently if you had another chance.

4. Outline a three-hour workshop which you can use to train people how to witness and how to encourage new Christians to grow in their faith.

17

The Ups and Downs
of Life

(SUCCESS AND FAILURE)

As Jim rose to speak, thunderous applause erupted in the church's sanctuary. The Sunday School's Christmas program had been a resounding success.

After Jim offered some closing remarks and the benediction, Bill Chamberlin walked up to him, and said, "Congratulations, Jim. That was the best Christmas performance I have ever seen. You ought to be really proud of yourself and your team members."

Although Jim responded with an appropriately humble thank-you, he could barely contain himself. The production had been out-standing. Jim wanted to pat himself on the back and shout with glee, "It was kind of good, wasn't it?"

SUCCESS

Jim knew, from past experience, that this kind of achievement would mean a great deal not only to him, but also to other people. It would:

- Encourage other team members.[1]

- Bless the people who participated.[2]

- Boost his confidence and give him a sense of accomplishment.[3]

- Build other people's confidence in him.[4]

- Bring him new responsibilities.[5]

- Bring him recognition and notoriety.[6]

- Produce new friends and additional support.[7]

- Encourage him to accomplish even more in the future.[8]

- Quiet the critical comments of some of his opponents.[9] In fact, now that Jim had them on the run,[10] he was tempted to gloat over his critics and those who said his ideas wouldn't work.[11]

The next day, Jim called Bob Sparkman to share with him the good news of his triumph. His friend and confident was pleased and congratulated him on the church's excellent program.[12] However, Bob also issued a warning.

"It's OK to savor your successes,"[13] said Bob. "However, as you do, remember a few things.

"Success is a very perishable commodity.[14] I'm sure that your church members will eventually remind you of an old sports adage which says: "You're only as good as your last victory."

"Success never yields perfection. So don't let up. There are still many things at your church that need to be improved.[15]

"Success is a two-edged sword. Although it has its advantages, it also its drawbacks. "Success heightens people's expectations. From now on, your church members are going to demand even more from you.

"Also, success can unite your enemies and lead to vigorous attacks.[16] This is especially true if your opponents are jealous of your accomplishments.[17]

"When a leader is successful, he's tempted to take credit for what God has done.[18] Secular leaders might say that you've been successful because of your leadership skills, tireless efforts, excellent training, and superior resources.

"If you begin to think that way too, you'll soon forget God[19] and how much He has contributed to your achievements.[20] In Deuteronomy 8, Moses gives us an important warning:

> When you have eaten and are satisfied, praise the Lord your God for the good land he has given you. Be careful that you do not forget the Lord your God, failing to observe his commands, his laws and his

decrees that I am giving you this day. Otherwise, when you eat and are satisfied, when you build fine houses and settle down, and when your herds and flocks grow large and your silver and gold increase and all you have is multiplied, then your heart will become proud and you will forget the Lord your God, who brought you out of Egypt, out of the land of slavery. . . . You may say to yourself, "My power and the strength of my hands have produced this wealth for me." But remember the Lord your God, for it is he who gives you the ability to produce wealth.[21]

"Success often carries within itself the seeds of failure.[22] Why? Because, after a victory, people tend to become overconfident, lazy, and complacent.[23] They develop bloated bureaucracies and cast their 'tried and true' programs and procedures in cement. Their adherence to tradition and their desire to preserve the 'good old days'[24] prevents them from being creative, taking advantage of new opportunities, and solving old deficiencies.

"So, if you want to survive your own success, you'll have to continually demand excellence, strive for improvement, and reformulate your organizations and methods to meet changing needs, circumstances and personnel.

"Watch out for temptations and troubles. They're bound to follow your achievements.[25]

"The lives of David and Solomon both exemplify this principle. While these leaders were young, they honored God. In turn, God blessed them. However, after they had reigned as kings for a number of years, they started to stray from God's commands.[26] They were spoiled by their own success.

"One of the greatest temptations that you'll face in victory is the sin of pride. When you're treated like you're someone special,[27] it's hard to retain your humility.[28] But you'd better hang on to it as tightly as you can, because an egotistical attitude will lead you to certain failure.[29] As the Bible says, 'Pride goes before destruction.'"[30]

By the time Jim and Bob finally finished their conversation, Jim was a little disappointed. He had hoped that Bob would be more effervescent in his praise. However, by now, Jim had learned to appreciate Bob's style, comments, and actions. Although they were a bit somber and preachy, they always had Jim's best interests in mind.

Before moving on to his next task, Jim wanted to record some of the tips that Bob had given him. So, he pulled out his leadership diary and jotted down the following ideas.

"What to Do After You Succeed."

- Praise God for your achievements.[31]

- Use your successes as witnessing opportunities to bring glory to God and turn people toward Him.[32]

- Recognize the contributions of your team members[33]— through public praise, private congratulations, thank-you cards, program notes, newsletter comments, and annual reports.

- Learn from your achievements. Ask yourself: "Why was I so successful?" Then, incorporate those elements into your other plans and activities.

- Keep the promises that you've made to God[34] and to other people[35] who have helped you reach your goals.

- Celebrate your victories with your team members.[36] The party after the Christmas program was as much fun as the program itself.

- Establish audio and/or visual records of your accomplishments.[37] For example, portions of the Christmas program's video could be shown in the new members class, in Sunday School classes, and at church anniversaries.

- Capitalize on your successes to launch new programs and ideas.

- Publicize your successes.[38] All of your triumphs may not be as visible as the Christmas program.

Highlight your team's quiet accomplishments in your staff meetings, church council meetings, and annual reports. Also, mention them in your casual conversations, sermons, and Bible studies.

FAILURE

A few days after the Christmas program Jim sat down at the kitchen table to compose his section of the church's annual report. The task proved more difficult than he had anticipated.

Jill could see that Jim was struggling for the right words that would summarize his first year at Bethel Church. She came alongside her husband and tried to encourage him. "Are you going to be able to limit yourself to just one page? After all, you've accomplished quite a lot since January. You've established a teacher training program, improved the church's facilities, revitalized the children's choir, and launched programs for single adults and deaf children."

"That's true," replied Jim in a somber tone. "However, I haven't done as much some other Christian educators in the area. Just look at Ray Billinger over at Sacramento Heights or Stanley Hodges over at Grace Temple. Both of them have nicer facilities, bigger budgets, and more dynamic youth ministries than I do."

Jill quickly realized that Jim was struggling not so much with his words as with his efforts. "Shame on you," she scolded. "You're always telling people to stop comparing themselves to others.[39] And, look at you now. You're not heeding your own advice.

"Besides don't be so envious of those fellows. They have problems that you don't even know about."

"What do you mean?" Jim asked.

"Did you know that Reverend Billinger has been paying so much attention to his church ministry that he's failed to minister to his own family? It may surprise you to know that he's getting a divorce and his son is on drugs.

"And, how would you define success? From what I hear, Reverend Hodges' youth program has a lot of glamour and glitz, fun and frolicking but it's almost devoid of Christian content. Would you call that a successful ministry?

"Isn't success knowing God's will and doing it? If so, I think you're succeeding admirably."

Jim was stunned by his wife's revelations. "How do you know so much about the lives of those pastors?" he wondered. "Maybe I need to get better acquainted with my colleagues."

"So, let me repeat myself," Jill continued. "The church's educational program has really moved forward under your direction. You ought to be pleased with your efforts."

"Maybe. However, this year hasn't been without its bumps and bruises," objected Jim. "I think of the times, for example, that I was so preoccupied with church work that I didn't really spend enough time with you or the girls. Clashes with church people like Mrs. Rutledge and Mike Todd often hurt my ministry. I've also experienced a number of setbacks like the Sunday School's 'February Flop' and Holly's sudden desertion.

"And then there are my goals. In quite a few cases, they haven't proved very seaworthy. Some, like my desire to get involved in a Master of Divinity program, have never made it out of the harbor. Others, like my attempt to get an athletic program started, temporarily capsized when I ran into unexpected storms. Still others, like my efforts to increase our Sunday School's attendance by 20 percent, haven't yet reached their port."

By this time, Jill was really getting frustrated. *How could Jim be in such a gloomy mood after he had put together such a terrific Christmas program?*[40] she wondered.

"So you're not perfect!" chided Jill.[41] "Let's face it. No one is—except God.[42]

"We all mess up from time to time. Even people like Abraham, Moses, David, and Peter failed. And, when they goofed, they did so in a big way.

"At least you're willing to admit your mistakes, Jim. Too many leaders think they're successful. But, in God's eyes, they're abject failures. They just haven't realized it yet.[43]

"There are also some people who know that they've failed but they deal with their failures inappropriately. Initially, they may try to cover up their sins and blunders, hoping that nobody will notice.[44]

"When that tactic proves insufficient, they start to play 'The Blame Game' like Adam,[45] Eve,[46] Aaron,[47] and Saul[48] did in the Bible. Their favorite scapegoats[49] are incompetent team members, unsupportive church members, and an unresponsive God.

"Then, if that ploy doesn't work, they excuse themselves by citing difficult and unpredictable circumstances: the equipment broke down or 'the weather was inclement'. Amazingly, they never blame themselves. They never admit that their defeat was a result of poor planning, procrastination, or the absence of contingency plans.

"If all else fails, some leaders simply pack their bags and leave. Their favorite motto is: 'The grass is always greener on the other side of the fence.'[50]

"Now, it's true. Unforeseen circumstances do come up, people do let you down and sometimes it's wise to start over again. But there are those who have turned excuse-giving and finger-pointing into a fine art because they use it so much.

"I'm so glad, Jim, that that's not your style. You believe in accountability[51] and accepting responsibility for your actions. That takes courage.

"By the way, aren't you leading the 'Early Risers' Bible study next week? Why don't you discuss the subject of failure with them? I'm sure you'll get a good response."

Jim took Jill's advice and designed a study around the topic: "Facing Failure." By the time he had finished his preparations, Jim felt sure that he had a dynamite lesson to share with his friends, a group of businessmen who came together each Monday morning from 6:00 to 7:00 a.m. to study the Bible.

However, when he announced the morning's theme, he was startled by their quick and negative reaction. Together they let out one loud, collective groan. "What a depressing way to start the week," complained Doug.

Jim let the shot just whiz past his head. "Actually," he said in a calm, matter-of-face voice, "I think you'll find the topic rather interesting and inspiring."

During the first half of the study, Jim's group used the following outline to study the life of King Manasseh and how this monarch dealt with failure.

1. Manasseh's Moral Failure (2 Chron. 33:1-9; 2 Kings 21:1-9,16)

2. God's Warning (2 Chron. 33:10; 2 Kings 21:10-15)

3. Manasseh's Punishment (2 Chron. 33:11)

4. Manasseh's Repentance (2 Chron. 33:12)

5. Manasseh's Restoration (2 Chron. 33:13)

6. Manasseh's Success (2 Chron. 33:14-17)

During the second half of the study, Jim asked the group: "OK. How does this passage apply to our lives?" The group's response was instructive.

"First of all, like Manasseh, you have to confess your sins to God and/or admit to people that you've made mistakes," said Clint Wagner. "And, let me tell you from experience, that saying 'I'm sorry' to one of your business colleagues, family members, or trusted friends is one of the hardest things that you can do. It makes you so vulnerable."

"I don't know if that's so bad," said Dan Rivers. "I think people appreciate leaders who aren't perfect and don't know everything. It makes them more . . . approachable."

"It also gives you a chance to encourage your workers," [52] said Doug Saxby.

"A lot of people see me for the highly successful, extremely wealthy man that I am now," he chuckled, tongue-in-cheek. "Most people don't know the problems that I've had to overcome or the mistakes that I've made climbing the so-called 'ladder of success.' However, when I tell them about my experiences—good and bad— they realize that they can be successful too."

"I have problems with that," said Mike Todd emphatically. "When you admit your mistakes to others, they often use those failures as weapons to hurt you. While we're assured of God's forgive-ness,[53] people aren't always so understanding."

"If people aren't willing to forgive you, don't worry about it," re-marked Clint. "You've done your part."

"I do worry about it, especially if my confessions are going to haunt me in the future," retorted Mike.

"Mike, you said that God will always forgive us when we confess our sins to Him," said Doug. "That's true. However, that doesn't necessarily mean that we're always going to get off 'scot-free.' I think whenever we fail, we're going to experience the consequences of our actions[54]—and we'd better realize that.

"Look at Manasseh in our passage. He reaped the fruits of his sin. In fact, even after he resumed his reign, his people wouldn't follow his righteous example because he had done such a good job of lead-ing them astray in the first place.

"Remember David? After he committed adultery with Bathsheba and had Uriah murdered, this powerful king had to pay the price for his wickedness, even though God forgave him.[55] In the end, David's actions cost him a son who died shortly after his birth and a son who died because he rebelled against his father.

"Inevitably, failures produce negative results. They damage rela-tionships; they produce stress and trauma;[56] they expose you to crit-icism and the ridicule of your enemies;[57] they instill fear in the heart of your workers;[58] they make people unwilling to help you out;[59] they turn people against you;[60] and they set you up for more fail-ures.[61]

"That's one of the reasons why we should try to avoid failure in the first place."

"Even though we may reap what we sow," Jim said, "I want to stress the fact again that God does love us. God is merciful. God treats us better than we deserve. And, God does forgive us, if we confess our sins to Him."[62]

"Our passage doesn't discuss this point," said Bill Chamberlin, "but I think it's important to perform an autopsy whenever we fail. We need to ask ourselves: 'What went wrong?' 'How did we get ourselves into this mess?' This is exactly what Jesus' disciples did when they couldn't heal a boy who was demon possessed.[63] Like-wise, Joshua analyzed his troops' defeat after they returned from the battle of Ai.[64]

"When you evaluate your failures, you may be able to trace the their source to sin,[65] laziness, poor communication,[66] insufficient faith,[67] inadequate planning,[68] poor organization or careless implementation."

"Or, you may discover that God has called you to do a task that will never result in success, as the world sees it," said Clint. "No matter. If God wants you to do it, you better obey Him. Isaiah faced that dilemma when God told him to speak to his own nation—a decidedly stubborn group of people who would never did listen to his message."[69]

"When you fail," added Dan, "there's another thing that you should do. You should learn from your errors.[70] Mistakes are too costly to waste. As my history teacher used to say: 'Those who fail to learn from history are bound to repeat it.'

"And, you really haven't learned anything unless you alter your ways[71] and try a new approach.[72] After the defeat at Ai, Joshua made some major changes. He dealt with the sin in his camp; he went out a second time, with a larger army; and he followed a new game plan which he had received directly from God."[73]

"Sometimes, you need to seek out expert help and advice before making those changes," suggested Bill. "A good consultant, counselor, or support group can help you with that."

"After a major setback, you may also need to take some time off, rest, exercise, and recharge your batteries,"[74] said Dan.

"But, you don't want to spend too much time wallowing in the 'if only's and 'what if's of self-examination," warned Doug. "Otherwise, you'll never take the last and most vital step. In order to completely recover from your failures, you have to leave those failures behind and move forward.[75] You have to focus on the future and seek out new opportunities.

PERSISTANCE

"Oh, I don't know. Sometimes I think it's just easier to quit," moaned Mike.

"Really?" asked Clint. "Is it really that easy to live with unfulfilled dreams, self-pity, regret, unresolved problems, negative memories, and a wounded spirit? I don't think so."

"Sure. Who wants to be a fireworks Christian?" agreed Dan.

"A what?" asked Mike.

"A fireworks Christian," repeated Dan. "That is, a quitter who burns brightly but briefly."

"What would happen if toddlers would suddenly stop trying to walk just because they had fallen down before?" asked Bill. "They'd become physical invalids. If we give up, give in or give out when difficulties come our way, we'll become mental invalids."

"Paul is a good example of someone who had a bulldog tenacity and a dogged determination to see things through to the end," added Jim.

"In his letter to Galatia, Paul *condemns* those who lacked persistence. He says: 'I am astonished that you are so quickly deserting the one who called you by the grace of Christ and are turning to a different gospel.'[76]

"In his letter to Thessalonica, Paul *commends* those who displayed persistence. He says: 'Therefore, among God's churches we boast about your perseverance and faith in all the persecutions and trials you are enduring?'[77]

"In his letter to Corinth, Paul *commands* us to be persistent in the Christian life. He says: 'Therefore, my dear brothers, stand firm. Let nothing move you. Always give yourselves fully to the work of the Lord, because you know that your labor in the Lord is not in vain.'"[78]

Bill chuckled. "Jim, it sounds like you're preparing a sermon on 'The Power of Patient Persistence.'"

"I plead guilty," offered Jim with his right hand raised. "You just heard a sample of my New Year's Eve talk. What do you think?"

Not wanting to wander too far astray, Clint said: "I think the thing that impresses me most about Paul is not that he preached persistence but that he practiced it. In the midst of sufferings, he sang, witnessed, and helped people who were in need. He could say in 2 Corinthians:

> We are hard pressed on every side, but not crushed; perplexed, but not in despair; persecuted but not abandoned; struck down, but not destroyed. . . . Therefore we do not lose heart. Though outwardly we are wasting away, yet inwardly we are being renewed day by day.[79]

"That's because he was goal-oriented," said Doug. "One of my favorite passages in the Bible is found is Philippians 3:12-14. In those verses, Paul says:

> Not that I have already obtained all this, or have already been made perfect, but I press on to take hold of that for which Christ Jesus took hold of me. Brothers, I do not consider myself yet to have taken hold of it. But one thing I do: Forgetting what is behind and straining toward what is ahead, I press on toward the goal to win the prize for which God has called me heavenward in Christ Jesus.

"That's an amazing statement, especially when you consider his circumstances. He spoke those words in the last years of his life. He could have said, like I hear some many senior citizens say, 'I'm retiring. Let the younger ones take over the work of the church.'

"Paul also uttered those words when he was in prison. Most of us would probably sulk in quiet resignation and say to ourselves, 'Well, that's the end of my ministry; there's nothing I can do now.' Not Paul. He used this time to encourage his fellow believers and witness to nonbelievers.

"Lastly, Paul made those comments after he had experienced a great deal of success. Yet he didn't have the attitude of Alexander the Great who reportedly complained: 'Woe is me. There are no more worlds to conquer.' And, he didn't possess the mind-set of the Pharisees who thought they had arrived because they knew so much about the law.

"Just the opposite was true of Paul. He was always looking for new ways to enlarge his ministry and to become more like Christ."

As the chime on the restaurant's clock began to announce seven o'clock, Jim said: "Well, I can see that our Scripture memory program is paying off. So let me close our study with one more Bible verse. It ought to encourage all of us as we continue to serve the Lord.

"In Galatians 6:9, Paul says: 'Let us not become weary in doing good, for at the proper time we will reap a harvest if we do not give up.'"[80]

POINTS TO PONDER

1. Why is it so hard for leaders to admit that they've failed?

2. Which is harder to handle: success or failure? Why?

3. Which failings should a leader confess and which ones should he avoid mentioning?

4. Are leaders who publicize their victories guilty of sinful pride? Why or why not?

5. What is the difference between a mistake and a sin?

6. When is it time to leave a church?

7. What kind of good things can come from failure?

PRACTICAL PROJECTS

1. Memorize Galatians 6:9; Psalm 37:23-24; and Isaiah 41:30-31.

2. Interview someone who has experienced success in their ministry. Ask them to tell you about three of their most memorable successes and what they learned from those experiences.

3. Interview someone who has experienced failure in their ministry. Ask them to tell you about one of their failures and what they learned from that experience.

Notes

Chapter 1—Evaluation

1. Josh. 2:1–24; see Num. 13:1–33; Judg. 7:9–15
2. Neh. 2:11–16
3. 1 Sam. 1:3–17
4. Luke 4:24
5. Matt. 9:28; 12:11–12, 26–27; 16:15; Luke 10:36; John 5:47; 6:67; 8:46; 14:9
6. Phil. 2:14–15b
7. Prov. 13:18; see also Prov. 9:8; 6:20,23; 15:10, 12, 14, 32; 27:17; 32:5–6; Ps. 141:5
8. Prov. 12:16; 15:1; 18:13; Jas. 1:19
9. Ex. 5:15–21; 14:10–18; 15:22–26; 16:1–3; 17:1; Deut. 1:19–46; Num. 14:1–10; 16:41–50; 20:2–5; 21:4–9; Neh. 2:17–20; 4:1–3, 7–8; 5:1–13; 6:1–14
10. Gen. 25:29–34; 27:1–45
11. 1 Pet. 2:12–22; 3:1–2, 15–17; 4:12–16
12. Prov. 15:1
13. Matt. 16:21–23; Acts 4:18–20; Neh. 6:1–16
14. Luke 23:34–41

Chapter 2—Goal Setting

1. Num. 13

2. Ps. 37:5
3. Matt. 10:38
4. Luke 14:25–23
5. Phil. 4:6
6. Prov. 15:29; Mark 11:24; John 14:13–14; 1 John 3:22
7. Luke 11:5–13

Chapter 3—Creativity

1. Alex F. Osborn, *Applied Imagination*, 3rd rev. ed. (New York: Charles Scribner's Sons, 1963), 286–87.
2. Matt. 5:13–16
3. Matt. 13:44–51
4. Luke 15:3–32
5. Gen. 1–2; Josh. 6; Judg. 7; Isa. 55:8

Chapter 4—Decision Making

1. 1 Tim. 4:12; 1 Sam. 17:33; 1 Kings 3:7–15; Jer.1:6–8
2. Rom. 12:1–2; Prov. 3:5–6
3. Pss. 40:8; 25:4
4. Jonah 1:1–12; Matt. 26:39
5. Luke 6:14; Acts 1:24
6. Mark 12:30
7. Luke 10:25–36
8. 2 Tim. 4:1–2; Matt. 13:13–17; Isa. 6:9–13; 42:16–17
9. 1 Cor. 1:17–2:5
10. Josh. 612
11. Judg. 7:1–8
12. 1 Sam. 17:38–40
13. Isa. 5:21; Prov. 9:10; Jas. 1:5
14. Prov. 11:14, KJV; See also Prov. 12:15; 15:22; 19:20
15. 2 Chron. 10:1–17
16. Dan. 6
17. 1 Kings 22:1–28; 2 Chron. 18:1–27
18. Deut. 18:21–22; 1 Kings 22:28
19. Matt. 28:19–20
20. Ps. 82:3–4
21. 1 Pet. 3:8

22. Eph. 6:10–12
23. Matt. 1:20–24; 2:19–23
24. Acts 9:10–19
25. Acts 10:9–35
26. Ex. 13:21–22
27. Matt 16:1–4; Luke 1:18–20; John 4:48
28. Acts 8:26–31
29. Acts 10:17–23; 11:7–11
30. Acts 13:1–3; 16:6–8; 20:22–24; 21:11
31. Jer. 7:24; Judg. 17:6; 21:25; Prov. 12:15
32. 1 Sam. 24; 26
33. 1 Sam. 24:6; 26:9–11
34. Isa. 6:9–10; 43:8
35. Isa. 6:8
36. Job 1:5; Dan. 6:10; Acts 17:2
37. Matt. 15:1–9; Acts 16:20–22
38. Gen. 16:1–16; 21:1–21
39. Ps. 27:14
40. Josh. 3:14–17
41. Jas. 1:6–8
42. Zig Ziglar, *See You at the Top* (Gretna: Pelican Publishing Company, 1975), 38.

Chapter 5—Planning

1. Ex. 7:14–11:10
2. Hag. 1:2–9
3. Eccl. 3:1–8, 17; 8:6; John 7:6–7; Gal. 4:4
4. Author unknown
5. Rom. 13:8; Prov. 22:7
6. Gen. 14:20; 28:22; Ex. 25:1–9; 35:4–36:7; Lev. 27:30–33; Deut. 12:6, 11, 17; 16:17; 1 Chron. 29:1–9; Prov. 3:9–10; Mal. 3:8–11; Mark 12:41–44; Acts 4:32–37; 2 Cor. 8–9; Phil. 4:14–19; Heb. 7:1–9
7. Based on a quote by J. Hudson Taylor as cited by Bill Gothard, *Men's Manual: Volume II* (Oak Brook, Ill.: Institute in Basic Youth Conflicts, Inc., 1983).
8. Matt. 14:13–21; Mark 6:30–44; Luke 9:10–17; John 6:1–14

9. Gen. 22:1–14
10. Phil. 4:19; Matt. 6:25–34
11. Ex. 16:1–17:7
12. 1 Kings 17:2–24
13. Eph. 4:20; Prov. 3:5–10
14. John 16:12–13
15. Luke 12:16–21
16. Jas. 4:13–15; Acts 18:21; Prov. 27:1
17. Prov. 16:3, 9, 20:24; Ps. 37:5

Chapter 6—Recruitment

1. Matt. 4:18–22; 9:9
2. Matt. 19:27; 10:37–39; Luke 14:25–33; 9:57–62
3. Ezek. 22:30; Luke 10:2
4. Ex. 3:1–4:18; Judg. 6:11–15; Isa. 6:1–8; Jer.1:4—10
5. Judg. 6:11–22, 36–40; 7:9–16; Ex. 4:1–9
6. Jonah 1:1–17
7. Matt. 19:16–22
8. Luke 9:57–62
9. John 6:66; Matt. 24:9–11; Luke 9:62; 22:1–6, 47–53
10. Phil. 4:19; Matt. 6:25–34; Gen. 22:1–14; Eph. 3:20; Prov. 3:5–10
11. Prov. 3:5–6; 16:3; 28:25; Pss. 55:22; 62:8; Heb. 11:6
12. Matt. 9:37–38
13. Matt. 20:20–28; Mark 9:33–35; 10:35–45; Luke 22:24–27; Phil. 2:4, 20–21; John 13:1–17; Gal. 5:13; Rom. 12:10; 1 Pet. 5:2–3
14. Matt. 19:27; 10:37–39; Luke 14:25–33; 9:57–62; Acts 20:35
15. 2 Tim. 2:2; Ex. 18:21, 25; 28:3, 6; Judg. 7:2–8; Acts 1:20–26; 1 Tim. 3:1–13; 5:22; Titus 1:5–9; 1 Sam. 16:1–13
16. 1 Cor. 1:26–29, 31; See also: 1 Cor. 2:1–5
17. Acts 4:13
18. 1 Cor. 12:1; 14:20
19. Phil. 4:6–7

Chapter 7—Training

1. Phil. 3:12–14

Chapter 8—Building Team Relationships

1. Gal. 6:2; Eccl. 4:9–12; Phil. 1:5
2. 1 Cor. 12:12–27; Acts 2:42–47; 1 Pet. 3:8
3. Col. 1:3–4, 9–12; 4:12–13
4. Ex. 32:7–14, 30–35; 15:22–25; Num. 14:13–20
5. John 17:1, 9–24; Luke 22:31–32; 23:34; 1 Tim. 2:5
6. Phil. 1:3–11; Col. 1:3–4, 9–12; 4:12–13; Rom. 1:8–15; 10:1; Eph. 1:15–23; 3:1, 14–19; 1 Thesss. 1:2–3; 3:10–13; 4:25; 5:17; 23–25
7. 1 Thess. 5:25; Eph. 6:18–19; 2 Cor. 1:10–11; Phil. 1:19
8. Jas. 2:14–26; 1 John 3:17–18
9. Acts 1:14, 24; 4:23–31; 6:4; 12:5,12; Col. 4:2–4, 12; Jas.5:13–18
10. Prov. 11:13; 20:19
11. Jas. 5:13–16; Eph. 6:18–20
12. Eph. 1:15–18; Phil. 1:3–11; Col. 1:3–14; 1 Thess. 1:2–3; 2 Thess. 1:3–12
13. Rom. 12:10b; Phil. 2:25–30; 1 Cor. 16:18; 1 Tim. 5:17
14. Gen. 29:28–30; 30:1, 4–7, 14–15; 37:3–4; 1 Sam. 1:1–7; 18:5–11
15. Luke 17:7–10
16. Gal. 1:10
17. Matt. 8:10b; 15:28; 25:21; Luke 7:37–39, 44–47
18. Rom. 1:8; 16:3–16, 19; 2 Tim. 1:16–18; Phil. 2:19–30
19. Matt. 5:9
20. Luke 10:25–37
21. Matt. 12:7; Hos. 6:6; Mic. 6:6–8; Isa. 1:11–17
22. Jas. 2:14–26; 1 John 3:17–18

Chapter 9—The Art of Speaking

1. Ex. 3:1–10; 4:10–12, 14–16; 6: 12, 30
2. Judg. 6:13–40; Isa. 6:1–8; Jer. 1:1–10
3. Acts 7:22
4. Jas. 1:22–25; 2:14–26; Luke 6:46–49
5. Gen. 9:8–17; Acts 10:9–23; Ex. 4:1–9; 7:1–12:13; 1 Kings 11:29–31; Isa. 20; Jer. 19:1–3, 10–11; Acts 21:10–11; Matt 6:26–30; 18:1–6; 21:18–22; 22:15–22; 27:50–51

6. Voltaire quoted by Dianna Booher, *The Confident Communicator*, 95.

Chapter 10—Communication

1. Gen. 11:1–9
2. Prov. 15:1, 4
3. 1 Sam. 16:7
4. Shakespeare, *Hamlet*. See also: Eccl. 3:1, 7; Prov. 1:5; 10:19; 11:12; 12:15–16, 23; Jas. 1:19–20
5. Prov. 11:13; 17:9

Chapter 11—Motivation

1. Ex. 5:1–18
2. Josh. 14:6–14
3. Ex. 32:30–32; Rom. 9:3; Phil.1:7–8
4. John 2:13–17; Ex. 32:19–32; 1 Kings 19:10; 2 Kings 20:2–3; 2 Chron. 31:20–21; Neh. 4:6; Ps. 42:1–2
5. Rom. 12:11; Matt. 22:37–38; Eccl. 9:10; Col. 3:23; Rev. 3:15–16
6. Matt. 23:1–4
7. 1 Cor. 4:15–16; Phil. 3:17; 4:9; 1 Thess. 1:6–7; 2:10–12, 14; 2 Thess. 3:7–9
8. 1 Cor. 11:1
9. Matt. 23:1–4
10. Matt. 15:7–9; 23:1–33
11. Matt. 15:14; 23:16, 24
12. Philem. 21
13. 2 Cor. 7:4, 14, 16; 8:7; 12:20
14. 2 Cor. 8:1–7
15. 1 Sam. 18:5–11
16. Gen. 37:3–4, 18–36
17. Matt. 6:1–5; 16–18; 15:1–20; 23:1–24
18. 1 Sam. 15:22–23; Isa. 1:11–17; Jer. 7:22–24; Hos. 6:6; Amos 5:21–27; Mic. 6:6–8; Matt. 9:13; 12:7; Mark 12:33; Ps. 51:16–17; 78:34–37; Prov. 21:3
19. John 16:7–11; Acts 16:14
20. Neh. 2:1–10
21. Matt. 2:1–12

22. Dan. 6:1–24
23. 2 Sam. 11:1–12:23
24. Rev. 3:15–16; Mark 12:30; Col. 3:23; Eccl. 9:10a; 1 Chron. 28:9
25. 1 Chron. 28:9; Ps. 139:2, 23; 7:9; Matt. 9:4; 12:25; Jer. 17:10; Prov. 24:12
26. Matt. 6:1–5, 16–18; 23:1–24; 2 Cor. 8:12; 9:7; Isa. 1:11–17
27. Matt. 9:1–8; 13:1–23; 21:31–32; 28:16–17; John 7:30–32, 40–43; 9:13–16; 10:19–21, 31–33, 39–42; Acts 4:1–4; 13:42–52; 14:1–7; 1 Pet. 2:6–8
28. Mark 10:17–22; Luke 9:57–62; Luke 14:15–24; John 6:66
29. Gal. 1:10
30. 3 John 9–10
31. Matt. 20:25b–26
32. 1 Pet. 5:2–3
33. Neh. 13:1–28
34. Ex. 32:15–35
35. Acts 5:1–11; Matt. 16:16–19
36. John 2:12–17; Matt. 16:21–28
37. 1 Pet. 2:13–21; 3:1–7; 5:5; Col. 3:18–4:1; Eph. 5:22–6:9; Rom. 13:1–7; Matt. 16:13–20; 22:21; 1 Tim. 2:2
38. Heb. 13:17
39. Eph. 5:22–6:9; Col. 3:18–14:1; 1 Pet. 2:13–3:7; 5:2–3; John 10:11, 15, 17
40. Ps. 23:1–2; Gen. 29:2–10; John 10:9b; 21:15–18
41. Ps. 23:3; 78:52–53; John 10:3–5; 1 Pet. 2:25; 5:2–3; Isa. 53:6; Jer. 50:6
43. John 10:11–13
42. John 3:16; 10:11, 14, 17–18; 1 John 3:16
44. John 10:4b, 14; Matt. 10:30; Luke 12:7
45. Ps. 23:2–3; Matt. 11:25–30; Isa. 40:28–31; Jer. 33:12
46. 1 Pet. 5:3
47. Ps. 23:4–5; 78:52–53; 1 Sam. 17:34–35; John 10:11–15; Acts 20:28
48. Luke 15:1–7; 1 Pet. 2:25; Isa. 43:6
49. Matt. 20:25b–28b; See: Matt. 23:11–12; Mark 10:42–45; Luke 9:46–48; 18:14; 22:24–27
50. Phil. 2:3–8

51. John 13:1–17; Luke 22:24–27
52. Isa. 55:8; 1 Sam. 8:1–20; Rom. 12:2; Jas. 4:4; John 17:11, 14–18; 2 Cor. 6:14–7:1; 1 John 2:15–17
53. Titus 2:14; 1 Pet. 1:1; 2:9; 1 Cor. 1:26–30; Isa. 43:10, 20; 44:1–2; 55:8

Chapter 12—Handling Conflict

1. Isa. 11:6–9; see Isa. 2:2–4; 35:9; 65:20–25; Ezek. 34:25–29
2. Gen. 4:8
3. Eccl. 7:9; Jas. 1:19–20; Prov. 14:29; 15:18; 16:32; 29:11
4. Matt. 26:69–75; 1 Pet. 2:21–25; 3:9; Prov. 9:7–8; Isa. 53:7
5. Matt. 26:47–56; 1 Sam. 25; Luke 9:51–55; Rom. 12:17; 1 Pet. 3:9
6. Jas. 1:19–20; Prov. 15:1; 24:29; Matt. 5:5
7. Jas. 1:19–20; Prov. 26:20–21
8. Prov. 10:12; 15:18; 17:14; 18:6–7, 19; Matt. 5:25–26
9. Gal. 5:22–23
10. Prov. 22:24–25; 1 Tim. 1:3–4; Titus 3:9
11. Prov. 26:28; 27:6
12. Prov. 27:17
13. Gal. 5:15, 19–21; 1 Cor. 1:10–13; Titus 3:9
14. Gal. 5:15; Matt. 20:20–24; Acts 15:37–40; Prov. 16:28; Mark 3:25
15. Prov. 16:7; Rom. 12:18; 14:19; 2 Cor. 13:11; Heb. 12:14
16. John 17:20–23; Rom. 12:16; 15:5–6; 1 Cor. 1:10; 1 Pet. 3:8
17. Ps. 133:1
18. Gen. 13:1–18. See also: Gen. 26:11–32; 29:21–30
19. Isa. 53:7; Mark 14:57–62; John 10:17–18
20. Matt. 26:47–54; John 3:16
21. 1 Pet. 2:13–3:7; Rom. 13:1–7; Eph. 5:21–6:1–9; Col. 3:18–4:1
22. Prov. 12:16; See: Prov. 19:11; 29:11
23. Matt. 7:1–5; Phil. 2:14; Gal. 5:15; Jas. 4:11–12; 5:9; Jude 14–16
24. Gen. 17:41–45; 26:12–25; 31:1–3; 22–23, 27; Acts 9:22–24
25. Ex. 1:15–2:3; Dan. 3:1–30; 6:1–28; Acts 4:1–31; 5:25–29
26. Mark 14:50; Prov. 24:21–22; Ps.101:2
27. Revised from Croft M. Pentz, *The Complete Book of Zingers* (Wheaton: Tyndale House, 1990), 274.

28. Rom. 12:17; Prov.15:1; 24:29; 1 Thess. 5:15; 1 Pet. 3:9
29. Luke 9:51–56
30. Luke 22:47–53; Matt. 26:47–56
31. Matt. 12:18–21; 16:59–68; 27:27–44; 1 Pet. 2:23
32. Prov. 13:14; 22:15; 23:13–14; 29:15, 17; Eph. 6:4; Col. 3:21
33. Acts 4:17, 21; Ezek. 3:17; 1 Sam. 17:41–47; 2 Chron. 32:9–21
34. Eph. 5:22–33; 6:1–4; Col. 3:18–20; 1 Pet. 3:1–7; Ex. 20:12
35. Heb. 13:17
36. Eph. 6:5–9; Col. 3:22–4:1; 1 Pet. 2:18–21
37. Matt. 22:17–21; Rom. 13:1–7; Titus 3:1; 1 Pet. 2:13–17; 1 Tim. 2:1–3; Num. 16:1–50
38. 1 Kings 21:1–16; 2 Sam. 11:1–27; Matt. 2:16–18; 14:1–12
39. 1 Kings 21:1–16
40. 2 Sam. 11:1–27
41. Matt. 8:26; 11:20–24; 14:31; 16:23; 21:12–13; 23:13–36
42. Neh. 5:6–13; 13:6–31
43. 1 Cor. 3:1–23; 5:1–5; 11:17–22; 14:20–40; 2 Thess. 3:6–15; Gal. 2:11–14; 3:1–6
44. Adapted from Arlo Grenz's "Learning to Love" manual, 1989, 52–53, 99–100.
45. Heb. 12:4–11; Prov. 3:11–12; Rev. 3:19; Eph. 4:15
46. Gen. 34:1–29; Dan. 6:1–28; 1 Kings 21:1–16
47. Rom. 12:17–19; Prov. 17:13; 24:29; Lev. 19:18; 1 Thess. 5:15
48. Acts 15; Gen. 30:25–43
49. Ex. 34:11–16; 2 John 7–11
50. Ex. 18:13–26; 1 Kings 3:16–28; Acts 15:1–35; 18:23–41
51. 1 Cor. 6:1–8
52. Acts 1:21–26; 15
53. Acts 15:36–40
54. 1 Cor. 5:1–2, 6; Heb. 12:6:10, 10:31; Acts 5:5, 11
55. Matt. 18:15–20; Acts 5:1–11; Rom. 16:17–18; 1 Cor. 5:1–13; 2 Cor. 2:5–11; Gal. 2:11–14; 6:1–5; Col. 3:16; 1 Thess. 5:12, 21–22; 2 Thess. 3:6–15; 2 Tim 2:22–26; 4:2; Titus 1:10–14; 2:15; 3:10; Jas. 5:15–20; 1 John 4:1–3; 2 John 9–11
56. Ezek. 3:18
57. Josh. 7:11–12; Num. 14:39–45; Acts 5:1–15; John 15:1–2
58. Eph. 5:25–27; 1 Cor. 5:7, 13

59. Jas. 5:19–20; Ezek. 3:16–18; Heb. 10:31

60. Acts 5:1–14; John 15:1–2

61. 1 Cor. 5:6–7; Heb. 12:15; 2 Tim. 2:16–18

62. Jas. 5:19–20; Heb. 12:10–11; Ps. 51:7–15; Matt. 3:2; 4:17

63. Jas. 1:15; 1 Tim. 5:21

64. 1 Tim. 5:19; Deut. 17:6; 19:15–20; Num. 35:30; Matt. 18:16; 2 Cor. 13:1; Prov. 3:30; 18:13; 1 Sam. 1:9–17

65. 1 John 5:16; 1 Tim. 2:1; 1 Sam. 12:23; Matt. 18:15–20; Ex. 32:9–14, 30–35; 34:8–9; Num. 11:1–2; 12:1–16; 14:10–25

66. Matt. 18:15–16; Luke 17:3; Gal. 6:1

67. 1 Cor. 6:1–8

68. 2 Cor. 7:8–10; Matt. 18:15

69. 2 Cor. 2:6–7, 10; Luke 17:3–4; 11:4; 23:34; Mark 11:25; Matt. 18:21–35; 6:12, 14–15; Eph. 4:32; Col. 3:13; Ex. 34:6–7; John 3:16

70. 2 Cor. 2:8; 1 Cor. 13; 14:1; John 3:16; 13:34–35; 15:12, 17; 1 John 3:16; 4:9–11, 16, 19; Eph. 5:2, 25; Col. 3:14; Rom. 12:10; 13:8–10

71. Luke 15:4–10, 20–24

72. 2 Cor. 2:7–8

73. Luke 15:11–32; Gal. 6:1; 1 Cor. 2:6–8; Acts 9:1–27

74. Jer. 31:34b; Isa. 43:25; Ps. 103:12; 32:1–2; Rom. 4:7–8

75. Mark 11:25; Luke 17:3–4; Eph. 4:31–32; Col. 3:12–15

76. 2 Cor. 2:9–11

77. Matt. 6:12, 14–15; 18:21–3; Luke 11:14

78. Eph. 4:32; 5:1–2; 1 John 4:10–11; Col. 3:13; Matt. 18:21–35

79. 1 Tim. 1:18–20; 5:19–20; Gal. 2:11, 14

80. 1 Tim. 3:2, 7, 10, 5:22–25; Titus 1:6–7; Jas. 3:1; Lev. 21–22

81. 1 Tim. 3:2, 7, 10; 5:22–25; Titus 1:6–7; Jas 3:1; Lev. 21–22

82. Luke 3:8; Matt. 3:8

83. Ps. 32:5; Prov. 28:13; 2 Sam. 12:13–14; 2 Cor. 7:8–10; Matt. 7:15–20; Acts 19:17–20; 26:20; Jer. 18:11; 35:15; 1 Tim. 1:12–17

84. Matt. 18:15–17; Prov. 1:23–33; 9:7–9; 13:1; 15:12, 32

85. 1 Tim. 5:20; Gal. 2:11–14; Matt. 18:17

86. 1 Cor. 5:5; 1 Tim. 1:18–20

87. Matt. 18:17; John 9:22; 1 Cor. 5:9–11, 13; 2 Thess. 3:6, 14–15; 2 Tim. 3:5; Titus 3:10; 2 John 10–11; 3 John 9–10; Neh. 13:1–3; Ezra 10:8
88. Luke 17:3; 2 Cor. 2:6–8
89. J. Carl Laney, *A Guide to Church Discipline* (Minneapolis: Bethany House, 1985).
90. Heb. 12:15; Eph. 4:31; Jas. 3:14
91. 1 John 4:9–10; John 3:16
92. Phil. 2:8; Eph. 4:1–3
93. 1 Pet. 3:18
94. Rom. 12:19; Ps. 37:1–2, 12–17, 20
95. Luke 6:35; Matt. 5:9–12, 45; Prov. 25:22
96. Prov. 16:7
97. Rom. 12:20; Prov. 25:22; Ps. 140:9–10
98. 1 Pet. 2:12, 15; 3:15–17; 4:14–16
99. 2 Thess. 3:14; Titus 1:13; Heb. 12:10–13; Gal. 6:1–2

Chapter 13—Problem Solving

1. Ezra 9:13
2. John 9:2–3; Prov. 11:17; 22:8; 1 Pet. 4:15; Gal. 6:7–8
3. Heb. 12:5–13; Prov. 3:11–12; 1 Cor. 11:28, 32; Gen. 3:16–19; Ex. 32:31–34
4. Gen. 4:8; 37:19–20; 1 Kings 21:1–16
5. Gen. 40:13–23; 1 John 3:17–18; Jas. 2:14–17; Luke 10:30–32; 16:19–21
6. Matt. 5:10–12; 10:16–25; Mark 13:9–13; John 15:18–21; 2 Tim. 3:12; 1 Pet. 4:12–19; Phil. 1:29; 2 Cor. 4:7–12; Dan. 3:8–30; 6:1–28
7. Job 1:8–22; 1 Pet. 5:8–9; Rev. 2:10
8. Josh. 7:20–26; Ex. 11:27–28; 12:12; Num. 14:18; Prov. 11:29; 15:27
9. Gen. 39:6b–20a; Acts 4:1–4, 8–12; 6:8–10, 12
10. Jas. 1:2–4, 12; 1 Pet. 1:6–7; Heb. 12:10–11; John 15:1–2, 8
11. Gen. 22:1–2; Heb. 11:17; Ex. 15:23–25; 20:20; Deut. 8:2
12. John 9:1–3; 11:1–4
13. Num. 22:21–33; Ex. 7–11; Judg. 16
14. 1 Kings 20:17
15. Job 5:6–7; 14:1; Matt. 5:45; 1 Pet. 4:12; John 16:33

16. Eph. 4:26; Matt. 5:23–26; Prov. 15:23; 25:11; Eph. 4:31; Heb. 12:15

17. Ex. 7:20–24; Dan. 6:8, 14–15

18. Luke 18:31–34; 24:5–8

19. Kenneth O. Gangel, *Feeding and Leading* (Wheaton: Victor Books), 150.

20. Rom. 8:28, KJV

21. Jas. 2:14–26; 1 John 3:17–18; John 5:5–7; Luke 5:18–20

22. Jas. 5:13–16; 2 Sam. 15:13–18; 2 Kings 20:1–6; 2 Cor. 12:7–10

23. Ps. 10:1; 22:1–2; 38:1–22; 42:9–10; 77:7–9

24. 1 Thess. 5:18; Phil. 4:6

25. Deut. 1:26–33; 3:21–22; 31:1–8; Josh. 1:5; 2 Cor. 1:10

26. Ps. 18:16–19; 34:17–19; 54:6–7; Jer. 39:17–18; 2 Tim. 4:16–18

27. Phil. 4:13; Ps. 46:1–2; 61:1–4

28. Isa. 49:13; Jer. 31:13; Matt. 5:4; 2 Cor. 1:3–5; 7:6

29. Ps. 23:4; 118:6–7; Isa. 43:2; Heb. 13:15b; Deut. 31:3–6

30. Gen. 50:20; Ex. 1:11–12; Deut. 8:15–16; Heb. 12:11

31. 1 Cor 12:26

32. John 6:66–69; 2 Tim. 4:16; Matt. 26:14–75; 2 Kings 9:30–33

33. 2 Cor. 1:3–7

34. Gen. 41:16; 45:4–7; 50:19–20; Dan. 3; 6; Acts 3; 4; 6; 7; 8:1–4; 11:19–21; 16:16–34; 21:27–22:22; 24–26; Phil. 1:12–16; 4:22

35. Acts 27:18–20; Matt. 24:16–21

36. 2 Cor. 12:7–10; Deut. 8:2–3, 16–18; 2 Chron. 7:13–15

37. 2 Cor. 12:7–10; Ps. 27:5–6

38. Deut. 4:25–31; Ps. 78:34–37; Isa. 10:20–21

39. Rom. 8:35–39; Job 13:15; Hab. 3:17–19

40. Heb. 12:2; Matt. 14:22–32

41. Matt. 6:25–33; Phil. 4:6–7; 1 Pet. 5:7

42. Ex. 14:10–13; Deut. 1:21; 3:2, 21–22; 20:3–4; 31:1–8; Isa. 12:2

43. Rom. 12:12

44. Jas. 1:2–4; Acts 16:22–25; Ps. 71:19–24; Luke 6:22–23; 1 Pet. 4:13

45. Ps. 23:4; 27:1; 46:1–2; Isa. 41:10

46. 2 Cor. 4:8–12, 16; 2 Thess. 1:4; Luke 21:19; 1 Pet. 4:19

47. 1 Pet. 5:7; Phil. 4:6–7; Ps. 25:15–22; 50:14–15; 55:16–17; Jonah 2:7; 2 Kings 19:15–19; Acts 12:5

48. Ps. 66:10–15; Judg. 11:30–31

49. Lam. 3:4–8, 44–45; Matt. 26:36–46; 2 Cor. 12:3–10; Ps. 22:1–2; 34:15

50. Ex. 5:20–23; 14:10–12; 15:22–25; 16:2–3; 17:2–7; Num. 11:1–13; 14:26–27; Deut. 1:20–21, 26–39; Job 34:37; Prov. 19:3

51. Ps. 13:1–2; 22:1–2; 28:1–2; 39:12; 42:9–11

52. 2 Kings 6:33; Ps. 39:21–22; 69:19–17; 102:1–2; 143:7

53. 1 Sam. 17:45; Ps. 20:7–8; 33:16–18; 44:6–8; 147:10–11; Isa. 31:1; Hos. 1:7; 10:13; Matt. 6:19–21; Luke 12:16—21

54. Jer. 9:23; 48:7; 49:4–5; 1 Tim. 6:17; Prov. 11:28

55. Zech. 4:6; 2 Chron. 16:8–9; Judg. 7:1–8; Ps. 33:16–18

56. Isa. 2:22; 30:1–5, 7; 31:1–3; Ps. 108:12–13; 118:7–9; 127:1; 146:3; Jer. 17:5; 2 Chron. 32:7–8

57. Isa. 5:21; Prov. 3:5, 7; Jer. 9:23–24

58. 1 Cor. 1:19–2:1; Acts 4:13

59. Ps. 27:13–14; 37:7; Isa. 8:17; Ex. 14:13–14

60. Ex. 14:10–22; 16:4–30; 1 Kings 17:8–16; 2 Kings 4:1–7; Neh. 4:8–9, 11–14, 16–21; Matt. 12:9–14; John 9:1–12

61. Josh. 6:1–20

62. 2 Kings 5:1, 9–15

63. Luke 1:37; Matt. 19:26; Jer. 32:17, 26

64. John 15:5

65. Rom. 8:31

66. Phil. 4:13, KJV

67. Prov. 3:5–6, KJV

Chapter 14—Delegation

1. Luke 14:25–27, 33; 8:5–8, 14; Hag. 1:1–4; Matt. 6:25–34; 8:21–22; 1 Cor. 7:25–35

2. Ex. 18:13–18; Num. 14:11–17

3. John 10:10b

4. Matt. 11:29

5. Matt. 11:29; Ps. 127:1–2

6. Ex. 18:13–26; Num. 11:14–17

7. Neh. 3:1–32; 7:1–3; 13:4–9, 30

8. Matt. 10:1–11:1; 14:15–21; 15:35–37; 16:16–19; 18:18; 21:1–7; 26:18–19; 28:18–20; John 4:1–2; 20:15–19; Acts 1:1–11

9. Acts 6:1–7; 13:3; 8:14; 15:22–33; 19:22; Rom. 16:22; 1 Cor. 4:17; 2 Cor. 12:18; Titus 1:4–5; 2 Tim. 2:2; Col. 4:7–8
10. 1 Tim. 3:6; 5:22; Gen. 39:2–6; 39:20–23; 41:37–40
11. Ex. 18:21, 25; 2 Tim 2:2
12. Prov. 2:2–6; 22:17–28; 23:12, 23; 24:5
13. Prov. 20:6; 25:19; Luke 16:10, 12; Eph. 4:1; 1 Cor. 4:2
14. Luke 14:25–27, 33; 9:57–62; 18:28; Isa. 6:9–10; Matt. 24:9
15. Mark 6:7–13; Luke 10:1–20
16. Ex. 17:8–13; Matt. 28:18–20; 1 Chron. 28:1–29:5
17. Gen. 16:5–6; Matt. 27:21–26
18. Neh. 13:1–31
19. Mark 9:14–32
20. Gen. 41:39–45; Num. 27:15–23; 1 Kings 1:28–48; 1 Chron. 29:22–24

Chapter 15—Time Management

1. Gen. 5:27
2. Josh. 10:12–14
3. Eph. 5:15–16; Col. 4:5; Ps. 90:12; 1 Cor. 4:1–2
4. Jas. 1:10–11; 4:14; Job. 7:6–7; 14:2; Ps. 37:1–2; 39:4–5
5. Luke 12:16–21; Prov. 27:1; Jas. 4:13–15; 1 Thess. 5:2–3
6. William Shakespeare, *Richard III* (Act V, Scene v).
7. Matt. 6:25–34; Phil. 4:6–7
8. Matt. 6:33
9. Prov. 6:6–11; 10:4–5, 26; 13:4; 20:4; 23:21; 24:30–34; Eccl. 10:18; Matt. 25:26–27; Rom. 12:11; 2 Thess. 3:10–12
10. Gen. 2:2–3; Ex. 16:4–5, 11–30; 23:12; Lev. 25:1–7; Neh. 15:13–22; Ps. 127:1–4; Isa. 40:28–31; Matt. 11:28–30; Mark 6:31
11. Hag. 1:5–6; Deut. 28:38–39; Lev. 26:20; Ps. 127:1–2; Luke 5:5
12. Gen. 19:27; 28:18; Ex. 34:4; Judg. 6:38; Job 1:5; Mark 1:35

Chapter 16—Outreach

1. Matt. 28:19–20; Acts 1:8; Rom. 1:16; Luke 12:8–9; Mark 8:38
2. John 3:16; 2 Thess. 1:6–9; Matt. 7:13; 8:11–12; 13:49–50; 22:11–14; 25:28–30, 41–46; Luke 16:19–31
3. John 1:35–45; 4:28–29, 39–42; Luke 5:27–32; Acts 4:18–20

4. Rom. 14:10
5. John 1:29–50; 4:28–29, 39–42; Luke 5:27–32
6. John 16:7–11
7. Matt. 10:19–20; Acts 4:7–12; Ex. 4:12; Neh. 2:4–5; Dan. 2:14–28
8. Deut. 4:9–10; 6:6–9; 11:19–20; 31:12–13; Ps. 78:1–8; Prov. 22:6; Ex. 13:8–10, 14–16; Eph. 6:1–4

Chapter 17—Success and Failure

1. 1 Sam. 14:12–23; 17:1–11, 50–52
2. Gen. 30:25–27, 30
3. 2 Tim. 4:7; John 19:30
4. Gen. 39:2–6, 8–9
5. Gen. 39:2–9; 41:25–40; 1 Sam. 18:5; 2 Sam. 5:2; Matt. 25:14–30
6. Ex. 14:31; Josh. 2:8–11; 6:27; 9:9–10; 1 Kings 4:29–31; 1 Chron. 14:16–17; Matt. 24:23–24; 9:27–31
7. 1 Sam. 17:48–18:4; 18:15–16, 28–29
8. Deut. 1:29; 3:21–22; 31:3–4; Josh. 1:5; 2 Cor. 1:10
9. Josh. 2:28–11; 5:1; Num. 22:2–4; 1 Chron. 14:16–17; Neh. 6:15–16
10. 1 Kings 20:18–21; 1 Sam. 17–51b
11. 1 Sam. 11:11–15; 2 Sam. 16:5–12; 19:14–23; 1 Chron. 10:8–10
12. 1 Chron. 18:9–10; 1Sam. 18:5–7; Ex. 18:9–12
13. Eccl. 5:18–20; 3:12–13; Isa. 65:21–23; Prov. 13:19
14. Hos. 9:11–12; Judg. 3:10–12; Isa. 23:6–12
15. 2 Chron. 20:31–33
16. Josh. 9:1–2; 2 Sam. 5:17
17. 1 Sam. 18:1–9; Acts 13:42–50; Gen. 26:12–16; 30:43–31:2–6
18. Rom. 1:21–23; Acts 12:21–23; 14:8–21; 3:11–16; John 1:19–29
19. Deut. 6:10–12; 8:18–20; 32:3–6, 15–17; Judg. 3:7–8; 8:33–34
20. 1 Sam 17:45–47; 2 Chron. 20:20–28; 26:3–7; 27:6; Ps. 1:1–3
21. Deut. 8:10–14, 17–18b
22. Hos. 4:7; 10:1–2; 13:6; Matt 21:6–11, 26:47–68; Gen. 9:18–21; 24:50–56; 41:29–31; Josh. 6:20, 7:2–5; 1 Kings 18:38–39, 19:1–4; 1 Sam. 30:16–17
23. Phil. 3:13–14; Rev. 3:17–18; Hos. 13:5–6

24. Ex. 14:10–12; Num. 11:4–6; 14:1–4; Acts 7:39
25. Gen. 39:1–20; Ex. 12:31–36; 14:9–12; Acts 6:1; Mark 1:9–13
26. 2 Sam. 11:1–12:25; 1 Kings 11:1–6
27. Acts 3:12–13, 16; 14:11–21; John 1:19–23
28. John 3:30; 1 Cor. 15:9; Eph. 3:8; 1 Tim 1:15
29. 2 Chron. 26:15–16; Isa. 2:9–17; Dan. 4:28–37; 5:20–23; Acts 12:19–23; 1 Cor. 10:12
30. Prov. 16:18–19; 11:2
31. Pss. 96:1–3; 106:1–2; Ex. 15:1–21; Judg. 5; 1 Chron. 16:8–36; Dan. 2:12–28; Luke 17:11–19; Rom. 1:21
32. Dan. 6:19–28; Acts 3:6–4:22; 14:11–21; Ex. 10:1–2; 13:8–16; 18:8–12; Gen. 33:5, 11; Mark 1:43–45; Matt. 5:16
33. Gen. 47:23–25; 2 Kings 4:36–37; 5:15; 2 Sam. 23:8–39; Phil. 2:19–30
34. 1 Sam. 1:11, 24–28; Eccl. 5:4–6; Ps. 50:14–15; 66:13–14
35. Josh. 2:1–24; 6:22–25; 1 Sam. 20:12–15; 2 Sam. 9:1–13
36. Luke 15:1–32; 10:17–20; Ex. 15:1–21; 1 Sam. 18:6–7
37. Josh. 4:1–9; 24:25–27; Ex. 16:32–34; 17:13–15; Deut. 27:2–6
38. Luke 7:14–17; Mark 1:27–28, 43–45; 6:14; Josh. 2:8–10; Ps. 145:4
39. John 21:20–22; Mark 9:33–37
40. 1 Kings 18:20–19:5
41. Matt. 5:48; 1 Cor. 15:42–55
42. Rom. 3:23; 1 Pet. 2:22; Heb. 4:15
43. Rev. 3:17; Prov. 13:7; Hos. 12:8; Matt. 7:21–23
44. Gen. 3:6–9; Josh 7:2–21; 2 Sam. 11:1–27; Acts 5:1–11
45. Gen. 3:12
46. Gen. 3:13
47. Ex. 32:22–24
48. 1 Sam. 13:6–14
49. Lev. 16:6–10
50. Ps. 55:5–8
51. 1 Sam. 22:22; Matt. 25:14–30; Luke 16:1–2; Rom. 14:12
52. Luke 22:31; 2 Cor. 1:3–4; Ps. 51:11–13
53. 1 John 1:9
54. Gal. 6:7–8; Job 4:8; Hos. 8:7; Prov. 22:8
55. 2 Sam. 12:1–3

56. 1 Sam. 1:2–8; 4:12–20; Lam. 1:2, 14, 16, 20; Neh. 1:1–4
57. 1 Sam. 1:2–8; 1 Kings 9:6–8; Ps. 22:4–8; Lam. 2:15–16
58. 1 Sam. 17:51–53; 1 Chron. 10:7
59. 2 Sam. 10:19
60. Lam. 1:1–2
61. Josh. 7:6–9
62. 1 John 1:9; 2:1–2, 12; Ex. 34:6–7; Pss. 32:1–5; 103:12; Isa. 55:6–7; Matt. 1:21; 18:21–35; Heb. 8:35; Heb. 8:12; John 3:16; 8:1–11
63. Mark 9:14–29
64. Josh. 7:1–12
65. Gen. 49:3–4; Num. 14:14–45; Deut. 11:16–17; 1 Sam 5:1–12
66. 1 Sam. 14:24–45
67. Deut. 1:19–40; Matt. 14:29–31; 17:14–21
68. Luke 14:28–32
69. Isa. 6:8–13; John 21:17–18; Acts 20:22–24
70. Prov. 26:11; 27:21–22; 2 Chron. 12:7–8
71. 2 Chron. 7:13–16; Zech. 1:3–4
72. Luke 5:4–11, 17–19; 1 Kings 13:33–34; 2 Kings 4:31–37; 1 Sam. 13:13–14
73. Josh. 7:1–8:29
74. 1 Kings 19:1–9; Ps. 32:3–5; Lam. 5:5
75. 2 Sam. 12:15–23
76. Gal. 1:6
77. 2 Thess. 1:4
78. 1 Cor. 15:58
79. 2 Cor. 4:8–9, 16
80. See also: Ps. 37:23–24; Isa. 41:30–31.